Seasons
of a
Woman's
Heart

A DAYBOOK OF
STORIES AND INSPIRATION

EDITED BY
Lynn D. Morrissey

STARBURST PUBLISHERS®
Lancaster, Pennsylvania

To schedule author appearances, write: Author Appearances, Starburst Promotions, P.O. Box 4123, Lancaster, Pennsylvania 17604 or call (717) 293-0939. Website: www.starburstpublishers.com.

CREDITS:
Cover design by Richmond & Williams
Text design and composition by John Reinhardt Book Design

Scripture taken from the HOLY BIBLE: NEW INTERNATIONAL VERSION®. NIV®. Copyright © 1973, 1978, 1984 by International Bible Society. Used by permission of Zondervan Publishing House. The "NIV" and "New International Version" trademarks are registered in the United States Patent and Trademark Office by International Bible Society.

To the best of its ability, Starburst Publishers® has strived to find the source of all material. If there has been an oversight, please contact us and we will make any correction deemed necessary in future printings. We also declare that to the best of our knowledge all material (quoted or not) contained herein is accurate, and we shall not be held liable for the same.

First Printing, April, 1999

ISBN: 1-892016-036
Library of Congress Catalog Number: 98-83167
Printed in the United States of America

With devotion to the Lord . . .
Soli Gloria Deo

With love to . . .
my mother, Fern, for inspiring the dream,
my daddy, Bill, for promoting the dream,
my husband, Michael, for sustaining the dream,
& my publisher, Sharon Hanby-Robie, for launching the
dream

With gratitude to my writing and/or speaking mentors . . .
Emilie Barnes, Jennifer Kennedy Dean,
Becky Freeman, Esther Goff, Florence Littauer,
Marita Littauer, Ruth McDaniel, Kathy Collard Miller,
Donna Mesler Norman, Susan Titus Osborn,
Bonnie Skinner, & Mary Whelchel

With appreciation for their assistance . . .
My *Lifeliner Prayer Partners*, & Chad Allen, Stan Baldwin,
Gail Boutelle, Connie Caruso, Peg Couch,
Kathy Ferguson, Rosemary Ganz, JoAnn Hanes,
Armené Humber, Diana James, Jo Manwarren,
John Reinhardt, Suzy Ryan, & Lela Vollmer

Contents

Introduction

The heavens declare the glory of God and so do earth's seasons. Seasons are God's signature, inscribing His invisible attributes in visual splendor.

Winter, spring, summer, fall; lushness, starkness; cold, warmth; dark, light; life, death, and life again—nature's seasons show the reality of God's existence and express the range of His creative power.

Like colorful greeting cards, seasons are God's cyclical salutations that brighten or comfort our days. We find their repetition reassuring. After a long winter, we are encouraged to know that spring, indeed, will return. We find their variety stimulating, surprising us with the brilliance of orange-flamed leaves or soft-shawling snow, draping bare branches.

As women, we recognize other seasons—internal seasons—spiritual seasons. Sometimes soothing, sometimes stormy, but always sacred, these are seasons of a woman's heart. It is in these seasons of growth or barrenness, joy or sadness, trial or triumph, busyness or boredom, fullness or fracture, solitude or sorority, that God etches the imprint of His character and presence on our hearts.

As women poised on the precipice of the twenty-first century with its looming uncertainty and turbulence, we often feel isolated, frustrated, and overwhelmed. Unlike nature's seasonal symphony performed in four perfectly repeated, harmonious movements, our heart-seasons often overlap in resounding discord. We lose the melody beneath the cacophony of our clashing roles and responsibilities.

We cover our ears to block the noise and confusion, but in the process, we no longer hear the music. And then, like a whippoorwill's trill in early spring, comes another harbinger of hope—the heart's cry of our sister of the heart—then another and another. Sisters who have gone before, now come alongside to sing with us in chorus.

God never intended us to sing solo in any season of life. As you read these true stories of fellow sisters of the heart, you will *take heart* and be encouraged by their example. You will laugh with their humor, cry with their sorrow, delight in their joy, and applaud their courage. And always, always you will be amazed at God, Who ultimately orchestrates their seasons and yours.

And because God is with you, writing His invisible attributes on your heart, you will have all you will ever need to live abundantly in any season. Because "it is only with the heart that one can see rightly; what is essential is invisible to the eye."[1]

Lynn D. Morrissey
Saint Louis, Missouri

---

[1]Antoine de Sainte Exupéry from *The Little Prince.*

Faith

Rescued on the Summit

BY PAMELA ENDERBY

God has designed prayer as an occasion when He and the Son will be glorified as the source and agent in doing good to His people.

—JOHN PIPER

*O*minous clouds sprawled across the sky as we pursued Mt. Baker's 11,000-foot summit in Washington state. We had crammed sleds, saucers, and four rambunctious children into our van for a family outing.

As we weaved around the mountain, huge snowflakes began to fall. The higher we ascended, the heavier the snow fell. The sight of a car, blanketed with snow, crawling down the narrow road alarmed me; but it inspired my husband to forge ahead. "Looks like the kids will be sledding," he cheered.

Suddenly, the van started to fishtail and our tires were spinning in place. The speedometer nose-dived to 25 mph . . .15 mph . . .10mph . . . then 5mph . . . Attempting to brake, we slid backwards.

Urgently, I turned to the children and commanded them to pray. "God, please keep us from going over the edge. Stop the van!"

The van's rear wheels stopped abruptly. We sat motionlessly, teetering on the edge of a 100-foot ravine, fearful that any slight movement would capsize us. With precision, John maneuvered the van to safety and parked along the roadside. The kids spent the afternoon throwing snowballs and sledding down the base of Mt. Baker!

I'm learning that the impact of prayer is immeasurable. It doesn't matter where I am or in what season—or if my prayers are long, short, loud, or soft. God's unlimited power is released when I place my faith in His ability.

> . . . if you have faith as small as a mustard seed, you can say to this mountain, "Move from here to there" and it will move. Nothing will be impossible for you.
>
> —MATTHEW 17:20

Thought . . . Is your faith small? Good! That's a start. It need only be the minuscule size of a mustard seed. Give it to God and watch it grow.

Bird Tracts

BY PAT DEVINE

Nature is a revelation of God.

—Henry Wadsworth Longfellow

It's early morning. I sit on the porch bird-watching and weighing my worries: a daughter undergoing radiation therapy for breast cancer; a son facing the possibility of two house payments.

I need to talk to God. I need to listen to God.

It's hard to hear anything except the crows having their morning "caw-cuss" at the feeder on the deck.

A reading from a few days ago tickles the edges of my mind, "Don't worry. Look at the crows; they do not plant seeds or gather a harvest, yet God feeds them." (So do we, though not intentionally.) "You are worth so much more than birds." *Oh*, I think, *I'm more important than a bird, especially a crow!*

God will provide. I'm just not sure *how* and *where* and *when* God will provide.

Maybe it will be less directly—like the way we put out seeds for the song birds and the crows come to help themselves, instead.

Pretty soon we are putting out scraps of bread and pieces of watermelon and seeds from cantaloupe, knowing the crows will eat it all. So now we are intentionally feeding the crows!

A lesson for the crows? Just go to the source and you will get what you need—and more. And a lesson for me? Just go to the Source—God will provide what I need and more. After all, He loves me more than He does the crows.

> Consider the ravens: They do not sow or reap, they have no storeroom or barn; yet God feeds them. And how much more valuable you are than birds!
>
> —Luke 12:24

Thought . . . Are you worried about providing for your physical, emotional, and spiritual needs? God is the source of *life itself.* Because that's true, He also possesses all the resources you need with which to live it! Just ask Him.

Just Fly a Little Higher

BY JOAN CLAYTON

Look out fear! Here comes faith!

—ANONYMOUS

As I walked across the street and toward the elementary school where I taught second grade, I sensed "aliveness" everywhere.

I hurried to my classroom in eager anticipation. The children would be there soon, and I had a sudden burst of enthusiasm.

"Did you see that blue jay?" a fellow teacher asked as she came dashing in. "Come see," she shouted.

We walked within ten feet of the tree where the blue jay was happily perched. We were so awestruck by his majestic countenance and marvelous singing, that we hardly noticed a large cat sitting at the base of the tree.

"Oh look," I whispered as the cat scurried up the tree. He crouched in the fork of some branches, trying to hide. "He's going to creep right out on that shaky limb!"

The blue jay showed no fear. As the cat finally came as close as he could, the blue jay decided that enough was enough! He stopped singing, faced his enemy and chided him most adamantly in a voice that we all understood!

Thus, having reprimanded the intruder sufficiently, the blue jay just "flew up higher" and resumed his beautiful song of praise.

The impact of what I had just witnessed began to take shape. I had been dreading the doctor's report. All of the *what ifs* had robbed me of sleep. Right then and there, I decided that I would not run in fear and panic. I would stand my ground. I would face the enemy and refuse defeat.

> You, dear children, are from God and have overcome them, because the One Who is in you is greater than the one who is in the world.
>
> —I JOHN 4:4

Thought . . . Is fear over what *might* happen in tomorrow's season robbing you of your joy? Don't borrow trouble that may not occur. Face reality—that God will be with you no matter what happens.

Moneybags

BY ELLIE KAY

Gain all you can, save all you can, give all you can.

—JOHN WESLEY

When it comes to money, there are basically two kinds of people—spenders and savers. Sometimes, these monetary characteristics are exhibited from an early season of life. For example, I was born six weeks early on December 28th, in time to save my dad a lot of money with another income tax deduction.

By the time I was in the second grade, I had my first thriving business. I found a hand buzzer in a box of cereal and charged my classmates for handshakes. The marketer in me convinced them that this was the greatest thrill since Neil Armstrong walked on the moon. It cost a girl *ten* cents to get buzzed and a boy (yuck!) paid *fifteen* cents. (I charged extra for the mental suffering of touching a boy's hand). I made around $10 in ten weeks—that's a *lot* of handshakes.

As I proudly displayed these earnings to my parents, my Dad tugged my braid and said, "Why you little *Moneybags*." They taught me to put $1 into the Sunday School offering plate. Naturally, I saved the rest.

One season led to another as that lesson took root, turning this *saver* into a *giver*. I learned that the sweetest dollar was the one I could give away. Years later, little "Moneybags" founded *Shop, Save and Share Seminars.* Now I teach thousands of people how to shop wisely and share their abundance with others in need. I discovered a wonderful truth—you can't out-give God. Now that's a tip worth saving!

She opens her arms to the poor and extends her hands to the needy.

—PROVERBS 31:20

Thought . . . Are you spending or saving your money for yourself, without tithing or sharing it? Your money belongs to God. Let Him determine its use.

How Big Is God?

BY LINDA EVANS SHEPHERD

If God is God, He's big and generous and magnificent.

—J.B. PHILLIPS

I was speaking to a class of five-year-olds, when a little boy raised his hand. "How big is God?" he asked.

"He's as big as you can imagine."

He asked, "Is He as big as a camel?"

"Yes," I replied, smiling. "God is bigger than a camel. He created camels."

"Is He bigger than a giraffe?"

"Even bigger!"

In frustration, Jon asked, "Is He bigger than the whole world?"

"Yes," I said, laughing. "God created the whole world. In fact, King David once said, 'His greatness no one can fathom! (Psalm 145:3)'"

Jon tossed his hands into the air, completely puzzled, and asked, "Then how can God fit into my heart?"

My eyebrows rose. "That's a hard one, but let me ask you a question. How big is your love for your mom and dad?"

Jon squinted his eyes and held his hands a foot apart. "About this big."

"But," I responded, "your heart is smaller than that. How can you fit all that love in there?"

Jon scratched his head. "I don't know."

I leaned forward, my eyes holding his gaze. "The way God fits into our hearts is the same way the love for our moms and dads fits into our hearts. A wise man once said, 'If you invite God into your heart, He'll find room to grow as He fills your heart with a love for Him.'"

I pray that you . . . may have power . . . to grasp how wide
and long and high and deep is the love of Christ,. . . that
you may be filled to the measure of all the fullness of God.

—EPHESIANS 3:17–19

Thought . . . Does God's love fill your heart? Make room
in it for God's Son, Jesus Christ. As you walk with your
Savior, God will increase your capacity to love Him.

The Good Fight

BY CORRIE TEN BOOM

Let me tell you the secret that has led me to my goal—my strength lies solely in my tenacity.

—LOUIS PASTEUR

*O*ften people say, "How good God is. We prayed it would not rain for our church picnic, and look at this lovely weather!" God is good when He sends good weather. But God was also good when He allowed my sister Betsie to starve to death in the German concentration camp.

When I was very discouraged there I remember telling Betsie I thought God had forgotten us.

"No, Corrie," said Betsie, "He has not. Remember His Word: 'For as the heavens are high above the earth, so great is His steadfast love toward those who fear Him . . .'"

The Lord in His love accepts us, and if we are obeying, will work through us, whatever our circumstances.

In Russia I met a woman dedicated to typing Christian books. She was paralyzed—only one finger could be moved. Yet she typed many Christian books. She read a great number of books. She had translated my books and given them to people.

Often we say we have no time and strength to work for the Lord. I was ashamed when I saw this woman.

Perhaps you think, "I don't have enough faith."

When the jailer at Philippi asked Paul and Silas, "What must I do to be saved?" they answered, "Believe on the Lord Jesus Christ." When you take this step you become a child of God.

This is the great beginning of the fight of faith. It is a fight of victory; the Lord throws open wide the door of faith's treasure-house of plenty and bids us enter and take with boldness.

When the Son of Man comes, will He find faith on the earth?

—LUKE 18:8

Thought . . . Do you have enough faith? However small it is, it is enough for God to use. Tell Him that you believe "a little." Then ask Him to overcome your remaining unbelief (Mark 9:24).

Always Good

BY TERESA ARSENEAU

God's gifts put man's best dreams to shame.

—ELIZABETH BARRETT BROWNING

*O*ur car was dead. No resuscitation was possible. We had only $800 in savings and were determined not to go into debt. We found a car that we wanted, but it was twice as much as we could afford. The owner wouldn't budge and, apparently, neither would God.

After three weeks of waiting, my husband Terry's brother drove us to look at something else, but it was a dead end. On the way back, Terry silently prayed, "Lord, is there another reason we have driven this far?" He opened his eyes, and there in a tiny car lot, so small we hadn't seen it previously, was the same style of car we had hoped to buy.

It was in excellent condition, had leather upholstery and every conceivable "extra," and was two years younger than the other. The next day a check came unexpectedly in the mail. That, coupled with our savings, gave us the exact amount needed to buy our new car.

The following week Terry heard that the first car we had wanted had transmission problems. If we had been able, we would have bought ourselves a $600 to $800 repair bill! The Lord knew that we wouldn't have waited on Him, so He withheld the cash to prevent us from making a big mistake.

God's blessings are neither always wrapped the way we think they should be, nor do they always arrive in the seasons in which we expect them, but they are always good—just as He is always good, whether or not we can see it.

> Which of you fathers, if your son asks for a fish, will give him a snake instead?
>
> —LUKE 11:11

Thought . . . Are you weary of waiting for that "special something" you've asked of God? Because God is good, believe that what He gives you will be best and will far surpass your desire.

Only a Slingshot

BY JO HUDDLESTON

All I have seen teaches me to trust the Creator for all I have not seen.

—RALPH WALDO EMERSON

One afternoon, I leaned over to get the newspaper from its delivery tube attached to our mailbox. Straightening up, I discovered a neighbor's giant of a German shepherd dog, planted like a fence post, standing in the street.

I followed his gaze and saw my eight-year-old daughter, Paige, coming down the street toward us. Immediately I gauged the potential graveness of the situation. If he chose to do so, this dog could tear my child apart like a rag doll.

All I had for battle between the dog and my daughter was the thin, small-town newspaper folded in my hand. I felt like David going against his giant with a skimpy slingshot.

"Paige, walk at the edge of the street," I said deliberately. "Don't run, just walk slowly toward the house." I was amazed at my own calm.

She walked past me and at last I stood between her and the dog. He turned, as if in slow motion, and squared his shoulders toward us. I walked backwards, one slow step at a time. The dog continued to watch me, but still had not followed us. Finally, we were inside. I closed the door and, gratefully, drew my daughter close to me.

Angels must have stood in the dog's way, just as an angel had blocked the way of Balaam's donkey (Numbers 22:21–36). I still cringe whenever I dwell for very long on what could have happened, yet I realize we both survived because of God's care and protection.

. . . I will fear no evil, for You are with me . . .

—PSALM 23:4

Thought . . . Do you immediately pray when you are afraid? If you do, with God's help, you can turn and face your fear head-on. Watch your "enemy" retreat!

Fear Not

BY VERDA J. GLICK

Courage is not the absence of fear, but the ability to carry on with dignity in spite of it.

—SCOTT TUROW

*A*larmed to hear the chickens flying, flapping, and squawking, I rushed to the chicken house. What could be wrong with our laying hens?

Somehow a tiny chick had found its way into the flock. As the curious chick moved about, the adult hens fled from it in terror. "Oh, you silly chickens!" I exclaimed. "Is that all it takes to frighten you?" Relieved at the easy solution to ending their distress, I caught the chick and put it outside.

But then I wondered, *Do I become fearful about equally small matters?* God has a completely different perspective than we do on the things that trouble us, and sometimes we fear when there is no need to do so.

Jesus' disciples feared death by drowning when a fierce storm tossed their boat. But the Master of the wind and the sea rode with them. Even in serious difficulty, He told them not to be afraid. Whether the problems facing us are large or small, Christ is near and reminds us, "Fear not."

Do not be afraid, little flock, for your Father has been pleased to give you the kingdom.

—LUKE 12:32

Thought . . . When you are afraid, do you run around like a chicken—fussing, flapping, and squawking—making much ado over nothing? Instead, find refuge underneath the wings of the Most High, Who promises to shelter you in times of trouble (Psalm 91).

God's Better "Yes"

BY KATHY TROCCOLI

What does a child do whose mother or father allows something to be done which it cannot understand? There is only one way of peace. The loving child trusts.

—AMY CARMICHAEL

Copper-gold sunlight pierced the green leaves, and deep tones of burgundy and brown emanated from the painting. Written on the bottom were the words of Ecclesiastes 3:1: "To everything there is a season, and a time to every purpose under heaven." I continued to stare at the painting as God's Word continued to fall over me like a warm blanket.

So often I question the Lord. I wonder when He's going to do something. I complain, mistaking the severe mercy of God for neglect. I feel forgotten. I think my prayers are falling on deaf ears, when all the while He is listening. He is often protecting me from my wants, waiting for my maturity to catch up with my desires. He is patient as I learn to desire His will more than mine.

Why is it so difficult to understand that God only wants the best for us? He's never lied to us. He never will. His promises can never be broken.

Next time you think you hear nothing in response to your prayers, don't assume God isn't listening. He may simply want you to rest in His shadow until He reveals His answer. When you hear no, there will always be a better yes. God is for you, and will work out everything in His will.

I pray we will grow in our faith.

For the revelation awaits an appointed time; . . . Though it linger, wait for it; it will certainly come and will not delay.

—HABAKKUK 2:3

Thought . . . Are you tired of waiting on God? Think of a time when He spared you disaster because He said, "No, not now." With time's perspective, you can understand His decision. Trust Him to make the best decision again.

The Secret of the Cloud

BY MARILYN KREBS

A rainbow is Heaven's promise in technicolor.

—ANONYMOUS

A few years ago, bold headlines in every local and national newspaper reported one flying accident after another. Around this time, knowing that I had family there, a friend offered me a free trip to California. She had won two airline tickets in a raffle and had planned to go with her husband but, at the last minute, he canceled.

"Is this a joke?" I asked suspiciously.

"I'm serious," she said. "If you want it, it's yours."

A week later, sitting at a window seat on a DC-10, my friend seated next to me on the aisle, I gazed out the window watching our luggage being loaded on the plane. Suddenly, headlines of the recent string of airplane tragedies flashed before me. Panicked, I turned to my companion and asked for prayer.

Once in the air, my anxiety returned. Glancing up from my book, I noticed through the window that in the previously cloudless sky, there was a fleecy white cloud. It seemed to be moving along with the airplane.

Looking closer, I saw a rainbow in the cloud and in the rainbow waxed the silhouette of our aircraft. "Look!" I said to my friend, pointing out the window. "What do you see?"

She looked, then replied excitedly, "I see a rainbow in that cloud, with the reflection of our plane in the middle of the rainbow!"

There was no mistake. God had met my need thirty-thousand feet in the air. I relaxed in my seat, confident that we would safely reach our destination, surrounded by God's protection.

Like the appearance of a rainbow in the clouds on a rainy day, so was the radiance around Him.

—EZEKIEL 1:28A

Thought . . . Are you afraid of doing something that you have not yet even experienced? Ask God for a promise, a Biblical "rainbow," that dispels your cloud of fear. Then take the plunge. Seasons of blessings often follow the biggest risks.

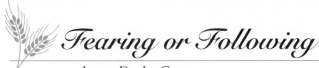

Fearing or Following

BY JUNE D. LACELLE

The sense in which a Christian leaves it to God is that he puts all his trust in Christ—trusts that Christ will somehow share with him [His] perfect human obedience . . .

—C.S.LEWIS

The Cabot Trail clings tenaciously to the outer edge of northern Nova Scotia. It unfolds an expanding panorama of rugged beauty for those who drive along it. The summer we drove the Trail, it had been all but washed away in places by pounding winter storms. Repairs proceeded where necessary along its length.

At one section, we stopped and gasped in horror. Instead of the road, we saw a narrow gravel track slanted into the side of the mountain on the left, and on the right, nothing but a sheer drop onto rocks and sea below. Our hearts sank. Was our long-anticipated journey over? We waited doubtfully, a few cars lining up behind us, an impassable stretch of road ahead.

Then a pickup truck appeared. The driver bounded out and stood before us, speaking with unruffled confidence. "You can go safely over this patch," he said, "but you must follow me *exactly*. Your tires must go where mine have been. You must not look at the drop-off, or at the narrowness of the way. You'll be all right if you fix your eyes on my truck as you follow, and go exactly where I go."

Taking a few cars at a time, he led us carefully beyond the danger to where the pavement was wide and smooth again.

After that incident, I thought about how we can trust God to lead us that exactly in seasons of peril. When the way is steep and danger lurks at every side, He alone can lead us safely home.

Whether you turn to the right or to the left, your ears will hear a voice behind you, saying, "This is the way; walk in it."

—ISAIAH 30:21

Thought . . . How do you follow God *exactly*? The Bible is God's road map for guiding your life. You can also receive God's instructions through prayer, as you both petition and listen.

The Utility Company or the Storehouse?

BY GOLDEN KEYES PARSONS

We give Thee but Thine own whatever the gift may be; All that we have is Thine alone, a trust, O Lord, from Thee.

—WILLIAM W. HOW

I stood in the doorway to the small kitchen of our little duplex where we had lived since relinquishing our spacious, custom-built home. We had been directors of a wonderful camp/conference ministry for ten years before the camp sold and we were let go. We were still struggling with all the accompanying issues that the unceremonious dismissal had brought with it—loss of home, careers, self-confidence. We had yet been able to find meaningful, gainful employment.

Seven years later, with the electric bill in one hand and our tithe check in the other, I knew my small paycheck from our church, where I worked, would not cover both. I asked my husband, "What are we to do? We don't have enough money for both!" My husband *knowingly* looked at me; we knew the answer. I breathed a prayer as I "took the tithe check to the storehouse."

Later in the day, one of the pastors called me into his office and asked, "How are things going?" I told him we were struggling financially a little, but that was all I said. As I left work that day, I found a sizable check from the church on my desk and a huge box full of canned goods for us in the hall. The pastor walked in with a twinkle in his eye and said, "Don't ask any questions—just praise God!" And I did! I praised Him for blessing our obedience.

> "Bring the whole tithe into the storehouse. . . . Test Me in this," says the Lord Almighty, "and see if I will not . . . pour out so much blessing that you will not have room enough for it."
>
> —MALACHI 3:10

Thought . . . Are you afraid that your obedience to God will cost you too much? He will bless those who follow His commands. But disobedience to God costs you everything!

Leap of Faith

BY JENNY YOON

You can do very little with faith, but you can do nothing without it.

—SAMUEL BUTLER

"*J*ump! Think of all the times God has been there for you!" someone shouted. With my heart pounding fiercely, I restrained myself from screaming, "No! He wasn't!"

Standing on the branch of a tall tree, strapped by ropes and on a belay, I was facing my last challenge of the ropes course. I had to jump toward a trapeze hanging at a high angle above me. As I was standing on the edge ready to jump, I repeatedly stopped myself by stretching my arms and bending my knees.

It was explained that the belay represented God's security. Despite the awareness of my outward protection, internally I did not feel secure. In the depths of my being, I did not trust God. I could only recall experiences where I perceived that God had abandoned me.

I was faced with the choice of either trusting God or relying upon my own strengths. Despite the feelings of fear, anger, and confusion, I yielded my will. I prayed, "God, I feel afraid and I don't know if You will be there for me, but I am going to trust You." At that moment, I took a deep breath, closed my eyes, and jumped through the cool, crisp air. I felt as if the breeze gently had lowered my floating body to the ground. I landed safely.

My faith and trust in God has grown through this experience. I can now confidently shout, "Yes! I will think of all the times that God has been there for me in every season!"

> If the Lord delights in a man's way, He makes his steps firm; though he stumble, he will not fall, for the Lord upholds him with His hand.
>
> —PSALM 37:23–24

Thought . . . Is God challenging you to risk a new "leap of faith"? Take the plunge. Just when you think you are going down, He will swoop down like an eagle, catch you, and carry you to new heights (Deuteronomy 32:11).

Home at Last!

BY MARILYN J. HATHAWAY

Heaven is not built of country seats, but little queer suburban streets.

—CHRISTOPHER MORLEY

*I*n the years when our three children were quite young and every day was an adventure, we made our home in Salt Lake City. During those days, any chance for a long weekend found us tramping somewhere in the vast wilderness of Southern Utah's wild and bewitching Canyonlands. Stretching each venture to its pinnacle, it was often late the final day when we reluctantly hitched our pop-up tent trailer to the Jeep and headed home.

Following a particularly ambitious weekend, young Peter was weary and restless. His usually doting sister had tired of reading to him and he was bored of exchanging rib pokes with his brother because "he *looked* at me." Turning his face towards the window, he whimpered several moments, then promptly fell asleep.

Many miles later we entered the Salt Lake Valley, exited the interstate onto Wasatch Boulevard, and swung onto the narrow winding lane that led to our canyon home.

As we drove down the slope to the creek, Peter awakened and, seeing the leafy arbor suspended over the car, cried out in jubilation, "Oh! *this* is where I want to be!"

For me, that moment foreshadowed our entrance into Heaven. Someday every living creature will fall asleep and, I believe, in the twinkling of an eye, the Christian will awaken at the feet of Jesus and cry out in exaltation, "Oh! *this* is where I want to be!"

Home, at last!

If we have been united with Him like this in His death, we will certainly also be united with Him in His resurrection.

—ROMANS 6:5

Thought . . . Do you often think of heaven? Because our focus is worldly—whether on our trials, triumphs, or trinkets, Heaven seems only a distant dream. Focus on its reality and the world loses its charm or threat.

Not One Ray of Light

BY JONI EARECKSON TADA

If the stars should appear just one night in a thousand years, how would men believe and adore?

—RALPH WALDO EMERSON

One summer, my family and I traveled to see a gigantic wonder called Carlsbad Caverns in the southwest corner of the United States. I clasped my mother's hand as the tour guide led our little group down into the cold, dark earth. When we reached the bottom of the pit, our guide turned out the overhead lamps so we could see, just for a moment, how thick the darkness really was below the surface of the earth.

Click! I gasped as oppressive and utter blackness enveloped me. Far beyond the reaches of natural rays of light, I could not even see my hand in front of my face. Panic seized me and I thrust my hand into the darkness to reach for my mother. In an instant, her hand was around mine, washing away my fear and anxiety. "Joni," she said, "you're safe. I would never lose you."

You probably have days that seem like deep, cavernous holes. Days when you can't find your way because of the darkness and you search for a single ray of light and see absolutely nothing.

Don't be alarmed. Remember that your walk is not by sight but by faith. And God, according to Isaiah 50:10, agrees with you: There are times when it's hard to see even a single ray of brightness in your circumstances. But even in the blackness, God promises you will find Him. Close. Near. He says, "You're safe, I would never lose you."

Let him who walks in the dark, who has no light, trust in the name of the Lord and rely on his God.

—ISAIAH 50:10B

Thought . . . Are you in the dark because of a trial, where there are no answers? Even a tiny pin-prick of light dispels the darkness. Look to Jesus Who is the light; He will reveal the truth.

The Real Joy of Christmas

BY BONNIE COMPTON HANSON

A perfect faith would lift us absolutely above fear.

—GEORGE MACDONALD

Oh, the blessing of Christmas music! After hearing a great Nativity concert, my husband and I almost floated down the street. But when we finally reached our car, parked on a dark side street, we quickly came back to earth. It wouldn't start!

Finally, after much effort, it sputtered into half-life, then chugged along barely fifteen miles an hour. The streets ahead seemed impossibly long and threatening—every shadow, every passing car seemed to shout, "Danger!" With the motor threatening to die at each stoplight, the six miles to the freeway seemed an eternity; we prayed every inch of the way.

But when we reached it—new worries! What if our car stalled in a lonely spot and we had to walk miles for help? Neither of us had worn warm enough jackets to protect against the now-biting wind. And I was wearing high heels!

Even with the car chugging and jerking, we were actually able to travel the entire fifteen miles to our exit before it finally slowed, sputtered, and died. Just as we had resigned ourselves to walking the last three miles, the motor resurrected to a slow rumble, a shudder, and then began creeping again.

Finally . . . we pulled up in front of our own home. We sat in the car for a minute, safe, exhausted, relieved—but overwhelmingly awed at the wondrous demonstration, mile-by-mile, moment-by-moment, of God's ever-surrounding love. What a precious experience of trusting and sharing with Him every minute of our hazardous trip. We had received our very own Christmas miracle!

Taste and see that the Lord is good; blessed is the man who takes refuge in Him.

—PSALM 34:8

Thought . . . Do you lose your peace when you encounter threatening circumstances? On that first Christmas, a child was born, Who is your Prince of Peace. Trust Him.

Hold Out a Light

BY DEBORAH HOLT

Hold out a light, the way is dark, no ray to guide yon struggling bark. Rough rocks are near, and wild waves roar; Hold out a light to show the shore.

—ADDISON HOWARD GIBSON

"*D*onna, show your light."

"Laura, please show your light."

I would often hear these paged announcements as I sat in my son's room when he was hospitalized. These were requests from the nurse's station to locate a nurse on the floor to respond to a patient's needs.

The announcement intrigued me whenever I heard it. I wondered how it would be if God, from his Heavenly P.A. System, called to me . . . "Deborah, show your light . . . please show your light." How would I respond?

I thought about that and, truthfully, I thought that I would say something like this: "Oh, dear Lord, please don't ask me to show my light. It is just a tiny flicker . . . it doesn't shine as brightly and strongly as others I have seen around me. I would rather keep it hidden here under this bushel basket so that no one will really notice how small and insignificant it is."

Then I imagined that God would smile and say to me . . . "Deborah, Deborah, please show your light. Your tiny flicker may be all that someone lost in the darkness may see. And to one in total darkness, even a tiny flicker appears as a bright, shining beacon . . ."

You are the light of the world. A city on a hill cannot be hidden. Neither do people light a lamp and put it under a bowl. Instead they put it on its stand, and it gives light to everyone in the house. In the same way, let your light shine before men, that they may see your good deeds and praise your Father in heaven.

—MATTHEW 5:14–16

Thought . . . How can you "shine your light" for Jesus? Oppose darkness by becoming blameless and pure. Shine like stars in the universe and hold out God's Word to a people who walk in darkness (Philippians 2:15).

I Can't See Him.
Is He There?

BY LUCI SHAW

It was less like seeing than being for the first time seen, knocked
breathless by powerful glance . . . I'm still spending the power.

—ANNIE DILLARD

*D*isappointment is part of our experience with God. We live
one day at a time, not knowing what will happen tomorrow. We
ache to have "the eyes of our hearts enlightened" so we can see
God, who is Spirit.

The Pacific Northwest is known for rains that fall steadily for
days and for clouds that shroud the landscape. Just a few miles
from the coast rise the Cascade Mountains and, spectacular among
them, Mount Baker, when we're fortunate enough to see it!

I wrote in my journal: "For weeks I drive my highway. The
mountains are on the map, but they might as well not exist, lost
as they are in fog. Then some strong air from the Pacific sweeps
away the mask, the sun shines cleanly, and Mt. Baker is seen to
be what it has been all along—strong, serene, unmoving, its profile cut clear against a sky of deepest blue.

"The mountains are getting whiter these days as snow covers
their gray blue peaks. Today I kept turning my eyes from the
road to glance at Mt. Baker, wanting to be overwhelmed again
by the spectacular view. It is heart stopping. I can never take it
for granted—I may not see it again for weeks.

"For me it's another picture of God. He's *there*, whether I see
Him or not. It's almost as if He's lying in wait to surprise me.
The wind is like the Spirit, sweeping away the fogs of doubt,
opening my eyes to the truth of the mountain's perfection, its
heartbreaking beauty."

The Lord our God has shown us His glory and His majesty, and we have heard His voice from the fire.

—DEUTERONOMY 5:24

Thought . . . Do you insist that "seeing is believing"? Faith
underscores that believing is seeing. When you search
for God with all your heart, you will find Him (Jeremiah
29:13).

Guidance

When Things Go Wrong

BY KAY ARTHUR

Don't ever say we have no opportunity to reach people. It is not that
the chances are missing, but we are missing the chances.

—CHARLES GUILLOT

I arrived at the airport five minutes late, but this was one plane
that was on time! God didn't hold the plane.

It was hard to "give thanks."

Yet, I know when I do not give thanks, I am walking in unbelief.

I wished I had control of the situation. I wouldn't have missed
the plane.

However, I would have missed what God had in mind.

What did He have in mind? A flight attendant who was hurting. A woman who had a form of godliness, but needed Jesus.

What else did God do so I wouldn't miss her? I finally got my
connecting flight, but that flight never went to Houston. They
routed us to Los Angeles.

I wasn't able to sleep. In the middle of the night, I was witness
to the most majestic light show I have ever seen. God lit up the
sky, showing cloud formations in a series of lightning flashes on
three stages.

One of the flight attendants came to gaze with me. All I could
say was, "Father, it's awesome! As the lightning comes from east
to west so shall the coming of the Son of Man be." The steward-
ess was listening.

She moved me to a row of empty seats where we could talk.
Then I knew why I had missed my plane—it was for her. All had
been arranged for one precious, confused, lost lamb.

When I was to give thanks rather than be stressed, I didn't
know why. But He asks us to walk in faith—to thank Him in faith.

Give thanks in all circumstances, for this is God's will for
you in Christ Jesus.

—I THESSALONIANS 5:18

Thought . . . Do you believe that God arranges all your
delays? Because He is sovereign, see interruptions as
opportunities to watch God work. Ask Him what He
wants to show you—whom He wants you to reach.

A Gift for Gretchen

BY ANN M. VELIA

The fear of God is evidenced in our lives by instant, joyful, and whole obedience to God . . . Anything else is disobedience. Delayed obedience is disobedience. Partial obedience is disobedience. Doing what God has asked with murmuring is disobedience.

—JOY DAWSON

I left the bank with five crisp $20 bills, one earmarked for my friend, Gretchen. I would slip it into her Bible at our Christmas Eve service with a note that read, "Get a few surprises for your kids."

Gretchen lived for her two toddlers. Her husband lived for the gambling tables, where he vainly tried to supplement his laborer's wages. I knew that the Christmas season would be bleak for her.

After I dressed for church, I took $20 from my wallet to enclose in an envelope. But then I felt God tell me, "Give it all to her."

I frowned. Gretchen didn't need $100 to buy trinkets.

Give it all to her? I began to argue with God. If I gave her a windfall, most of it surely would end up on a poker table.

"All of it," the Lord repeated.

I didn't like the idea. But I clipped $100 to my note.

After service, I drove Gretchen home and waved goodnight. With a sudden pang, I realized that she might not find my note before Christmas.

I was wrong.

The telephone rang as soon as I walked into my house. "I didn't want to spoil your Christmas, so I didn't tell you that we're on eviction notice. Our landlord told us to get out by December 31st unless we were caught up with our payments. And we were $80 short. Thanks to you, now we still have a place to live!"

And thanks to God, Gretchen had $20 left to buy a few toys!

This service that you perform is not only supplying the needs of God's people but is also overflowing in many expressions of thanks to God.

—II CORINTHIANS 9:12

Thought . . . When you obey God do you do so fully, immediately, and joyfully? It's easy to obey when you realize that God fully, immediately, and joyfully provides for you.

God Always Has a Better Idea!

BY PHYLLIS WALLACE

The journey of a thousand miles begins with one step.

—LAO-TSE

*G*od always has a better idea! To reveal His plans for me, God had to delete from my brain's hard drive things like my grade average, a teacher's advice to drop out of school, and neon lights screaming, "You're not smart, slim, or clever enough!" No big deal for God. A formidable challenge for me. He had the work all lined up. I simply kept in touch with His request line. My requests, of course.

One summer, my sister and I vacationed in a Michigan cottage. While "putting up" fruits and vegetables, we listened to her Christian tape series on womanhood. I bought that series from her, and the workbook we'd finished together.

First Sunday back, I noticed the church bulletin: "Needed: Women's Bible Study Leader." I thought, "That wouldn't be me!" But all week came the thought, "No coincidence that you not only worked through the series, but also bought it. Invite women, push the 'on' button, and hand out workbooks."

First a little Old Testament "fleece" . . . I told Pastor if ten women responded, I'd scrape out my house for them. Imagine my relief when only seven called. Pastor reminded, "Sunday isn't over yet!" Three more called!

That was the shaky beginning of a petrified wife and mom stepping out in faith to introduce people to Jesus Christ. God prepared me for what I do today, as host of a nationally syndicated women's radio broadcast, through the ten years I served that group which grew to one hundred women from fourteen different church backgrounds. God always has a better idea!

In his heart a man plans his course, but the Lord determines his steps.

—PROVERBS 16:9

Thought . . . Do you fear taking a leap of faith? No big deal. Take one step at a time, instead, letting God equip you each step of the way. All things are possible with Him.

In the Name of the Lord Our God

BY DOLLIE HARVEY

Where God guides, He provides.

—ANONYMOUS

"That little car will never make it all the way to Pennsylvania pulling that trailer!" Despite this continual warning from family and friends, we continued to load the U-Haul trailer with all our worldly goods. God had called us to be rural missionaries in the mountains of Appalachia and today was moving day.

With the tiny Studebaker Lark loaded to the roof, Tom and I and our two children climbed in, waved good-bye to our parents and siblings, ready for our great adventure of following God's direction. The Lark gave one mighty lurch, and the trailer hitch slammed to the ground. The trailer's weight had yanked the bumper right off the car!

We spent a desperate afternoon trying to find some other means of getting our household goods to Pennsylvania. Nothing we could afford was available.

About to give up, Tom and I went into the house to pray. He reached for a Bible and it fell open at Psalm 20. Verse 7 almost jumped off the page: "Some trust in chariots, and some in horses, but we trust in the name of the Lord our God."

"That's it!" Tom shouted. "That little Studebaker 'chariot' is going to make it to Pennsylvania in the name of the Lord our God!" He bolted on the bumper, installed a different kind of hitch, and off we went.

We sang all the way, and as the mountains grew higher and higher, it seemed the little Lark sang along with us: "I think I can, I think I can. . . ." We knew HE could.

Some trust in chariots and some in horses, but we trust in the name of the Lord our God.

—PSALM 20:7

Thought . . . Are you trying to do the impossible, trusting in *your* strength, alone? Trust in God's *name*. When you trust in His name, you trust in Him. With Him, nothing is impossible.

Bearing One Another's Burdens

BY CORRIE TEN BOOM

The prayer that we find hardest to comprehend, namely, the intercessory, Jesus took most easily and naturally for granted.

—FRANCIS J. MCCONNELL

What a joy it is to know that the Holy Spirit leads us when we have an opportunity to counsel people.

I once had a talk with a student who suffered from nervous tension. Although the Lord performed a miracle of liberation, the boy still seemed rather absent-minded. Then the Lord guided my approach.

"Will you do something for me?" I asked. "I have a problem. My prayer time is so attacked by the enemy. As soon as I start to pray, all kinds of thoughts distract me."

"There was a time when unclean thoughts came into my heart the moment I would concentrate on praying. But this is past. Now they are clean, practical questions, such as 'At what time must I speak tomorrow? Who is taking care of transportation?' All very good thoughts, but they hinder my concentration for prayer. Will you pray with me that the Lord will make me free and protect my prayer time?"

He did, and his prayer was something unusual—so dedicated, so understanding, so full of love. He showed a real burden for my problem!

"I am sure you have a ministry of intercession," I told him.

"I believe it, too," he answered.

At that moment I saw that his absent-mindedness was gone. He was free. He became a real prayer partner from that day on. The moment he started to do something for another, he was free from self, with all its complications. And my prayer life was healed.

Therefore confess your sins to each other and pray for each other so that you may be healed.

—JAMES 5:16A

Thought . . . Have people said, "I wish I could help you in ministry." Ask them to pray. It will be the best gift they can give you and themselves!

26

Wrong Number

BY BONNIE COMPTON HANSON

Whate'er we leave to God, God does and blesses us.

—HENRY DAVID THOREAU

*W*hen I answered the phone, a woman's voice on the other end asked, "Is this the doctor's office?" Immediately I was irritated. My husband has a Ph.D., but lots of people assume he is a medical doctor. "No," I almost barked. "This is a private residence."

"B-But, isn't this (714) 751-7824?" Something about her voice softened me. "Yes, dear, but it's my home phone number. My husband isn't a physician." I started to hang up, but suddenly God said, "Keep talking!" "Look," I added, "are you having an emergency?"

"Yes!" she cried. "It's my daughter, Jill, who's visiting me. She has cancer, and she's suddenly worse. I've got to reach her doctor out there in California. What should I do?" "From where are you calling?" "St. Louis, Missouri." "St. Louis?" I gulped and grabbed the phone book. "Now, honey, give me your doctor's name and I'll look up the number for you." She seemed near tears.

"Oh, thank you. My poor daughter!" After I gave the number to her, God said, "Pray with her." *Pray with a stranger over the phone? What if she gets angry,* I wondered. "Look," I hesitated, "is it all right if I pray for you and your daughter?"

"Oh, would you, please?" After I prayed, she sobbed, "Oh, my dear! You don't know how much this means to me. God must have given me your number!"

Yes, and, oh, how He blesses us when we go where He leads us, "wrong numbers" and all!

The Lord will guide you always . . .

—ISAIAH 58:11

Thought . . . How often do you rush ahead and ignore the Holy Spirit's *prompting*? Don't ignore Him, as you would a "wrong number." Obey His "call" and minister to those to whom He directs you.

The Right Road

BY DiAnn G. Mills

Though our chosen path isn't paved with yellow bricks, we still hope it will lead us home.

— Max Lucado

*R*ecently I accompanied my husband on a business trip to Delaware. Our son joined us and he and I elected to take a day-trip to Philadelphia. After an exciting and eventful day of rummaging through the historic section of the city, we drove back to Delaware.

My son, age fifteen, navigated while I drove. At one point he saw a sign indicating our exit. He informed me of this, but I continued driving on the same road, preoccupied with my own thoughts.

Again, he stated, "Mom, we need to take this exit." I continued on my own path, thinking he couldn't possibly be right. A third time his voice raised and I clearly heard his agitation. "Mom, you have to get over now, or we will miss the exit!"

I kept right, certain that he was wrong. After taking a bridge into New Jersey, paying a toll, and then turning back again towards Delaware, my son asked why I hadn't listened to him.

"It didn't *feel* right," I replied, and it truly didn't. Needless to say, my family will never let me forget that foolish incident.

Now I realize how ridiculous and stubborn my remark actually was. It strikes me as indicative of people today. I wonder how many stubborn people will miss eternity because the road to heaven didn't *feel* right? I am determined to travel the road of faith, based on the fact that only the death of Jesus Christ paves the way to heaven.

But small is the gate and narrow the road that leads to life, and only a few find it.

—Matthew 7:14

Thought . . . Have you accepted Jesus Christ as your Savior and Lord? Jesus says that He is the way, truth, and life and that no one can come to God, except through Him (John 14:6). Jesus is the *only* way to heaven!

A Collage of Blessings

BY SYLVIA DUNCAN

I fear no foes with Thee at hand to bless.

—HENRY FRANCIS LYTE

The thought of visiting a baby in the pediatric intensive care ward at a large children's hospital was making me squirm. It would be easy to stay home. *I am too soft-hearted for this trip,* I thought. I could not be a strong support person. The hospital visit would remind me of the terrible things that happen to God's innocent children. My heart sank low. The injured baby would be alone today if I did not take her mother, a non-driver. After praying for strength and insight I decided, reluctantly, to go to the hospital.

When we arrived, the baby was sleeping restlessly. Although it was not the season for carols, her mother began to sing, "Away in a Manger." When she came to the words, "Bless all the dear children in Thy tender care," I looked away to prevent tears. And as I did, I saw that God had produced a collage of blessings for me—the staff who provided His tender care to the sick children. There were doctors, cleaning staff, nutritionists, and nurses bustling. Not one was idle.

My mind calmed. I realized that although our foes continue to be diseases, accidents, and genetic defects, God is at hand to bless with remedies and skilled workers. Blessings abound daily. I had begun the day asking for insight. I was shown that when troubles abound, so do blessings.

Blessed are the pure in heart, for they will see God.

—MATTHEW 5:8

Thought . . . Can you face what you consider to be unpleasant for the sake of helping another? In so doing, you will find many blessings in disguise.

Hearing God

BY IRENE CARLONI

God guides us, often by circumstance.

—F. B. MEYER

On a warm Sunday afternoon last summer, our church held a baptism at the beach. I was there to take photos. The pastor gave instructions to those who were to be baptized. We prayed, and then everyone went to the water's edge.

I was wearing shorts, so with camera in hand, I waded into the ocean up to my knees. The rest of the people went into deeper water. To get a better photo of the baptisms, I decided to move a few steps to the side, when a strong wave hit me and I fell. I was surprised when I realized that I was sitting in water up to my neck.

Suddenly, I felt the powerful undertow of the receding wave pulling me deeper into the ocean. Instinctively my hand reached down into the sand to brace myself, but the strong undertow was still pulling me.

Panicked, I gasped for a breath of air. In that instant, I heard a still small voice inside of me say, "Wait until the next wave comes and then you will be able to stand up."

I glanced at the horizon and saw the waves. I was ready. When the next one washed over me, it pushed me upright and I walked safely out of the ocean.

I marveled at how God is with us all the time and guides us when we open our hearts to hear Him. Sometimes we hear Him at the most unexpected times.

He who belongs to God hears what God says. The reason you do not hear is that you do not belong to God.

—JOHN 8:47

Thought . . . In this season of life, is the powerful undertow of trials or sin dragging you under? Ask God to show you His way of escape and when He tells you what it is, take it. He will not let you drown.

When Opposition Comes . . .

BY DIANNE E. BUTTS

"God only knows what's going to happen next."
"Yes . . . and that's enough."

—*Touched by an Angel* Flip-Calendar 1997

I slumped into my favorite chair, dropped my shoes by my feet, and clicked on the lamp.

I was running late for another leadership training session which was to prepare me to lead a Bible study discussion group. I felt totally inadequate for the job, hating being the one in charge. And no matter how much I tried, I didn't seem to be catching on or fitting in. I felt disconnected. Inadequate. Alone. I wanted to quit.

I wrestled silently. *Maybe I had made a mistake. Maybe I wasn't supposed to do this job. Maybe I had misunderstood what the Lord wanted me to do.*

Just then, I noticed a paper lying on the table under the lamp's glow. I recognized it immediately.

"Expect opposition," my trainer had said. "Whenever we say 'yes' to serving the Lord, opposition comes." Her words had prompted me to write down all the reasons I had felt the Lord was telling me to say yes—thoughts that stood out in a recent Bible study, my prayers to be involved in helping people study God's Word, doors that had closed, this door that had opened . . .

Reviewing my notes convinced me again that I was doing exactly what the Lord wanted me to do in this season. And because He wanted me to lead the study, He would give me the ability to do it.

I turned off the lamp, slipped on my shoes, and headed out the door.

He has caused His wonders to be remembered; the Lord is gracious and compassionate.

—Psalm 111:4

Thought . . . Are you questioning that your current "assignment" is really God's will because it is difficult? List the reasons you initially took the challenge. If God's will is reinforced, then *expect* Him to equip you to finish the task.

Eating Humble (Raisin Cream) Pie

BY LENAE BULTHUIS

The doorstep to the temple of wisdom is a knowledge of our own ignorance.

—CHARLES H. SPURGEON

For me, beginning a day without seeking God's guidance is like eating humble pie—raisin cream, to be specific.

Whenever I rely upon my own wisdom, I am reminded of my first attempt to make raisin cream pie. Although I had never made meringue before, I was not about to ask for anyone's advice.

I simply followed the recipe to a "T"—easy as pie. That evening, I proudly set my raisin cream pie in front of my husband, Mike. He said, "Well, it doesn't look like raisin cream pie." But, after a few bites, he decided that it did taste like it!

Seeing my anxious expression and in an effort to encourage me, he took another piece. And still later, he deliberately ate another. It was only after the third piece that Mike dared to ask, "What's all this slimy stuff on top of the pie?" "That's meringue," I answered. "Usually my mom's meringue is really fluffy," Mike said. "How long did you beat it and bake it?" I swallowed slowly and asked, "Beat it? Bake it?"

It only took one raw-meringue pie for me to realize that my culinary skills needed help. Realizing my dependency upon God's help for guidance, however, has not been as easy to learn. When the meringue of life is three-feet high, my pride stubbornly sloshes through it and I lean on my own wisdom. Inevitably, God lifts me from my sticky situations, and reminds me again that the perfect recipe for wisdom begins with Him.

If any of you lacks wisdom, he should ask God, Who gives generously to all without finding fault, and it will be given to him.

—JAMES 1:5

Thought . . . In what area are you relying upon your own wisdom? Humbly ask God for His insights. He will never fault you and His counsel will never fail you.

A Gentle Nudge

BY VICKEY BANKS

The strength and happiness of a man consists in finding out the way in which God is going and going in that way too.

—HENRY WARD BEECHER

I have always loved to write. As a little girl, I would write my name over and over again. As a teenager, I wrote long letters to friends and began to keep a diary.

As I entered the season of adulthood, I began to journal during my daily devotional time. Once I became a mother, I kept journals for my children. I also wrote many encouraging notes to friends. I began to feel that God had some additional plans for my writing, but I had no idea what.

One day, I felt God's gentle nudge. I was seated next to a businessman who wrote a monthly letter to his employees. He mentioned that he was writing that month about Great Britain's Princess Diana, who had just died. I told him I had been so touched by her death that I had written about it in my journal. He immediately began to question me about what I wrote. "Give him a copy of your entry," I could almost hear God audibly say.

Feeling slightly silly, I later handed this respected businessman a copy of what I had tearfully written late one night as reports revealed that the Princess had died. That led to my being given the opportunity to write a monthly newsletter for the gentleman's employees. Those newsletters opened the door to having my first pieces published. It was just a nudge, but it was a nudge in the right direction, and I followed it.

You guide me with your counsel . . .

—PSALM 73:24

Thought . . . Have you been waiting for God to reveal His direction in neon lights? He often speaks in a quiet voice, through little nudges. As you follow each nudge, one by one, you will arrive at the destination He desires for you.

Steps in Time

BY MARIE ASNER

Such sweet compulsion doth in music lie.

—JOHN MILTON

*M*y mother was a music teacher by day and dance band musician by night. I wanted to play lively dance tunes, but she gave me classical or "church music" to play, instead. I "escaped" by accompanying the high school choir, for then mother couldn't comment about the type of music I was playing.

The summer after high school graduation was designated as the "trip to Europe." We saved for two years to be able to go.

My mother was the hit of the trip, able to play dance tunes on any piano at a moment's notice. Where was there a place for me? Dad's younger sister suggested an outing for the two of us. We drove to a nearby town, stopping at a centuries-old church. My aunt told me to "try out the organ," and I did. The medieval building didn't deter me. I felt at home and before I knew it, I had played for an hour.

As I rose to leave, my feet naturally fit into footprints worn in the stone near the bench. How many organists before me had stepped there? From that moment on, I knew I was one of them! Now I have retired, entering a new season after forty years "on the bench." It took a trip to Europe, but God's purpose for me became evident just as my family knew that it would.

I will instruct you and teach you in the way you should go;
I will counsel you and watch over you.

—PSALM 32:8

Thought . . . Do you feel unsure of God's calling? Trust Him to unfold it, one step at a time. Gladly accept this time of preparation so that you will be ready when His call comes!

The Potter and the Clay

BY CYNTHIA HEALD

Be generous in your self-surrender! . . . Be glad and eager to throw yourself unreservedly into His loving arms, and to hand over the reins of government to Him. Whatever there is of you, let Him have it all.

—HANNAH WHITALL SMITH

The older I get, the more I realize I'm not going to be permitted to live my life on my own terms! God is in the continual process of using all things to mold my life.

I had plans to fly to Louisville and meet my mother. We agreed to meet in the baggage claim area. I learned that my flight was delayed, which meant I would miss my connecting flight and arrive several hours later than scheduled. I began to worry about mom. I pictured her waiting in the baggage area, alone and bewildered.

To my surprise, the gate agent whisked us to another airline, and within minutes we were airborne. I realized that once we landed, we would transfer to another terminal to make our connection. There was no way we could make the flight. *Lord, I can't believe this is happening!* I protested. *This is totally frustrating!*

There was a second surprise. In Phoenix, an agent greeted us to escort us to our connecting flight, being held for us. Once again, within minutes we were on our way, and I was able to meet mom on time.

This was not how I had designed my day, but it was God's plan. He is the potter, and I am the clay. He was creating something in me through this experience. My trust was strengthened in His sovereign power to go before me and be with me. I realized worry accomplishes nothing. My life was reshaped with praise, for I knew my God was *for* me.

Woe to him who quarrels with his Maker . . . Does the clay say to the potter, "What are you making?" . . .
—ISAIAH 45:9

Thought . . . Are you still controlling your life? God is the Potter and you are the clay. Let Him mold you into the person He wants you to become. You will end up in much better shape!

Beloved Child

BEVERLY J. ANDERSON

So, then, God is greater than our heart (I John 3:20). Far greater is He who defends me than that which accuses me; indeed, infinitely greater. God is my Defender, while my heart is my accuser.

—MARTIN LUTHER

*D*riving the freeway toward home, I reviewed my day. Everything I had planned went wrong. I had carefully crafted the morning meeting's agenda. The committee acted like it didn't exist. I had looked forward to meeting friends for lunch. They had a conflict and canceled. I had an appointment to clarify issues and work on a shared project. Nothing I said seemed worthwhile.

Watching the road but not the scenery I usually enjoyed, I repeatedly accused myself of being inept and incapable. I remembered where I should have done better or where I had failed to plan adequately. Every moment of preparation and execution that I scrutinized, I found wanting. My self-esteem lay in shreds by my own hand.

Without bothering really to notice them, I passed vistas of magnificent pines and snow-capped distant mountains. I felt God's gentle inner voice interrupt my downward-spiraling thoughts by saying, "But you are My beloved child and I love you in spite of your weakness. Lean on Me."

Tears coursed down my cheeks. A wonderful warmth flowed over me. I hadn't measured up to my expectations. The plans I had didn't work to my satisfaction, but God still loved me. And He loved me enough to tell me.

Then, I felt I heard, "Let's look at your day together." Starting at the beginning, I saw it with a whole new perspective and actually laughed at points.

Now, I've chosen to plan my day more prayerfully and to listen for God's guidance throughout the day instead of seeking His rescue at its close.

For God did not send His Son into the world to condemn the world . . .

—JOHN 3:17

Thought . . . Have you met with unfulfilled expectations in this season of life? Your plans may not be God's. He'll show you what to do and enable you to do it.

Ministry Happens

BY PATRICIA A.J. ALLEN

Life is the art of drawing sufficient conclusions from insufficient premises.

—SAMUEL BUTLER

When God called me to relocate to western North Carolina, I had visions of touching the lives of countless thousands of people for Jesus. Although I'm a regular type of person, when I felt the inner calling of God to relocate, I drew glorious pictures in my imagination. That vision grew beyond reason.

Then we moved and life got hard. Rather than reaching the masses for Christ, I encountered a waiting season of twelve long years before God involved me in ministry. My lifestyle changed and changed again as I absorbed differences in culture. I had always lived in a service community. Now, I lived in an industrial area, where people thought and worked differently. Even their speech patterns were different. Opportunities to share Christ were basically reduced to random words of grace spoken to strangers in grocery stores!

Then, a counselor at the college I attended referred a journalist to interview me as part of promoting the college in the community. I read the published article which began, "In 1982, Patricia Allen met Jesus . . . " The writer quoted my support verse and gave the Scriptural reference. She told how God had changed my life.

Because of that article, I realized that God had encouraged four large counties full of people, showing them His strength, love, and the fullness of His provision. Many people told me how my words had impacted them. In His own magnificent way, God did far more than I thought I had to do alone!

As the heavens are higher than the earth, so are My ways higher than your ways and My thoughts than your thoughts.

—ISAIAH 55:9

Thought . . . Do you feel the burden of trying to accomplish your ministry single-handedly? Try to remember that the ministry is ultimately God's. Allow Him to accomplish it through you in His time and in His way.

Worth the Wait

BY SANDRA PALMER CARR

... if the work is His, the responsibility is His ...

—HANNAH WHITALL SMITH

I answered the telephone cheerfully and the sweet voice on the end of the line was an elderly lady from church. After her initial greeting, she asked, "Honey, do you work?" "I feel like I do," I answered. "Well, I mean outside the home," she clarified.

Then she described the need for some "young blood" on the steering committee to reorganize the women's ministries. I was forty. I had been asked to join the committee in seasons past, but always declined because of conflicting areas of service. I felt that I should decline again, but I decided to pray for a clear answer as others continued to ask me. I promised to call back the next week.

The decision was difficult. Was God speaking too softly or was I not listening attentively enough? With a husband, two active sons, ages fourteen and eleven, and my own involvement in music and drama ministry, how could my schedule hold one more commitment?

As a younger woman I had learned to say "yes" too quickly to requests for service and sometimes lamented my hasty responses when pressures mounted. This time I would wait on God.

A full week's events clarified my decision. I said "no" to the committee again. But I knew I was saying "yes" to God's will. And what a thrill to learn that three gifted women, whose children were grown, felt called to work together to restructure the women's ministries. God blessed my waiting and their willing efforts with fruitfulness and shared joy.

The Lord will guide you always ...

—ISAIAH 58:11

Thought . . . Are you willing to wait on God before saying either *yes* or *no* to a ministry opportunity? He will answer. Never launch forward nor remain behind without knowing His will.

Habits

BY MARLENE BAGNULL

Make me a blessing, make me a blessing. Out of my life may Jesus shine.

—IRA B. WILSON

My husband had been on a new job for seven miserable weeks. Each week seemed worse than the previous one. When Paul learned that no one was able to work well with his boss, he wasn't surprised.

Every morning Paul woke up long before the alarm with a knot in his stomach. As his mind rehearsed the tasks before him that day, he was filled with dread.

"Oh God," we prayed together, "please give Paul a good day today." But despite our prayers, Paul wasn't having good days. He was finding it increasingly hard to get along with his boss and increasingly hard to please him.

"It's going to be a great day," Paul said one morning as he left for work with a big grin on his face. "My boss isn't going to be in today." We both laughed. Then, suddenly, we saw the bad habit we were forming.

Instead of practicing the principles of Philippians 4:8 and thanking God for the admirable qualities his boss did possess, we had been focusing only on the negatives. We had been grumbling instead of praising, doubting God's leading to this new job instead of trusting. And when we prayed, we prayed *about* Paul's boss, but we never prayed *for* him. We had never asked the Lord to give his boss a good day!

Amazing changes began to take place, especially in us, as we replaced our bad habit of criticism with the good habit of daily asking God to bless his boss.

I urge, then, first of all, that requests, prayers, intercession and thanksgiving be made for everyone, for kings and all those in authority . . .

—I TIMOTHY 2:1–2

Thought . . . Are you experiencing conflict with someone? Don't complain. Pray. It is difficult not to empathize with someone for whom you are praying.

The Divine Appointment

BY MARILYN HEAVILIN

Jesus . . . wants us to see that the neighbor next door or the people sitting next to us on a plane or in a classroom are not interruptions to our schedule. They are there by divine appointment. Jesus wants us to see their needs, their loneliness, their longings, and He wants to give us the courage to reach out to them.

—REBECCA MANLEY PIPPERT

I checked my bags at the curb and went into the airport. I began thinking, *You don't have one of your books with you. You need to have a book.* The feeling became so strong that I walked back through the airport and found my briefcase. I got two copies of my book and went back into the airport.

Once on the airplane, I was seated next to a man who commented that he wished the weather had been better in California. I asked, "Are you here on business or vacation?"

The man started to answer, but his eyes filled with tears. "I was here to bury my son."

I pulled out my book as I said, "Sir, I don't know if you believe in divine appointments, but you've just had one."

This man poured out his heart to a total stranger. Since my children's deaths I have become more sensitive to God and to others. Before their deaths I probably would have been too occupied to have heard God's voice telling me to go and get a book, let alone to have responded.

A bereaved parent asked if I wished I could bring my children back. I thought, *I would love to have them back, but I would never want to be the Marilyn I was before they died.*

Through my children's deaths, I have learned that life is not just about living; it is about caring, loving, hurting and dying. As we walk through these different experiences of living and of dying, we are friends.

You discern my going out and my lying down; You are familiar with all my ways.

—PSALM 139:3

Thought . . . Do you avoid small talk? Consider each interruption a divine intervention—an opportunity to share Christ—probably your *only* chance with a stranger!

Maturity

Seasoned Gifts

BY JANET CHESTER BLY

A wise man will make more opportunity than he finds.

—FRANCIS BACON

*W*e'd just heard a series of sermons on spiritual gifts. My mind buzzed with ministry possibilities.

Mildred, an elderly friend, passed me in the hall and I greeted her. *She doesn't seem her usual perky self,* I mused. *I wonder if something's wrong?*

"How are you really doing today?" I asked.

She clutched my arm in appreciation. "Oh, I'm doing just fine, thank you. Only . . . "

"Only, what?"

Her eyes searched mine. "You're young, active, able to do things—I don't begrudge you that—but I still have just as strong a desire to serve God as ever in this season of life. Only difference is, there's nothing I can do—is there?"

"Sure!" I answered, but I couldn't think of a thing at the moment. I promised to pray.

One day, I got a call from Mildred.

"Janet, do you know where I can find Christian storybooks?" Her words spilled out with excitement. "You know those children I've complained about in that new apartment building behind my house? The ones always running through my garden making noise? Several of them were playing in my front yard. I decided to pull a chair on the grass where they were and read awhile. Before I knew it, all three sat quiet as can be beside me while I read out loud."

"You know what? They've been coming back every afternoon and bringing their friends. Today I had a dozen! Now I've run out of books."

We rejoiced at the Lord's provision of an unexpected ministry opportunity right outside her front door.

They will still bear fruit in old age, they will stay fresh and green.

—PSALM 92:14

Thought . . . Have you retired from ministry because you feel useless? Search your neighborhood for opportunities. The list is as endless as God's leading.

Trail of Blessed Memories

BY GLENDA SMITHERS

The way is dark, the road is long; Help me, dear Lord, far I cannot see!
Give me a light to guide me on; Teach me with patience to follow Thee!

—ANONYMOUS

*P*op and Clipper will always walk beside me. Pop, the grandfather who taught me the joy of the early-morning cruise through the grass-carpeted trails, put it this way: "a jaunt through the outdoors for a bit of body freedom!"

As a child, I didn't care where my grandfather explored as long as he took me. Pop's canvas army pack, with its worn leather straps, stood packed and ready to go in the corner of Grandma's kitchen. Clipper, the spaniel, napped on twenty-four-hour sportsman's call.

Invariably grandmother fussed if I went along with Pop, especially if it were raining or snowing. However, she always acquiesced if I wore two pair of heavy socks and Pop's long underwear.

Clipper knew everything. Mound grouse and meadow-dwelling quail could not trick him. Clipper and Pop never got lost.

But one summer day I did! The track ran pale but, nonetheless, continued to lure me through the woods. I heard the song of a whippoorwill, beckoning me like notes from a wooden flute. Then the patch of red-berried cat briar caught my fancy. And soon I was lost. I must have circled the area dozens of times before I finally fell exhausted to the ground. Clipper found me. Pop prayed a thank you prayer as he carried me all the way back home.

Sometimes the powerful pull of the past is enough to draw us steadily through each day. And always, unexpected blessings fall like leaves when I explore untrodden trails with my own grandchildren. Pilgrimages with a ten, six, and three-year-old are routed carefully with repetition and a youthful instinct for adventure. Of course, prayer always goes along. Pop and Clipper would expect that.

The memory of the righteous will be a blessing . . .

—PROVERBS 10:7

Thought . . . What wonderful memories with your grandparents can you update for your own children? The past enriches the present and will enhance the future.

That Kind of Love

BY JANE FOARD THOMPSON

We need love's tender lessons taught as only weakness can; God hath His small interpreters; The child must teach the man.

—JOHN GREENLEAF WHITTIER

*T*ears blinded me as I nuzzled her fuzzy head one last time, placing my sleeping granddaughter in my daughter's arms.

"I'll be back soon!" I assured. With a final wave and an attempt at a brave face, I proceeded down the boarding ramp, my precious ones disappearing from view. Yet I knew that I would not soon forget the imprint my first grandchild had made on my heart. I could almost still feel her warmth and softness.

At 30,000 feet, and aching with loss, I opened my Bible and read Isaiah 49:15: "Can a mother forget the baby at her breast and have no compassion on the child she has borne? Though she may forget, I will not forget you!"

Sighing, I laid my head back on the seat. Suddenly, I understood that God understood *my* feelings. He loves me the way that I love Corri. He hovers over me as I sleep, waiting to shower me with love and care as soon as I open my eyes and seek Him. He aches when I cry in pain and comes to my aid when I'm scared and calling for help. He yearns for my closeness when I wander away.

Reading Isaiah assured me that God loves me even more than I do my grandchild. Jesus is as anxious to come back for me one day as I am to return to Corri. Because of my new granddaughter, God's timeless lessons took on new depth. What promises! What love! What a God!

For You created my inmost being; You knit me together in my mother's womb. I praise You because I am fearfully and wonderfully made; Your works are wonderful, I know that full well.

—PSALMS 139:13–14

Thought . . . Can you fathom the depths of God's love for you? The awesome love you feel for your child is but a dim reflection of God's love for you. He loves you so much that He gave His only precious Son to die for you, so that you might spend eternity with Him.

44

A Smiley Face from God

BY JOYCE E. TOMANEK

Peace! Peace! wonderful peace, coming down from the Father above;
sweep over my spirit forever, I pray, in fathomless billows of love.

—W.D. CORNELL

My elderly mother who lived with us was bedridden, paralyzed, and unable to speak or swallow after a series of strokes. I cared for her at home with the help of home health professionals.

Torn between caring for her and trying to do justice to my dear husband, Frank, there was never a time when I was with one that I didn't yearn to be with the other, as well. It was one of those seasons in life when there just wasn't enough of me to go around.

I grieved as I watched Mom lie there, wondering how much she knew and what she would say if she could talk. Was she in pain? There was no way to know. Clearly, she was approaching death.

One day as I went outdoors to drive the half-mile to our rural mailbox, I looked up through the bare winter trees into a bright sky. I caught my breath, hardly believing what I was seeing. I blinked and looked again.

There, suspended in the brilliant blue expanse, was an upside-down rainbow!

"Frank! Come look!" He saw it, too. I wasn't seeing things! We held hands and watched it together.

Warmth flooded me—and comfort and peace. That big *smiley face* in the sky just had to be from God! It was as if He were reminding me that He was with me . . . and with Mom, as well. It was as if He were saying, "Keep smiling, Joyce. Everything is going to be okay."

Your love, O Lord, reaches to the heavens, Your faithfulness to the skies.

—PSALM 36:5

Thought . . . How can you find peace when those you love are ill? Wrap yourself and them in the blanket of God's sovereignty. He is in control and loves us, no matter what happens. He promises comfort to those who call on Him.

"Leaf" It up to God!

BY PHYLLIS WALLACE

The only thing I don't like about middle age is that you eventually have to leave it!

—DORIS DAY

"Let's make like a tree and leaf!" I recall my kids' jingle each fall—when our Ginkgo drops her spectacular yellow leaves, like so many petticoats, as if to say, "That's it! My turn to rest." A sight so stunning, I don't touch it for a week. I enjoy tea in my garden, regally enthroned on this soft carpet, writing and watching butterflies on the phlox and hummingbirds hanging on hollyhocks.

Fall teaches me about weathering this "season" of my life, a time to rest and store up, as my body cries, "Not so fast!" I mostly ignore the message, because I don't embrace loss. All four kids are "twenty-something." Yesterday they were teens. Is it easier? Maybe, except for the "loss" part. I wish I'd realized how much I liked it sooner!

God seasons me. My roots are nourished by His Word to risk. Skip rushing the net for set point and enjoy the game. Skip the "me" focus to risk loving someone unloveable. Contentment lingers longer in the fall of life. The longing to be somewhere else doing something else subsides. It feels good to just "be," aware the Lord is with me always. Perhaps I'll be like the Oak, last to lose its leaves. But I know it's coming, so I stay rooted. My parents' love of life, serving the Savior, graciously models loss. My kids lovingly reach back from their corners of the world. God shows me that loss is do-able, if I just "leaf" it to Him!

At least there is hope for a tree: If it is cut down, it will sprout again, and its new shoots will not fail.

—JOB 14:7

Thought . . . Are you experiencing loss? Think of it as a time of transition into a new, more fruitful season. Pruning always precedes a bountiful harvest.

46

The Hummingbird Parable

BY DR. KATHRYN PRESLEY

Grow old along with me! The best is yet to be, the last of life, for which the first was made.

—ROBERT BROWNING

The last season of life is perhaps the sweetest, yet it is also perilous: both physical and mental strength wane, loved ones die, and some aging saints succumb to bitterness and despair. This September, I learned a lesson from the hummingbird.

Sitting on my quiet porch above Lake Somerville, I struggled with loneliness and a sense of futility, when suddenly the air was filled with the whirring of tiny wings. Ruby-throated hummingbirds were preparing for their long journey to South America. Fiercely competitive, their tiny, militant beaks clashed as they frantically drew nectar from honeysuckles and fought for space at the feeder.

Hummers must feed constantly to consume up to fifty percent of their weight in sugar daily, and their arduous journey seems impossible for fragile bodies. No wonder they work so valiantly to store up energy for their flight.

We also have a difficult pilgrimage to make. Loss of independence, terror of strokes or Alzheimer's disease, the fear of burdening children, these can cause anguish as we grow older. But the Rock of my salvation has promised never to leave nor forsake me. "Even to your old age and gray hairs I am He . . . Who will sustain you (Isaiah 46:4) . . ."

Like the hummingbird, I am determined to draw "honey from the rock," not only to strengthen me for my journey, but to sweeten me in days of sorrow and affliction.

He gives strength to the weary and increases the power of the weak. Even youths grow tired and weary, and young men stumble and fall; but those who hope in the Lord will renew their strength. They will soar on wings like eagles; they will run and not grow weary, they will walk and not be faint.

—ISAIAH 40:29-31

Thought . . . Do you fear growing older? Do not fear. The Sovereign Lord has assigned your days. Find strength in Him and "feed" on His Word for sustenance.

Broken

BY FRAN CAFFEY SANDIN

Let me not neglect any kindness, for I shall not pass this way again.

—ANONYMOUS

*W*hen the telephone rang at 5:30 A.M. on a cold, dark December day, my physician-husband answered. From his questions and the concern in Jim's voice, I learned that his eighty-five-year-old widowed mother had fallen in her apartment, breaking her left wrist. Jim reassured our beloved "Grandma," then dressed quickly and took her to the emergency room.

I felt compassion, then wondered . . . *How would I manage my busy schedule and take care of her, too?* My empty nest was alive with activity: I played the organ at church and worked full-time as a nurse at my husband's office to cover an employee's vacation. Fragrant evergreens and twinkling lights had enticed me with Christmas festivities. Writing deadlines called from the calendar.

At first I resented the time spent washing Grandma's clothes, cooking, shopping, and assisting with her personal needs. Then something happened. One day as I tiptoed to reach for a jar on the grocery shelf, an inner voice whispered, "You are not doing this for Grandma, you are doing it for ME."

I had never thought of that. *Yes, Lord, I am shopping for You.*

When I stopped focusing upon myself and broke through a season of selfishness, caring for Grandma became a unique opportunity to serve God. He gave me extra strength and multiplied my efficiency. Grandma and I prayed, chatted, and laughed together. Soon my *burden* became a cherished blessing.

Whatever you do, work at it with all your heart, as working for the Lord, not for men, since you know that you will receive an inheritance from the Lord as a reward. It is the Lord Christ you are serving.

—COLOSSIANS 3:24

Thought . . . Do you resent caring for an elderly relative? Serve her as you would the Lord, and your heart will be filled with compassion.

Virtual Reality

BY PAQUITA RAWLEIGH

To do is to be.—PLATO

To be or not to be.—WILLIAM SHAKESPEARE

Do be, do be, do.—FRANK SINATRA

I asked my mother-in-law to help with some of my work at the office. She was reluctant in her agreement to help because of the new office equipment. She preferred an old typewriter and a sensible chair to our computer and new executive chair.

Showing her how to set the swivel handles on the chair, I left her to experiment and find a comfortable seating position. As soon as I left the room, the chair started to roll backwards. Mom did the most logical thing possible to stop her regressive progression; she grabbed onto the desk drawer. Unfortunately, the drawer also had smooth rollers.

From the hallway I heard a crash! I rushed into the office to find my mother-in-love lying on the floor, her feet up in the air—and a drawer in her lap. Unharmed, she looked at me with a twinkle in her eye and asked, "Don't they call this Virtual Reality?"

Isn't life similar? As soon as we get too comfortable with a new situation, we're flat on our backs—facing a new season of life. Whether we are in season or out of season, we still need to know truth. To experience genuine reality, we go to the source of all wisdom—and I don't mean an ancient philosopher or the latest software. The source of all truth is found in God and His Word. After all, the foolishness of God is greater than the "wisdom" man has to offer. As Christians, we have more than virtual reality—we have the ultimate reality, God Himself!

> But God chose the foolish things of the world to shame the wise; God chose the weak things of the world to shame the strong.
> —I CORINTHIANS 1:27

Thought . . . Are you searching for truth? Society says it doesn't exist or, at best, is elusive. It says everyone must find her *own* truth. Truth exists in a person, Jesus Christ (John 14:6), and His Word is true (John 17:17). Measure all you think against God's truth. Anything else is a lie.

Short Loss, Long Gain

BY JUNE D. LaCELLE

Earth's best does not compare with heaven's least.

—F.B. MEYER

*T*he doctor's voice was kind, but his words were grim. "Your heart valves are changing as the years advance." I hated to hear it.

The years—how was it fair that my quota was so nearly gone? I had enjoyed those years so much as they passed, first meandering forward, then gathering speed as they rolled downhill. I wanted them to keep rolling along smoothly, but not at breakneck speed!

And whatever happened to "lived happily ever after"? Life seemed to be sinking to the finish. Where was the point? Was aging nothing but a bad joke?

"You have an option," the doctor said. "Keep exercising." *As if this old clay could fool the years and renew its youthful vigor by my pummeling it,* I doubted.

Then I remembered: *I have more than an option, I have a certainty! God put His own guarantee on it. By Jesus' death and resurrection He opened heaven for people like I. He gave me a reason for living and hoping, no matter how tightly time and illness may squeeze me.*

"I like it here," I told the doctor. "I may not want to leave when the time comes, but something better is waiting."

After the narrow season that separates time and eternity, what wonders will open before us? I'm not looking forward to the journey; death is a dark mystery. But I know that heaven stands beyond, brighter than our imagining. Time is short; I can't hold it. Heaven is forever. And the Lord will eternally hold me in His gracious hand.

> But our citizenship is in Heaven. And we eagerly await a Savior from there, the Lord Jesus Christ, Who . . . will transform our lowly bodies so that they will be like His glorious body.
> —PHILIPPIANS 3:20-21

Thought . . . Are you afraid of death? If you know Christ as Savior, death is not your enemy, but your friend, ushering you into His eternal presence. Realizing life's brevity can also help you live more fully, appreciating every day as a gift and opportunity to reach others for Christ.

Letting Go of Loss

BY CLAIRE CLONINGER

In youth we learn; in age we understand.

—MARIE EBNER-ESCHENBACH

How do we deal with the pain of loss? Where do we go with our confusion, outrage, grief?

I have been contending with a small loss this year that has to do with my body. I enjoy jogging every day and have entered a number of amateur races over the years. When I first began running more than fifteen years ago, I could knock off a ten-kilometer race in around fifty-four minutes. These days the exact same distance is more difficult and takes much longer. This is a minimal loss, but I hate the fact that I have slowed down. It signifies that I am growing older.

The Lord has been showing me a way of surrendering this loss to Him. When I feel the sting of growing older, I stop and surrender the decades of my life to Him.

"Lord," I say, "I give you my fifties, sixties, seventies, eighties, nineties. However many years You desire to give me, I give back to You. You already know the number of my days. They were a gift, and I now return them. I surrender all the losses that will come with these years as well as all the joys, for I know You to be a God of love, and I can trust You with them."

A sweet peace comes to me when I surrender this area of loss to God and feel Him take hold. The sting goes out of letting go.

All the days ordained for me were written in Your book before one of them came to be.

—PSALM 139:16

Thought . . . Have you surrendered to God the seasons of your heart and of your years? Change your perspective on aging by considering every new year as a special gift in which to serve God.

Aged to Perfection

BY GRACIE MALONE

I desire no future that will break the ties of the past.

—GEORGE ELIOT

*M*other slipped her arm in mine as we walked down the long corridor and into my 103-year-old grandmother's hospital room. Standing by the bed, I felt overwhelmed by the sight of her frail form, barely visible beneath the sheets. *Mama has lived entirely too long,* I thought. *Why doesn't she give up? Why doesn't God take her home?* But soon my perspective changed.

Like a hen hovering over her brood of chicks, my mother fluttered and fussed over Mama. She washed her face with a warm cloth, brushed her hair, and applied lotion to her gnarled hands. I overheard Mother speaking tenderly, "Everything's okay. I'm here. I love you." I thought about my rich heritage from these two women, and suddenly 103 years didn't seem enough.

Later, my fear of the future faded as I read, "He who dwells in the shelter of the Most High will rest in the shadow of the Almighty. He will cover you with His feathers and under His wings you will find refuge; His faithfulness will be your shield and rampart." I thanked God for His promise to those who love Him, "With a long life I will satisfy him, and let him behold My salvation (Psalm 91:1,4, 16)."

I pictured Mama, my mother, and me huddled together under God's wings like three old wet hens in a storm. I imagined the warmth and security I would feel snuggling in the soft feathers close to the heart of God, feeling every heartbeat. The thought of it was enough to make me feel safe and confident.

One generation will commend your works to another; they will tell of your mighty acts.

—PSALM 145:4

Thought . . . Do you fear old age? Is it hard for you to watch loved ones growing older? Rest in the sovereignty of God. He numbers your days and He has a purpose in each and every one. When He calls you home, the timing will be perfect.

Mother No Longer Sings Solos

BY MARLENE BAGNULL

Age is not decay; it is the ripening, the swelling of the fresh life within that withers and bursts the husks.

—GEORGE MACDONALD

When I was little, every Thursday I went to choir practice with Mother. The director allowed me to sit next to her and encouraged me to sing along.

I beamed with pride. My mother was the best soloist in the choir! I leaned against her and tried to imitate her voice, but almost always mine squeaked on the high notes she sang so clearly.

Mother held the music and turned the pages. When I got lost, she pointed to the right note.

Tonight I picked up Mother at her apartment and took her to choir with me. Her voice is no longer strong. It cracks on the high notes and slides off key. She isn't asked to sing solos anymore.

Mother's hands get tired holding the music. She forgets to turn the pages and loses her place. I think about the doctor's prognosis. Mother has a dementing illness similar to Alzheimer's disease. She is not going to get better, and it is only a matter of time before she gets worse.

Suddenly, my thoughts are interrupted by the words we are singing. I feel God's presence. He reminds me that even though we grow old and weary, He never changes. He never stops loving us. He will be with us always in each of life's seasons.

I glance at Mother. She may no longer understand the words she is trying to sing, but I know His Spirit is touching hers. He will allow neither death nor life to separate her from His love.

Therefore we do not lose heart. Though outwardly we are wasting away, yet inwardly we are being renewed day by day.

—II CORINTHIANS 4:16

Thought . . . Is it terribly difficult for you to watch a loved one's decline? Do whatever you can to be of help, but most importantly, entrust him to God; He promises His presence, protection, and comfort, despite our age.

Capable Hands

BY DOLLIE HARVEY

Keep your words soft and sweet. You may have to eat them!

—ANONYMOUS

I'm generationally challenged. Born too late to be a "builder"—that heroic group who survived the Great Depression and marched off to World War II to preserve our freedoms—I was born too soon to be part of their offspring generation, the "Baby Boomers."

Like others caught in this time-warp season, I bemoaned the world's fate left in the hands of upcoming generations, the "Busters" and "Generation Xers"—with their pierced noses and navels, rap music, and half-mast baggy pants. They were rude, crude, and tattooed. The future looked grim, indeed.

Recently my mission-director husband and I were invited to *Moody Bible Institute* for a missions conference. While there, he underwent major emergency surgery.

I was alone in Chicago. The students at *Moody*, all "Generation Xers," quickly came to my rescue, with daily prayer bands on our behalf, housing, laundry, and transportation back and forth to the hospital—they took care of everything I could possibly need! One student came to the hospital the night of the surgery and, handing me a wad of dollar bills, said, "Just in case you need a Coke or something . . ." They surrounded me in the cafeteria to pray and stopped me in the halls for updates on the surgery.

Most importantly, they totally changed my attitude about their generation. I think we "old-timers" are going to leave this world in some very capable hands!

> Don't let anyone look down on you because you are young, but set an example for the believers in speech, in life, in love, in faith and in purity.
>
> —I TIMOTHY 4:12

Thought . . . What is your overall attitude towards the *younger generation?* Instead of criticizing, why not *mentor* a young person, instead? Both you and she will learn from each other.

Root-Bound

BY BETTY J. JOHNSON

Let all blessed old things stay, but let the clutter of our heads and hearts be removed, that new inspirations and new affections may come in to gladden our lives.

—CHESTER BURGE EMERSON

"Hey, Honey, look at this bush. I'd say it's root-bound and ready for transplanting," my husband commented during our Saturday morning landscaping project. His comment and the sight of the twisted roots triggered an inner question: Do we as human beings become root-bound by sameness, routine, and monotony?

Staring at the house in which we had lived for the past eighteen years, I wondered if a newer, smaller house would be more appropriate for our empty-nest season. Or, perhaps it was time to fulfill our dream of building a cabin by a lake somewhere.

My mind shifted to our relationships with family and friends. Did being root-bound stifle growth in others as well as ourselves? Instead of calling someone from our usual group to play golf this weekend, perhaps we could invite the new neighbors to join us.

Finally, my mind struggled with the concept of being spiritually root-bound. Even though being rooted in Christ Jesus was our goal, busyness and routine often choked our spiritual growth. Suddenly, I felt excited about watering our spiritual garden with fresh ideas and new small groups.

I reached for my husband's hand. "Hey, Honey, let's take a break and discuss making some changes. Perhaps God used that root-bound bush to teach us important lessons."

See, I am doing a new thing! Now it springs up; do you not perceive it? I am making a way in the desert and streams in the wasteland.

—ISAIAH 43:19

Thought . . . Are you so rooted in routine, that the thought of a transplant seems painful? Grow shallow roots so that you are ready for change when God initiates it. But always stay deeply rooted in Him and His Word.

Summer Tents

BY CYNTHIA SCHNEREGER

Just a few more days left for toiling, just a few more nights, dark and cold, then our tents will be folded forever—we shall trade them for mansions of gold.

—ETHEL MEADOWS

*K*im, Don and Janet died this summer, having touched our lives in ways as diverse and unique as snowflakes or sunsets. Each left something precious behind: Kim—three growing kids deeply in need of a Christian mother; Don—a daughter and son-in-law awaiting a final adoption, and Janet—a wheelchair-bound husband of twenty years, dependent on her for his very freedom, and perhaps his personal dignity, as well.

Our boys set up their tent in mid-June, intending to dwell in it for the duration of the summer. At first it stood proudly, but today I glimpsed its sagging outline from my August window: its once-proud sides flattened, its roof caved in and who-knows-what lying abandoned inside . . .

The Bible informs us that our bodies are like tents. Temporary. Frail. Inherently devoid of life. But our spirits indwell these lodgings for a time, just as my boys spent a season in their beloved tent. And then time passes. Car accidents and cancer happen. Our tents lie discarded. No one's home anymore.

But hope endures. Just as my boys' abandoned tent can surely be set up again next summer, so our bodies will be raised one future day. In the twinkling of an eye our earthly tents will be left behind, only to be replaced by permanent homes in a far better garden. Old relationships will be renewed: mothers with children, grandparents with grandchildren, husbands with wives—dwelling eternally in a season of joy.

Now we know that if the earthly tent we live in is destroyed, we have a building from God, an eternal house in heaven, not built by human hands.

—II CORINTHIANS 5:1

Thought . . . Are your physical aches, pains, and illnesses getting you down? These are *temporary* conditions. Take joy that in Heaven your body will not only be perfect, but it will last *forever!*

Let's Face It

BY MARILYN MEBERG

Courage is never to let your actions be influenced by your fears.

—ARTHUR KOESTLER

When I first moved to California, I was excited about walking the beach as my exercise routine.

One morning, I was making my way down to Main Beach when I noticed a Doberman trotting some distance behind me. I was the only one on the beach, and the dog was not on a leash. That made me nervous. Dobermans are known to be fierce. I picked up my pace. So did he!

The dog was gaining. Within a short time, I was moving at a full-on run. So was he.

I knew within moments he would be upon me. So I abruptly stopped and turned to face him. He was delighted. He came bounding up, tail wagging and eager to be petted. I stroked his face and then dropped onto the sand with exhaustion and relief. Together, we arrived at Main Beach, with his stopping repeatedly to wait for me.

I have metaphorically applied that story to my life many times.

After my husband died, I didn't think I could handle money matters like taxes, interest rates, and investments. I had no choice but to face the fear. I have learned it won't leave me dead on the beach to read a tax form.

Dashing ahead of the Dobermans of life leaves me breathless and scared. Facing them with faith in my heart allows me not only to trust God but to experience victory.

> The Lord is the stronghold of my life—of whom shall I be afraid?
>
> —PSALM 27:1B

Thought . . . Does fear paralyze you? When you call its bluff, often whatever has haunted you will evaporate. And if it doesn't, remember that God is greater than fear. When He is *for* you, who or what can be against you? They simply pale by comparison.

Faith

BY PAQUITA RAWLEIGH

To see a world in a grain of sand and a heaven in a wild flower, hold infinity in the palm of your hand and eternity in an hour.

—WILLIAM BLAKE

"We have the results of your tests," the doctor's words sounded ominous. This was her second pregnancy and it had been a difficult one. "The baby is in stress." The medical professionals said that a decision would have to be made—to continue the pregnancy or terminate it.

We held our breath as the obstetrician finished his report, "The baby could be mentally slow or have spina bifida." My daughter-in-love, a new Christian, cried out, "What should we do?" It was the most terrifying and stressful season of our lives. As we prayed our way through this decision, we cried, "Lord, Thy will be done. Help us Lord!"

Peace flooded our hearts and, in one accord, we instantly knew—this baby was God's gift to us. This child was a bit of heaven, no matter what the rest of the pregnancy brought. I was in God's waiting room, learning to hold infinity in my hand.

My grandchild was delivered and, once again, we awaited the test results as two tiny punctures were made in his back. As the doctor entered the hospital room, he told us the results. "He's all right. The holes at the base of his spine are closed."

We praised God for His faithfulness. Yet, somehow, we knew that if the test results would have been different—God's will still would have been just as faithful.

My grandson is an active, handsome four-year-old. As he bounces off the walls, his shorts cover two tiny scars at the base of his back—permanent reminders of God's grace.

Jesus looked at them and said, "With man this is impossible, but with God all things are possible."

—MATTHEW 19:26

Thought . . . Are you willing to trust the outcome of any situation to God? You can because He loves you unconditionally and promises that every situation will work out for your good, to make you like Jesus (Romans 8:28–29). Trust Him.

Against All Odds

BY CAROLEE REISCH

A little faith will bring your soul to heaven, but a lot of faith will bring heaven to your soul.

—DWIGHT L. MOODY

"I give up! I'm just tired of living."

I kissed him gently and said, "Pop, please say you don't mean that."

Pop would soon celebrate his one-hundredth birthday. For more than twenty years my prayer had been, "Lord, please don't let Pop die without knowing You." I knew that in his late-life season, it would be against all odds.

Pop is one of those rare people who is just naturally good. He felt no need for repentance. Pop believed that simply being good would open heaven's gates to him.

Praying silently, I asked God to break down the barriers of deception.

I praised the Lord as I watched the wall of unbelief begin to crumble as Pop searched for answers to his question, "Will I ever see your mother again?"

Fear and doubt disappeared as the Holy Spirit began to minister to Pop's spirit. One day he said to me, "Carolee, I don't understand something. When I listen to the news on television, I can't hear what they say. But when I'm tuned in to a preacher, I can hear every word." Pop had been almost totally deaf for many years, hearing only through the assistance of hearing aids.

One evening God's Spirit led Pop's nurse to ask him to pray the prayer of faith with her. He said "yes" to Jesus and we rejoiced over a salvation that was, by human standards, against all odds.

The Lord is not slow in keeping His promise, . . . He is patient with you, not wanting anyone to perish, but everyone to come to repentance.

—II PETER 3:9

Thought . . . Have you given up praying for a loved one to receive Christ? We are commanded to pray to the God of all hope. He loves your beloved more than you and with Him, nothing is impossible.

Little Things Do Mean a Lot

BY ANN M. VELIA

Better shun the bait than struggle in the snare.

—JOHN DRYDEN

*W*e love the place we have picked as our retirement home, a
spot in the sunny New Mexico desert. With lots of open land, I
decided to dedicate a small portion as a food garden. The first
season yielded a bumper crop of tomatoes and green beans and
a few undersized, but very sweet cantaloupe.

That fall I spaded sand over the withered vines and settled
back to enjoy our new neighbors: jackrabbits, cottontails, quail,
and assorted squirrels that moved into our neighborhood in great
numbers as winter descended.

We decided to interact, setting out birdseed, carrots, nuts, and—
a favorite with spotted rock squirrels—flour tortillas for our visi-
tors.

The next spring I again planted tomatoes, beans, and cantaloupe. But every plant that poked its head above ground disappeared as soon as our tiny guests discovered it. Our friendliness
to the little critters cost us our garden.

I have found that it is also "little critters" that trouble my Christian walk in every season—seemingly inconsequential traits that
hardly merit the label of "sin," but which eat away at spiritual
vitality.

For example, indifference to problems which, contrary to
popular wisdom, don't go away when they are ignored; or nosi-
ness: prying into matters over which I have no legitimate control and dispensing unsought advice; thoughtlessness, laziness,
tardiness, and disorder, which trouble relationships and hinder
my effectiveness as the Lord's ambassador.

Feeding these traits, rather than discouraging them, costs me
my fruitfulness as Christ's disciple in the harvest into which He
has sent me as co-worker.

> Catch for us the foxes, the little foxes that ruin the vine-
> yards, our vineyards that are in bloom.
> —SONG OF SONGS 2:15

Thought . . . What little things are you tolerating this
year, which you didn't last? Uproot them now so they don't
threaten your growth in the Lord.

Let Go!

BY LYNN D. MORRISSEY

October is the fallen leaf, but it is also a wider horizon more clearly seen. It is the distant hills once more in sight, and the enduring constellations above them once again.

—HAL BORLAND

After the "surprise" birth of my daughter, Sheridan, I wrestled with God over leaving a twenty-year career. It was a wrenching decision, but the Lord pried loose my grip.

As I walked in autumn woods, God guided my decision through the example of colorful leaves, clinging tenaciously to branches, struggling to hold on. Then, as if by some knowledge of God's command, with each gust of wind, they simply let go, entering a graceful waltz, pirouetting with abandon in the breeze. I "heard" God's inaudible command, "Lynn, let go!" and gave my employer notice, committing to enter whatever dance God was choreographing.

Times of depression, doubt, and loneliness ensued. I was a "winter tree," stripped of lush foliage of professional purpose, accolades, and friendships. Yet I knew that though the tree looked dead, it lived; its life wasn't in its leaves, but roots. As I rooted myself in God, I'd bear future fruit.

Trees don't sin by complaining. They bloom in season; and in times of barrenness, their leafless limbs raise in praise to their Maker. Stripped of foliage, they have an unparalleled opportunity to behold stars shining like brilliant jewels between their branches.

I decided to behold life's "stars" I'd been too blind sided to see—blazing constellations of blessings, lighting my darkness—more time to share with my daughter and to pursue my dream of writing.

When, like the autumn leaf, I let go, I entered the beauty of God's dance—finally free to follow Him only, not mammon—experiencing that the only gulf into which I could fall was the palm of my Partner's hand.

He is like a tree planted by streams of water, which yields its fruit in season and whose leaf does not wither. Whatever he does prospers.

—PSALM 1:3

Thought . . . To what are you clinging against God's will? Let go and experience the beauty and joy of release.

Blow a Bubble

BY KAREN KOSMAN

Know you what it is to be a child? . . . It is to believe in love, to believe in loveliness, to believe in belief; it is to be so little that the elves can reach to whisper in your ear; it is to turn pumpkins into coaches, and mice into horses, lowness into loftiness, and nothing into everything, for each child has its fairy godmother in its soul.

—Francis Thompson Shelley

One of God's most precious gifts in this season of my life is the privilege of being a grandmother. To share special moments with my granddaughters is a blessing. Some of those moments teach them about God's love and helping others, while others allow the child within me to surface.

One such occasion occurred when they accompanied me on a trip to Hemet to help a sick friend. On the way home we listened to Christian music. Each of us shared her happiness over our friend's recovery.

Then Staci and Breanna asked, "Grandma, can we have some bubble gum?"

"Sure and I'll have a piece, too."

"Grandma, you like bubble gum?"

"Certainly I do."

"Can you blow bubbles?"

"Of course." Both girls chimed in together, "Blow a bubble, Grandma!"

"Watch this," I said. Then I blew a gigantic bubble.

"Wow! Staci, look at Grandma's big bubble," Breanna announced.

Then disaster struck as a breeze blew in from the open car window. Kablooey! My bubble became a sticky facemask. Laughter filled the car as I tried to clean up the mess.

Then Breanna made a profound statement. "Grandma, you're old, but you're really young." My granddaughter recognized and appreciated the little girl in me. It was a precious moment that we've never forgotten. It was also a sticky lesson.

Children's children are a crown to the aged . . .

—Proverbs 17:6

Thought . . . Are you aware of the little girl who still resides within? Spend time with a child and re-learn the lessons of belief, wonder, discovery, delight, and innocence.

Trials

What Does God Ask of You?

BY JONI EARECKSON TADA

Jesus is all the world to me, my Friend in trials sore.

—WILL L. THOMPSON

Not long ago I was forced to lie in bed flat on my back for a month in order to heal a couple of stubborn pressure sores. That meant canceling a few important appointments and missing some critical deadlines. It meant days of the same old routine: A bed bath. Dressing the wounds. Leg exercises. Breakfast. Waiting. Lunch. Napping. Dinner. Being read to. Prayers and then sleep.

At times it was hard to hold depression at bay, and I was tempted to think, "Now come on, God, none of my Christian friends seems to be faced with these faith-challenging tests. Aren't you asking a bit much?"

Just what does God ask of us? Deuteronomy 10:12 sums it up neatly. All God asks for is . . . everything. If we feel like a martyr faced with heart-wrenching trials, perhaps we're concentrating too much on what God asks of us and not enough on what God has given us.

Is "everything" too much? Think about what God has given you. How much did He hold back? Anything? Of course not. In fact, He gave more than everything. "He who did not spare His own Son but gave Him up for us all—how will He not also, along with Him, graciously give us all things (Romans 8:32)?"

If we're faint-hearted, remember that God has promised us power to help us do all that He asks of us. Even if it is everything.

And now, O Israel, what does the Lord your God ask of you but to fear the Lord your God, to walk in all His ways, to love Him, to serve the Lord your God with all your heart and with all your soul.

—DEUTERONOMY 10:12

Thought . . . Have you given Jesus everything except your body? Remember that when your body is tired or sick, Jesus understands how you feel because He sacrificed His human body for your sins on the Cross.

Nevertheless, Afterward

BY DR. KATHRYN PRESLEY

Afflictions are but the shadow of God's wings.

—GEORGE MACDONALD

No seasons of a woman's life are more instructive than those we live in the Valley of the Shadow of Death and Affliction.

We had prayed for God to conform our family to the image of His Son, forgetting that that might mean polishing, grinding, and cutting. The painful process began in earnest in 1974: sudden death, Alzheimer's disease, cancer, and financial disasters; they came fast and furious.

We learned to dread the telephone's raucous ring. There were nights that we simply knelt around the coffee table and wept before the Lord. Our children were ready for college and my greatest fear was that their faith might be destroyed. However, both of them sailed through the seventies on campuses where chaos reigned, while many of their friends turned away from God.

Today, our children are parents of teens and pre-teens, and I asked them recently why their faith remained strong, why their anchors held (hoping, of course, that they would attribute it to "godly parents")! My son's answer startled me.

"Oh, I don't know, Mother," he said, frowning in concentration. "But I think it was that terrible time when we had to depend on the Lord for everything. In all those tragedies, He always met our needs, though sometimes at the last moment and in ways that we would not have expected. I've never forgotten that."

It takes my breath away! Adversity had not destroyed my children's faith, but strengthened it.

For our light and momentary troubles are achieving for us an eternal glory that far outweighs them all. So we fix our eyes not on what is seen, but on what is unseen. For what is seen is temporary, but what is unseen is eternal.

—II CORINTHIANS 4:17-18

Thought . . . Have you and your family endured horrendous trials that have drawn you closer together and to God? Tests prove the reality of your faith. It is often in adversity that you most experience God's presence and power.

His Magnificent Stained Glass Window

BY SUSAN TITUS OSBORN

The Engineer of the universe has made me part of His whole design.

—LEIGH NYGARD

The vase slipped from my hands and crashed on the kitchen floor. The cut roses lay neatly on the counter, but the crystal jar I had intended for their use was shattered. I could never mend it.

Most of us experience a time when our lives are splintered like that vase. A number of women lose a spouse or child. Others suffer from illnesses or personal problems.

How do we react in crisis? A few do nothing because problems overwhelm them. Other women allow God to use those opportunities to strengthen their faith and shape them in His image.

We can accept God's help, or we can remain on the ground—shattered, bored, hopeless, questioning, rationalizing. The decision is ours.

God created each woman to be unique. He wants us to allow Him to pick up the fractured slivers representing our lives. He will mend and reshape them, once again making us whole.

The stained glass windows of magnificent cathedrals are examples of what can be done with broken glass. If we allow Him, God will use us to form the pieces of His *magnificent stained glass window.* He places each fragment of glass in the perfect place He has chosen.

Each segment of glass depends on every other part for the picture to be complete, but it takes God to hold us together.

Next time you have a chance, observe a stained glass window. Watch the sun piercing through each unique pane of glass. Then notice how many shapes and sizes are necessary to form the whole.

Now you are the body of Christ, and each one of you is a part of it.

—I CORINTHIANS 12:27

Thought . . . Is your life shattered? Give the shards of pain to God to rearrange into a stained glass design. Others will be attracted by your vulnerability, realizing that you can still be beautiful, even having been broken.

Whose Am I, Anyway?

BY ARMENÉ HUMBER

Faith is standing on the fact that God has designed me flawlessly for His purposes in the universe when I feel everything about me is one big mistake.

—PAMELA REEVE

What in the world do I think I'm doing? I asked myself. I was driving to my first consulting job since resigning as a medical sales representative just a month earlier. The idea of packaging my experience and knowledge to work as an independent consultant had seemed like a great idea *then.* But now I wondered if I could really help any small company overcome the obstacles of the healthcare market.

Needing confidence, I instinctively touched my lapel pin. It was a beautiful alabaster lily that my husband had given me as a reminder of the Scripture God had used over the years to forge a healthy identity from my badly damaged self-esteem. "You are a lily (Song of Songs 2:2)," He had told me repeatedly until I finally began to believe that I could do whatever He gave me to do. But this job seemed too big and I had major doubts.

Circling the parking lot, I faced the mounting tension of not finding a parking place. Then, finally, I spotted a car pulling out of a space at the door of my appointment! "Thank you, Lord," I whispered as I pulled into it and turned off the ignition. I glanced through the windshield, then looked again and burst into loud laughter.

There, in full bloom immediately beside the office door, was the largest clump of brilliantly blooming Calla lilies I had ever seen! And in that moment, I knew that I could do anything *through Him!*

I can do everything through Him who gives me strength.
—PHILIPPIANS 4:13

Thought . . . Do you know any LILIES . . . Ladies In the Lord In Every Situation? Christ lives *in* you. And when you face difficulties in *His* strength, you can do anything in any season or situation!

Wearing Love

BY WHITNEY VON LAKE HOPLER

Wise men appreciate all men, for they see the good in each.

—BALTASAR GRACIAN

*O*nce again, my sister-in-law, Terri, and I found ourselves at a family event, uncertain how to make conversation. As we stared at each other across our mother-in-law's living room, I thought of how our previous attempts to develop our relationship had ended in mutual irritation. We were polar opposites: she loved shopping and socializing; I enjoyed frugality and solitude. She didn't understand my passion for writing and I didn't relate to her zeal for cooking. And that was just the beginning!

In the silence, I studied the purple blouse Terri was wearing. That, at least, was one thing I could appreciate. "I like your blouse, Terri," I said hesitantly. "Purple is my favorite color." A smile flashed across her face. "And I like your necklace," she told me. "It's simple, and that's what makes it so elegant."

After that day, we slowly found other small things to appreciate about each other, all of which helped us begin to share something much larger—Christ's love.

. . . clothe yourselves with compassion, kindness, humility, gentleness and patience. Bear with each other and forgive whatever grievances you may have against one another. Forgive as the Lord forgave you. And over all these virtues put on love, which binds them all together in perfect unity.

—COLOSSIANS 3:12-14

Thought . . . How do you break the ice with someone you must see occasionally, but with whom you have no rapport? Make an effort to pay her *just one* compliment. Your genuine kindness will be a welcome surprise and open the door for further conversation.

With Christ in the Storm

BY BETH MOORE

Faith never knows where it is being led, but it loves and knows the One Who is leading.

—OSWALD CHAMBERS

*W*e can be in God's will and still go through terrible storms. Christ loved the disciples, yet "made" them get into the boat when a storm was coming. They were where they were supposed to be and still experienced turbulence.

One of my family's worst storms occurred when Michael, the child we raised for seven years, left our home to return to his birth mother. We received countless cards and letters which were a great comfort to us. Many attributed our loss to Satan and our storm to spiritual warfare. We understood because it was clearly the easier explanation—albeit not necessarily accurate.

God was clear in His message to us. We knew without doubt that Michael's return to his birth mother was the will of God. We were certain God was directing the events.

Christ calls us to walk by faith through storms. It seems a big requirement until we realize that He walks on the water during our storms. God has placed all things under Christ's feet—including waves that break relentlessly against us. He is in charge. He is right there.

Christ walked on water before He calmed the storm. If He had simply calmed the storm, the disciples would have missed His majesty.

We want Christ to hurry and calm the storm. He wants us to find Him in the midst of it first.

A furious squall came up, and the waves broke over the boat, so that it was nearly swamped. Jesus was in the stern, sleeping on a cushion.

—MARK 4:37, 38

Thought . . . How are you handling this stormy season? Jesus may not stop the rain, but He reigns in the midst of the storm. Because He is in control, You can rest in Him.

Mysterious Journey

BY MARY ANN HAMILTON

Each of us has a special role in God's plan, a job nobody else can do. Make the most of your mission and of yourself.

—THE CHRISTOPHERS

There is one final purpose for which God has created you. Until you discover it, your life is a mystery that unfolds only one day at a time. Prayers are answered in ways that you cannot understand, their meaning becoming clear when you least expect it.

Polio dropped a shroud over my life forty-five years ago when I was a young wife and mother of four youngsters. Those children were nurtured by a mother who could do nothing but love and cherish them. With paralyzed arms and respirator-supported breathing, I relied on God to help raise these little ones. I never considered future rewards.

Two years ago I faced open-heart surgery to replace a faulty heart valve. When no local doctors could give me any hope of surviving the surgery, I chose to travel to St. Louis, Missouri, where a polio specialist had his practice.

"If you want to come here," the doctor encouraged, "I'll put together a team of excellent doctors and we'll get you through this."

For six weeks, our children, like guardian angels, took turns flying to St. Louis to bolster their dad in his bedside vigil, boosting my courage and extending their love tenfold.

When we initially left home on my possible "journey of no return," my fear was replaced by faith as I noticed a brand new sign shining beside the highway: It read, "TRUST JESUS." I put my life in *His* hands at that moment. My fear vanished and the mystery of His loving purpose surfaced in countless ways throughout my season of recovery.

Each one should use whatever gift he has received to serve others, faithfully administering God's grace in its various forms.

—I PETER 4:10

Thought . . . For what purpose has God created you? It may now be a mystery, but God wants to help you solve it. If you ask, He will reveal His plan, moment by moment or giant step by giant step. Trust His methods and timing.

Looking to Him

BY VERNETTE F. FULOP

Silently now I wait for Thee, ready, my God, Thy will to see; open my eyes, illumine me, Spirit divine!

—CLARA H. SCOTT

"*I* can't see!" I cried. "Everything is blurry in my left eye." We were at the missionary conference grounds nestled among the mountains near Lake Nojiri, Japan. A local doctor had cauterized my eye and prescribed medicine, but nothing had helped. Now my right eye was beginning to water. "You had better take her to Tokyo," he urged my husband.

"Please, Lord, send us to the right place and remove my fear. It's so awful not to see," I prayed as we drove down the dusty, bumpy roads. My brother-in-law lived at an air base where they sometimes accepted missionary emergencies. It was Sunday and we headed to the emergency room. The doctor on call "happened" to be an eye specialist!

I had contracted a virus. He said that if we had delayed any longer, my eye would have surely ruptured. After his treatment of several days, I could see again. It was wonderful!

I couldn't help but think of how the Lord had guided our path to Tokyo and to exactly the right physician. Words of a familiar hymn kept ringing in my heart as we drove back home: "Open my eyes that I may see, glimpses of truth Thou hast for me . . ."

I need not fear when seasons of danger or disease come, because God will help me if I call upon Him.

I lift up my eyes to the hills—where does my help come from? My help comes from the Lord.

—PSALM 121:1-2A

Thought . . . When you are distressed, do you immediately reach for the telephone to call a friend for advice? Call upon God first. Allow Him to direct your steps.

Stronger When Broken

BY BARBARA CURTIS

How else but through a broken heart may the Lord Christ enter in?

—OSCAR WILDE

I had finally finished unpacking. To celebrate, I gathered my four sons and trekked to the farthest pasture on our new country property to fly a kite.

The day was sparkling, the wind just right. Running quickly, I tugged at the kite string. Suddenly, I was flat on the ground looking into Joshua's worried eyes! He had run behind my legs and I had fallen over him. Reaching up to reassure him, I felt a searing pain in my left arm. My hand was dangling from the wrist at an angle that made me sick to see.

I'm a baby when it comes to pain. Carrying my left hand with my right, I bawled all the way back to the house and all the way in the ambulance to the hospital.

Through the summer season in a hot, heavy cast from fingers to shoulder, I worried that my broken wrist would never be the same. Would I still be able to be the mommy that I needed to be?

Finally, as the doctor was sawing off the cast, I asked him how I could compensate for my weakened joint.

"Oh, you don't have to worry," he said, laughing. "When a broken bone heals, it lays down more bone material. This wrist will be stronger than the one that was never broken."

Ah! Just as in the spirit! When I am broken, God is faithful to heal—but more . . . He leaves me stronger than before.

Heal me, O Lord, and I will be healed . . .

—JEREMIAH 17:14

Thought . . . As you recall trials, can you rejoice? Though you may never wish to repeat feeling pain, you can thank God for His presence and the life-lessons that you never would have experienced otherwise.

 # How, Not If

BY DORIS C. CRANDALL

Stop thinking IF. Next time trouble strikes you, avoid the word if.
Focus on the dynamic word how. Don't run away from your problem.
Face it. Then fight it out.

—NORMAN VINCENT PEALE

I tiptoed into the kitchen to fix lunch for my husband. I didn't
want Lottie, my older sister who had had a stroke, to hear me or
I knew that she'd come to assist me. Her *help* really tried my
patience. She couldn't use a knife and could get burned easily
on the cooktop. Having a disabled helper was new to me. *Lord,
if only, if only . . . my husband had a longer lunch hour*, I thought.

Then, thud-drag, I heard Lottie's right foot dig into the carpet and force her wheelchair toward the kitchen.

"I've got it under control," I said, "I won't need help." The
disappointed look on her face stabbed my heart.

I can't stand this, I thought. Reaching into the refrigerator, I
noticed the crisp head of lettuce. A thought struck me—Lottie
can tear this lettuce into bite-sized pieces for a salad!

Another thought struck me, but this time it didn't come entirely from me. I'm certain God spoke to my heart, "Plan meals
so there will always be something Lottie can prepare. For start-
ers, she can stem strawberries with a spoon."

And that day, God started a work of compassion in my heart
that I have never forgotten.

Be kind and compassionate to one another . . .
—EPHESIANS 4:32

Thought . . . Do you know disabled people whom you
could involve in your life in some *tangible* way? Just
your taking time to notice and show kindness, could
make all the difference in their lives.

The Three Locks

BY CORRIE TEN BOOM

My chains fell off, my heart was free. I rose, went forth, and followed Thee.

—CHARLES WESLEY

*Th*ree times in my life locks were closed and, after a time of
imprisonment, opened again.

The Lord made me learn that, for a child of God, a pit can be
very deep, but always below us are the everlasting arms.

The first lock left me in a cell in solitary confinement for four
months. Fellowship with the Lord was so precious that I wrote
to friends, "Please never worry about me; it may be dark, but the
Savior provides His light."

My sister Betsie, in a different cell, wrote, "This horror has
come from God's loving hands to purify me."

The second lock closed in Vught concentration camp. I wrote,
"We are in God's training school continually protected by extraordinary providence. God knows the way; we are at peace."

The third lock closed in Ravensbruck, the terrible concentration camp. For Betsie, the lock was opened when the Lord
took her to Him.

For me the door opened to a wide world where I became a
tramp for the Lord, going wherever I could tell that when the
worst happens in the life of a child of God, the best is yet to be.

Whom the Lord makes free, is free indeed—that I saw in the
lives of people behind the locks of bondage to drugs, alcohol,
and smoking.

Self is a tight lock. Sinners were in spiritual prison because
self was on the throne of their hearts. Liberation came when
Jesus cleansed the heart with His blood. He came to the throne,
and self went on the cross.

The Lord sets prisoners free.

—PSALM 146:7B

Thought . . . Is there still a closed lock in your life? Jesus
is the key Who is willing to set you free! Turn to Him.

Right Here

BY DIANNE E. BUTTS

Each of you has been given a specific mission. You and I often feel inadequate to the task, but I learned a long time ago that the . . . assignments God has given me cannot be [done] quite as well by anyone else.

—SALLY E. STUART

"I'm sorry, I don't accept speaking engagements," I informed the nice lady on the phone. That was the third call this week asking me to speak to a special group or at a school and I was beginning to wonder if the Lord were trying to tell me something.

Lord, do You want me to say yes to these speaking opportunities? I prayed as I hung up the phone, setting it down on my writing desk.

The Lord and I had been through this conversation many times before. I had never been able to overcome "stage fright"— my extreme panic, shaking, and shortness of breath resulting from even the *thought* of being up in front of people. My inability to control it frustrated me. *If only I could conquer it . . . If only I didn't have this problem in the first place,* I wrestled.

Why won't You heal me of this, Lord, I asked for the zillionth time. *If you would, I could be out there speaking . . .*

Before I had finished my thoughts, in one of those rare moments when His answer came to my mind so quickly that I knew it must be His, I felt Him say, "Because if I did, you'd be out there speaking. I want you here."

Here . . . Here for this season . . . I looked around at my little writing desk and at all my writing projects sprawled across it.

Without further hesitation, I picked up my pencil and went back to work.

For we are God's workmanship, created in Christ Jesus to do good works, which God prepared in advance for us to do.

—EPHESIANS 2:10

Thought . . . Is the way blocked for you to pursue a certain ministry? God, alone, opens and closes doors. If the door remains shut, continue to do God's work with all your heart right where you are. You are in the right place.

Hope

BY TERESA ARSENEAU

You don't have to know why God let you be hurt. The fact is, God knows and that's all that counts. Just trust Him to work things out for good, eventually, if not right now.

—JONI EARECKSON TADA

*M*ost of my life I have kept personal journals, but I had never thought of naming these books seasonally as some people do—until 1994. My mother had died, my father was planning to remarry within a month of her passing, my marriage was falling apart, and our teenage sons had rebelled against God. The tension in our home could be cut with a knife.

My diary entries had dissolved into angry, desperate scrawlings of hatred for life. My supreme wish was that I would go to sleep and never wake up.

Then the Lord directed me to put away that book and start afresh with a new journal named *Season of Hope*. It seemed ridiculous, but I did it. I determined to fill this book only with hopeful thoughts, even when I felt despondent.

Despair gradually began to lift and a miraculous healing took place in my marriage and family. Although not all things changed, the way I viewed them did.

I now recognize God's hand of mercy in my father's new marriage and even in my mother's death. My sons are still going their own ways, but if there is one thing I have learned, it is this: The Word of the Lord is sure and true and His Promises are unfailing. And because God is with me, I always, always have hope.

I pray also that the eyes of your heart may be enlightened in order that you may know the hope to which He has called you, the riches of this glorious inheritance in the saints and His incomparably great power for us who believe.

—EPHESIANS 1:18-19A

Thought . . . Are you harboring depression and anger because of your circumstances? Concentrate, instead, on the God of all hope, by reading His Word and keeping a *hope journal*. Though your situation may not change immediately, you will be at peace in the midst of it.

No One Likes Me

BY MARY HAKE

God loves us the way we are but He loves us too much to leave us that way.

—LEIGHTON FORD

*R*ushing in the door after school, I had collapsed into my mother's arms, sobbing, spilling out my devastating news. Another fourth-grader had told me, "No one really likes you."

Shocked at this revelation, I lost all self-confidence and began to doubt my worth. I wanted desperately to have friends. Not understanding what had brought about their rejection, I developed an inferiority complex.

This struggle continued throughout my school years and into marriage and motherhood. I knew that my husband, Ted, truly loved me, although I could hardly believe he did.

When I learned of Christ's great love and free offer of salvation, I eagerly embraced it. I now understood that God loved me, but I still felt He must have made a mistake in choosing me. I couldn't accept myself the way I was.

I began attending a ladies' Bible study. Other women were friendly, but I was certain that they couldn't really like "messed-up" me. Even when others assured me that they appreciated me, I couldn't convince myself of their sincerity.

Several years after becoming a Christian, I attended a ladies' retreat. Following her evening message, the speaker directed small groups to pray for each person. I shared my "secret" and accepted the women's prayers.

Suddenly, I could feel my burden slip away. The sense of inferiority I had carried for such a long season had vanished completely and instantaneously!

Freed from this overwhelming encumbrance, I could now better accept and minister to others because my focus was no longer on myself. How I thank God for this inner healing.

So if the Son sets you free, you will be free indeed.

—JOHN 8:36

Thought . . . Do feelings of inferiority plague you? Find your self-worth in Christ, Who loved you enough to die for you. Then tell others that He loves them, too.

Rainbow in Winter

BY LUCI SHAW

The soul would have no rainbow had the eyes no tears.

—JOHN VANCE CHENEY

Such a simple, unremarkable moment. A dark, rainy day in late winter. My granddaughter Lauren, six, painting at a table near a window, quite unconscious of my scrutiny of her.

But the promise I received as I watched her laying the wet colors down on paper felt potent, as real to me as the covenant the Lord God made with Noah after the Great Flood.

He promised Noah that He would never again destroy by water all the living creatures on the earth. What I received in a child's painted rainbow was also a promise of life—that the days would lengthen, that the joy of spring and green would return, and that once again God would paint His iridescence wherever the sun shone on the rain's falling moisture. It is only when the two work together—sun with rain, joy with tears—that we see the glowing ribbon of a rainbow and the promise that comes with it.

Restore us to Yourself, O Lord, that we may return; renew our days as of old.

—LAMENTATIONS 5:21

Thought . . . Are you experiencing a season of despair? Take comfort in knowing that God loves you so much that He collects your tears in His bottle (Psalm 56:8). He will transform every tear into a rainbow because of His promise—that though weeping may last for the night, joy comes in the morning (Psalm 30:5).

EDITOR'S NOTE: Ms. Shaw wrote this piece several months following her husband Harold's untimely death from cancer.

Contrasts

BY LUCI SHAW

The dark is as real as the light; God allows us to experience both so we will know the difference.

—LUCI SHAW

*L*ast spring my journal recorded a sudden change: "All the rain, sleet, melting ice, and warming southerly winds mean that there is too much water for the sodden ground to absorb—and there's no place for it to go. Every ditch and furrow and stream brims and glitters with water. As I travel the country roads I see the sky reflected in places I've never seen it before!

"Each night the temperature dips. Frost catches and controls the flooding until the next day. But during last night's darkness the level of the river dropped dramatically, leaving the saplings along its banks collared with lacy scallops of ice, with the black water churning away two feet below."

Contrasts—warm to cold, high to low, shadow to brightness, smooth to rough—without each we lose the meaning of the other. Without struggle and storm the slick, sunlit days would dream along, serene and unremarkable, taken for granted. Without the dry, hopeless stretches in our emotional or spiritual seasons we might get bored with blessing; grace might seem stale.

Change and renewal dance into our lives dynamically, intersecting the humdrum, with its flatness and decay. I praise my Creator for building into our universe some extraordinary excursions into the unknown, for planning the contrasts and shifts of seasons, for the infinity of space as well as the gentle glow of light shining through a leaf or the wood grain in a floorboard.

I am the Lord, and there is no other. I form the light and create darkness . . .

—ISAIAH 45:6B–7

Thought . . . In what season of life are you now? Savor every season as God's extraordinary gift, brimming with opportunities to experience His variety, grace, and renewal. Even seasons of trial can bring great blessing.

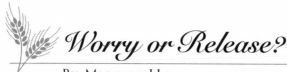

Worry or Release?

BY MICHELE HOWE

Our bodies have been constructed to withstand an enormous amount of stress and pressure . . . if. If we don't lose the one essential ingredient. Hope.

—CHARLES R. SWINDOLL

When my daughter's facial "ticks" became more apparent and persistent, we finally headed to a neurologist. His diagnosis was what we had long suspected: Tourette's Syndrome. While Corinne's condition is mild, there are times when she is unable to sit quietly without her hands, feet, or both moving to some sort of internal rhythm. Other days, she makes a consistent auditory sound of which she seems blissfully unaware.

On those days when Corinne's condition is painfully obvious, it hurts us all. As her parent, I worry about each season of her life—her present condition and her future handling of this disorder as an adult. Not surprisingly, my own emotional well-being greatly influences the type of day our family experiences.

I cannot fathom what the coming years will bring for Corinne—or for myself, for that matter. Yet, right now I can follow what Jesus lovingly instructed so long ago, "Do not worry about tomorrow . . . " When I choose to allow God to hold my worries in His capable hands, I am released to use my own hands to bring new hope, love, and comfort to those around me. I can only fully give to others when I let go of my anxious thoughts.

It is ironic to realize that in God's economy, my "letting go" is what ushers in His wealth of courage, strength, and resolve. Releasing my worries is the only act worthy of God's love.

Say to those with fearful hearts, "Be strong, do not fear; your God will come . . ."

—ISAIAH 35:4

Thought . . . Are you experiencing a season of worry? Release your worries to God through prayer, leaving room for His peace to flood your soul. You have His promise that it will (Philippians 4:6–7).

Learning to See

BY GAYLE CLOUD

If only we knew what miracles precede us on even the most ordinary of days.

—KEVAN CLOUD

I was raised in the Church and learned lots of Scripture, but I discovered the difficulty was in applying the Word. I especially had a lot to learn from those children of Israel who wandered forty years in the wilderness!

During a particularly trying time of my early married life, I found myself with two young children and a husband with a shaky job situation. As God would have it, I was reading through my Bible and came across those Israelites right about that time. They grumbled about everything: food, water, circumstances, etc., yet God *always* supplied their needs. They should have been grateful to escape the Egyptians and see God's miraculous hand extended on their behalf, but instead they complained.

I, too, had complained to God about my circumstances. I was no different from those Israelites! I, too, had seen miracles of His provision. I had to admit that God had a wonderful sense of timing and I was thankful that He had awakened me. I determined to feel blessed instead of acting grumpy.

Then my circumstances changed, as well. My husband got a better job and we went on to other seasons of life, but I have never forgotten the lesson God showed me: the Bible is filled with folks just like I who learned the lessons I often need to learn. Maybe I can learn from their experience and bypass the grumbling next time—or better yet, rejoice in the midst of trials!

Rejoice in the Lord always. I will say it again: Rejoice!
—PHILIPPIANS 4:4

Thought . . . Is grumbling your cup of tea? In the end, it is a bitter brew. Why not keep a joy journal, noting daily *at least one* thing for which you can be grateful. Noticing just one of God's blessings often leads to recording a whole litany of praise.

Revived by Love

BY PAMELA ENDERBY

The more hopeless and helpless we feel, the more we must believe that there is someone far greater than we, someone who loves us, who wants to take over our lives for our blessing and our fulfillment.

—ELISABETH ELLIOT

The alarm jolted me awake. Sluggishly, I pulled myself up and attempted to meet with God. After spending the night changing soiled bedding and nursing Anna's fever with tepid water, Scripture sounded just as dull as it appeared on the page.

Exercise will revive me, I reasoned. As I pumped my legs on the health rider, my indignation escalated and, finally, exploded. "Lord I have nothing to give to You or to anyone else. I'm always the one giving to others. Don't expect anything from me today." After a few more pushes, my remorse quieted my anger. I sat motionlessly and wept, "Please help me, Lord."

I ambled into the shower and dropped my head under the pulsating water. To my surprise, I felt I heard God whisper, "I don't need or want anything from you; just give me yourself." *Myself?—angry, tired, and full of self-pity? Why would He want me?* I wondered.

He reminded me of how Anna had interrupted my sleep; yet I had tenderly cared for her. Likewise, He wanted to embrace me now, tired and defeated as I felt.

Cautiously, I opened my clenched fists. His warm embrace melted my reluctance and I offered Him my heart as it was, filled with selfishness and anger. This gesture became my gateway to life that day.

I'm learning that raw honesty unlocks the door to my closed heart, allowing God to reach in and touch my deepest needs. In my seasons of surrender, He pours on me an abundance of peace and patience, love and strength.

> But now He has reconciled you by Christ's physical body through death to present you holy in His sight, without blemish and free from accusation . . .
>
> —COLOSSIANS 1:22

Thought . . . Is Jesus knocking on the door of your heart? Unbar the lock of resistance through honesty. You will experience peace because you will have welcomed the Prince of Peace.

Serendipity

Everything I Need

BY KAREN O'CONNOR

Our Creator would never have made such lovely days and have given us the deep hearts to enjoy them unless we were meant to be immortal.

—NATHANIEL HAWTHORNE

As I hiked to the top of Half Dome Mountain, I had an experience that forever changes the way I view God's presence. This was a trip I wanted to take for years so I planned every detail. I hiked weekly to build my endurance, learned about tents and sleeping bags and stoves and dehydrated food. On the morning of our ascent I awoke early, eager to get started. I wanted to experience it fully, with no regrets.

Halfway up the steep rock face, I did something I never thought I could. I stopped, turned around, and stood facing out. There was no room for a false step so I held onto the cable. Then I took a deep breath and looked!

In front of me—everywhere I gazed—was a visual feast of massive pines hovering over giant cliffs and majestic peaks jutting into the deep blue sky. I could scarcely take it in. It was so much more than I had expected. I thought, this is a holy place. God is here. I had been so caught up in the physical details of the trip that I had not thought about the spiritual impact. "Oh God," I prayed, "thank You for Your presence here—in the trees and peaks and boulders, waterfalls, and flowers. Everything I need and want—physically and spiritually—is right here with You."

I didn't need lovely clothes, a new car, theater tickets, or a gourmet meal.

God was here with me—in this wild place—meeting my every need and desire. How could I not notice His presence!

If I go up to the heavens, You are there; if I make my bed in the depths, You are there.

—PSALM 139:8

Thought . . . Is God all you want? Sometimes He'll remove all your worldly trappings to show you that He is all you really need. In fact, He is greater than any of your desires.

Parachute Answers

BY LINDA EVANS SHEPHERD

Afflictions are but the shadow of God's wings.

—GEORGE MACDONALD

I drove upon the scene of a car crash and my mind flashed back to my own car accident, several years before. I remembered hunching over the limp body of my baby daughter, wondering if she would live or die. The sound of sirens jolted my thoughts to the present.

"Jesus," I prayed, "those people need your help! Show them how much You love them."

I was startled when my four-year-old son shouted a prayer of his own. "Jesus!" he pleaded, "put on Your parachute and get down here!"

Looking skyward, I could picture Jesus and a multitude of angels gliding toward the rescue operation on wings of heavenly silk.

Suddenly, the memory of my own tragedy changed. Instead of seeing myself alone on the side of the highway, crying over my injured daughter, I realized that Jesus had been by my side, but at the time of the accident I had been unaware of His presence.

As I replayed the scene in my mind, I could almost see His arm around my shoulders. I could imagine the compassionate expression on His face as I cried out to Him for help.

King David said, "The Lord is near to those who have a broken heart (Psalm 34:18)."

While I waited ten months for my daughter, Laura, to awaken from her coma, I was never alone. God was always with me, even in a season when I could not recognize His presence.

He will cover you with His feathers, and under His wings you will find refuge.

—PSALM 91:4A

Thought . . . Do you need to feel Jesus' presence in this season of tragedy? Cry out to Him. He promises to comfort those who mourn and to offer peace beyond understanding (Philippians 4:6–7).

With an Everlasting Love

BY GRACIE MALONE

Love so amazing, so divine, demands my soul, my life, my all.

—ISAAC WATTS

*H*omebound for several months with a serious and painful illness, I struggled to keep my spiritual equilibrium. I had dedicated my life to God and thought that we were friends, but now when I needed Him most, I felt forsaken and alone. "God, why did this happen to me?" I asked. "Do You love me? Have I sinned?"

The next morning I read Jeremiah 31:3, "I have loved you with an everlasting love."

Today I marvel that I had the audacity to challenge the Almighty. But I'll never forget my reaction to reading that verse. "No, You don't!" I yelled. In a fit of frustration, I grasped a handful of pages and tried to rip them out of my Bible, but they were sewn in too tightly, and I was too weak. I slammed the Bible on the night stand and sobbed.

Later, our eight-year-old son, Jason, asked, "Mom, what are we having for supper?"

"Oh, I don't know. But, you know what I wish?" Jason shook his head, then I finished my thought, "I wish I were well enough to cook chicken and dumplings for you."

"And chocolate pie!" Jason added.

"Yeah," I agreed, "and chocolate pie! As soon as I am well, Jason, as soon as I am well . . . "

That evening the doorbell rang. Unaware of our conversation, one of my friends stood at the door bearing a gift in a big steaming pot: chicken and dumplings! Before my husband, Joe, could set the table, another friend arrived with dessert. Yes, a chocolate pie!

As I took a bite of the warm dumplings, sampled the pie, and sipped coffee, I thought,

You do, don't You? You do love me with everlasting love!

. . . with everlasting kindness I will have compassion on you . . .

—ISAIAH 54:8

Thought . . . In this difficult season, do you think that God has forgotten you? As a reminder, He has "engraved" you eternally on the nail-scarred palms of His Son, Jesus (Isaiah 49:25).

The Christmas Gift

BY LYNN D. MORRISSEY

If we're tuned to epiphanies—those guiding flashes of sacred insight—they happen, usually when we need them most.

—SUE MONK KIDD

In the still of winter, death's darkness enveloped me. Birdless, leafless trees and my father's incurable kidney disease testified to death's stark reality. I was consumed with worry, unable to experience God's peace and to trust His provision for my father.

As I dropped off Daddy at the dialysis center for the third time during Christmas week, I was struck by the poignancy of a naked little tree, bravely defying winter's onslaught. It was a painful reminder of my father's frailty and failing health.

Then suddenly, as if dropped from heaven, a beautiful, red-breasted robin alighted on one of its branches, adorning it like a ruby Christmas ornament. In the bleak winter season, I was amazed to see this little harbinger of spring. I praised God for this unexpected Christmas gift of hope, and for the precious gift of time—another day with my father.

Most of all, I praised God for His most lavish Christmas gift, His precious Son, born into this world of sin and death. He would die for humankind on a naked tree and rise victoriously from a wintery tomb. He would defy death and usher in new life, the springtime of eternity.

Instantly, I stopped worrying. God flooded my heart with peace and the knowledge that no matter what happened to Daddy, he would live eternally with Him.

Where, O death, is your victory? Where, O death, is your sting?

—I CORINTHIANS 15:55

Thought . . . How can you have the courage to face terrible trials? Turn to Jesus. Through His crucifixion and resurrection, He overcame the power of death and provided the promise of eternal life. He promised victory!

God's Budget Plan

BY SHARON P. MOORE

For it is in giving that we receive.

—ATTRIBUTED TO SAINT FRANCIS OF ASSISI

In this financially constrained season, with a large family and a limited budget, I rarely bought new clothes. One summer, though, with money I had saved, I shopped for a blazer to wear in the Christian school office. It had to be warm, match my other clothes, *and* be in my price range.

I still had the special shopping money when I heard missionaries from our church speak of needs overseas. As well as working in a hospital office and teaching Bible classes, they operated a guesthouse for traveling missionaries, many with young children.

I first saw "The Doll" on yet another shopping trip for a blazer. She was on the missionaries' "wish list." She was exquisite, with curly black hair, thick lashes, a pink dress, matching socks, and white kid shoes. Her price tag marked her as a doll about which little missionary girls could only dream.

"That money was for you, Honey," my husband protested, when he saw the doll. "What about your blazer?"

"I have a little bit of money left," I answered. "I can make one."

But summer ended and I sat at my desk in the school office before I found time to sit at my sewing machine.

The Lord was working, though. That fall, He produced not one, but three blazers—red, black, and beige, each with matching skirt. They were gifts from friends unaware of my need.

I was overwhelmed, but not really surprised. God's blessings are always far greater than our budget plans!

. . . If someone takes your cloak, do not stop him from taking your tunic. Give to everyone who asks you . . . Do to others as you would have them to do to you.

—LUKE 6:29-31

Thought . . . Is the Lord prompting you to give sacrificially? Quite often, He will give you something far greater in return. But, regardless, the satisfaction you will receive in making someone happy will far surpass your sacrifice.

88

Blackbird Ballet

BY BRENDA WAGGONER

He stands at the windows of the easily overlooked and the unlikely, tapping at the pane. He beckons us to places of encounter where we learn how well He understands the language of our hearts.

—KEN GIRE

On a blustery January Sunday afternoon, I stood at the kitchen sink peeling potatoes for an early dinner. A Vivaldi oboe sonata in B flat major played on the stereo. Glancing out the window, I caught sight of a large flock of blackbirds flying in for a landing behind our house. As the adagio transitioned into an allegro, the birds gracefully lowered their little bodies onto the ground as if choreographed with deliberate precision to fit a classical ballet. After a few minutes of quiet chatting and searching out a winter day's feeding, the birds arose in magnificent unison, flew a few feet to the left, then turned their sleek black bodies in the opposite direction and slowly departed. The allegro section of the sonata melted into a largo as I watched the birds flying at a distance, shimmering like a generous handful of black glitter sprinkled across the cold, gray sky.

In the least likely of places—our own back yards—God speaks to us, displaying His majesty and grace in everyday, seasonal settings. How tenderly He calls us to Himself. In the quiet moments, He comes.

Sh-h-h-h.

Can you hear Him?

The heavens declare the glory of God; the skies proclaim the work of his hands.

—PSALM 19:1

Thought . . . Do you detect the sacred in the secular?. . . magnificent in the mundane? . . . Omnipresent in the ordinary? When you open your eyes to see the Creator in creation, your world will shine with splendor. You will never be the same.

Five Little Angels

BY KATY PENNER

Children are not casual guests in our home. They have been lent to us temporarily for the purpose of loving them.

—JAMES C. DOBSON

*S*tuff! Stuff! Stuff! I sat in the midst of tons of stuff, wondering what to take home, what to trash, what to give away. Decisions made me weary! Photographs and significant letters could go into the burgundy suitcase. But what of this book of poetry with its lovely photographs, so comforting on many a lonely day? Would I want this musty, moldy book with its yellowed pages displayed on my coffee table in Canada? These towels, dishes, pots and pans should go to my house help, I decided. Just as I labeled them, my reverie was interrupted by the shuffling of little bare feet coming through the kitchen.

Quietly, without a word, without the usual greeting, five little girls, ages three to five, came in, sat down, and said, "Just keep on working, Mama. We have just come to sit with you for awhile."

And so they quietly sat there for about ten minutes. Suddenly my *stuff* did not seem that important. I realized that friendships and relationships were much more precious. Then, in beautiful harmony, the girls sang all four verses and the chorus of a little Lingala song, "Jezu azali awa," which means, "Jesus is here with us."

After a little talk and a short prayer, as quietly as they came, they slipped out! Tears trickled down my cheeks. How could I be so concerned about stuff when there were relationships waiting to be nurtured? This was a holy moment. I had been visited by angels!

See that you do not look down on one of these little ones. For I tell you that their angels in Heaven always see the face of my Father in Heaven.

—MATTHEW 18:10

Thought . . . Are people more important to you than possessions? You can tell by how much time you spend with each.

A Different Outlook

BY SYLVIA DUNCAN

So absolutely good is truth, truth never hurts the teller.

—ROBERT BROWNING

The entryway to the grocery store was crowded on the day before Thanksgiving. I concentrated on my shopping list, trying to block out the noise of cash registers and excited children.

As I selected a shopping cart I saw a man with a cane, assisted by a young woman. He paused to look out through the gleaming plate glass window, illuminated by the late afternoon sun. Then I heard his strong voice as he exclaimed, "This is the day the Lord hath made. Look at those chrysanthemums!"

"Come on, Dad. We don't have time for that kind of stuff," said the woman impatiently. "I still have to take you to the doctor's this afternoon." She tried to lead him on, almost pushing him in her embarrassment about his quoting the Bible aloud in this crowded place.

Then she noticed several of us gazing out the window at the parking lot which had been landscaped recently. Her arm relaxed on her father's shoulder and she stopped. We had all walked by the flowers in the sunshine a few minutes ago. Now we noticed them in a new way.

"Thanks," I said softly to the man. He had shown courage by praising the Lord publicly in this Thanksgiving season in an everyday situation. It is something I don't do very often.

He said to them, "Go into all the world and preach the good news to all creation."

—MARK 16:15

Thought . . . In what ways can you naturally praise God in public, drawing attention to Him? An easy place to start is noticing His glory in nature. Your comments might be the catalyst to prompt a non-believer to *see* God.

Apples of Gold

BY REBECCA BARLOW JORDAN

A well-timed word has the power to urge a runner to finish the race, to rekindle hope, to spark a bit of warmth, to renew confidence when problems have the upper hand.

—LAWRENCE J. CRABB, JR. AND DAN B. ALLENDER

*W*ith mixed feelings, I walked away from the chartreuse Sunday School classroom, painted by ambitious thirteen-year-olds the year before.

Today had been my last opportunity to teach these girls God's valuable truths. Yet, like a misguided arrow, my commitment, and theirs, had fallen short. I had seen no evidence of growth. Had I affected even one teen? In this season of life as a young teacher and minister's wife, all I could see was failure—so much left to do and no time to accomplish God's work for these girls.

As I trudged up the stairs of our dingy, stucco church basement, one of my shy eighth graders met me halfway. She tossed a hand-written, crumpled note into my hand. Like a child playing hide and seek, she quickly turned away, apparently embarrassed at her impulsive gesture. I carefully unfolded the note. There, among a garland of artistic flowers, were three words in bold print and underlined: **THANKS FOR EVERYTHING**! Other encouraging words followed. Like the ten lepers Jesus had healed, only one had returned to say "Thanks!" But it was all that I needed.

Seasons of drought affect us all. But I am glad that Heaven often sends us a visible shower of encouragement—*God with skin on*—to remind us that our work is not in vain. Each time I feel discouraged, that student's simple words of gratitude still shine in my heart like a harvest of golden apples.

A word aptly spoken is like apples of gold in settings of silver.

—PROVERBS 25:11

Thought . . . Do you speak *apt* words of encouragement in times of need? If you put your words *in writing*, the recipient can enjoy them again and again in any season.

Patterns for God

BY GWEN ELLIS

My life is but a weaving betwixt my God and me; I do not choose
the colors He worketh steadily. Not till the loom is silent and the
shuttles cease to fly, will God unfold the pattern and explain the
reason why.

—GRANT TULLER

The most vivid memory I have of my grandmother is of her
stabbing a needle in and out of a quilt held by a hoop.

She first cut fabrics into shapes. Some were dark, some brilliant. She knew what she was creating. She could see the pattern and understood the need for contrast.

Grandma put pieces of our lives into her quilts. There were
scraps left after cutting a baby dress, tag ends of a dress, or a
shirt. Skillfully, she joined them into quilt patterns.

She was an artisan of scraps and castoffs and made something beautiful.

I'm fascinated by the intricacies of the patterns, the colors
chosen. I step back to view the whole, and the pattern emerges.
The reason for the choice of colors is obvious.

Our lives are like patchwork quilts. When we view the pieces
of our lives—joys, sorrows, health, illness, marriage, obedient
children, willful children—often we can't see the pattern. We're
so close to what's happening we can't see the whole. But the
Ultimate Quilter, Father God, is at work. From our vantage point
we can't see that God is creating something beautiful, but He is.

Trust that God knows what He's doing and that someday
He's going to let you see the pattern of your whole life. Then
you'll understand why the dark times were necessary to bring
out the beauty of the whole person you are becoming. You'll be
glad you let Him choose.

We know that to those who love God, who are called according to His plan, everything that happens fits into a
pattern for good.

—ROMANS 8:28 (PHILLIPS)

Thought . . . Is your life filled with darkness, chaos, and
broken pieces? Let God create a mosaic from life's
shards and let Jesus, the "Sonshine," in.

The Glory of God

BY PAULINE RAEL JARAMILLO

A moment's insight is sometimes worth a life's experience.

—OLIVER WENDELL HOLMES

I locked the classroom door and walked across the parking lot. It was Friday and I was anticipating a quiet, relaxing weekend at home. Moments later, I was sitting forward, gripping the steering wheel as I inched my way up the mountain. It was snowing heavily.

When the car began to slide sideways, I decided to park and walk the rest of the way. I opened the trunk to get my snow boots. They weren't there! My daughter had borrowed them and must have forgotten to return them. I looked at the snow accumulating on top of my high-heeled shoes and slammed the trunk lid shut.

My anger grew with each step. "How dare she forget!" I said, fuming. "She's restricted for a week. Two weeks! Wait till I see her."

Finally, I paused to catch my breath. I leaned against a fence post and suddenly looked up. Snowflakes brushed their gentle caress on my cheeks and playfully caught on my eyelashes. They tickled the tip of my nose as they melted. I laughed and held out my hands amazed by the detail and beauty of each and every snowflake.

My daughter met me at the door, my boots in her outstretched hand. "I'm sorry I forgot, Mom." I set the boots on the floor and without a word drew her outside. We stood hand in hand for several minutes watching the snowflakes glide gently to earth. My anger was completely forgotten as we observed that "the heavens declared the glory of God . . . " in this exquisite wintry season.

The Lord is slow to anger, abounding in love and forgiving sin and rebellion.

—NUMBERS 14:18A

Thought . . . How do you handle anger? It's easy to let it melt like falling snow when you realize how much the Lord has forgiven you and how slow He is to become angry.

Hidden Strengths

BY ARMENÉ HUMBER

As Christians we are called to be healed helpers, moving not out of strength, but out of weakness.

—David A. Seamands

I couldn't believe it. There on the driveway huddled over a small pile of dried leaves were my two young sons, obviously trying to set the leaves on fire by angling their new magnifying glass over them to catch the sun's rays. I watched through the curtains as they patiently held the glass up to the sun and waited for fire. A few minutes later, a tiny stream of smoke rose from the leaves, followed by flames that quickly devoured them.

Satisfied that the fire had burned itself out, I turned from the window, entering the powerful stillness of one of those life-changing "God-moments." The Lord seemed to whisper, "What if you were to think of that magnifying glass as your weakness, the one you keep in your pocket, hidden because of the pain and embarrassment it brings you? What if you were to take it out into the open and focus it toward Me, angling it so that I, the Son, could shine through it? Do you realize how My power, focused through it, could ignite and consume all those situations about which you are struggling? Do you want to trust Me and give it a try?"

Twenty-two years later I still remember that magnifying glass and remind myself that my seasons of weakness are usually the very points at which God works most powerfully. Then I take the weakness out of hiding and angle it honestly up to Him again. And I am consumed with His strength.

Not that we are competent in ourselves to claim anything for our ourselves, but our competence comes from God.
—II Corinthians 4:5

Thought . . . Can you consider your weakness an asset? Instead of struggling with seasons of inadequacy, common to all, see them as opportunities to learn God's greatest lessons—to experience His greatest power.

God Is Always Ready

BY JENNIFER KENNEDY DEAN

Suppose prayer is primarily allowing ourselves to be loved, addressed and claimed by God. What if praying means opening ourselves to the gift of God's own self and presence? What if our part in prayer is primarily letting God be giver?

—MARTIN SMITH

God knows what you need before you ask Him. Before you call, He has prepared the answer. You may be caught off guard in your need, but God is not. The purpose of your supplication is not to inform God. The purpose of your supplication is to accept that which God wants to offer.

One day one of my sons had an embarrassing incident occur at school. I was told about it by a neighbor who happened to see it. As soon as I heard, I knew that he needed to be encouraged and loved and would need me to help him put it into perspective. All day I planned how I could help him when he came home from school. I was not only prepared, but eager to help.

To my surprise and disappointment, he did not tell me about it right away. I had determined that I should wait until he brought it up. It was several days before he told me. During those days I was longing to give him what he needed. I waited eagerly for him to give me access to his need. It was during those few days that God told me, "This is how I feel when you do not turn to Me in every need. I am overflowing with love toward you and long for you to come to Me and accept My provision for every detail of your life. I have everything prepared and am only waiting for you to ask."

Your Father knows what you need before you ask Him.
—MATTHEW 6:8

Thought . . . Though you realize that God knows your needs, have you considered that He longs for you to tell Him, because He loves you and desires intimate interaction with you? Prayer's purpose is more for developing a relationship than for submitting requests.

# Beware of the Bear

BY KATHLEEN HAGBERG

Judge a tree from its fruit; not from the leaves.

—EURIPIDES

*A*month into his new paper route, my ten-year-old son, Paul, received a late-evening telephone call. "I'm sorry," my son whispered, "I guess I forgot."

"Hurry, mom, we gotta go now," Paul insisted. "Mr. Ware is real mad that I forgot to give him his paper. And he wants it . . . RIGHT NOW!"

Past paperboys had warned Paul to *beware of the bear*. Not only had Paul been shorted one paper, but he had overlooked, of all customers, Mr. Ware the Bear!

We dashed off to the convenience store to purchase a paper. Paul ran inside leaving me to wonder if the route were worth such aggravation.

As we pulled into Bear's driveway, a shadowy figure peered out from behind the curtain. As Paul sprinted up to the house, I surveyed the weed-infested garden, unmown lawn, and lopsided shutters. What else, I thought, could you expect from a surly *old bear*. As the front door cracked open, Paul was greeted by an eruption of canine howls.

My son quickly returned clutching an envelope. "What's that?" I asked suspiciously, my defenses braced for a nasty note. Paul unfolded the note and a crisp five dollar bill fell into his lap. He read aloud the surprising contents, "This is for all the times you did it right."

That night this humbled mother relearned an old lesson. For the umpteenth time I was reminded not to judge others by appearances, not even *bears*.

The Lord does not look at the things man looks at. Man looks at the outward appearance, but the Lord looks at the heart.

—I SAMUEL 16:7B

Thought . . . Are you judging people by their appearances or actions, like books by their covers? Be friendly and "open them up" in conversation to discover how uniquely God has made them for all seasons.

Jesus at the Wheel

BY CATHY CLARK

Nothing is, or can be, accidental with God.

—CROFT M. PENTZ

The thrill of my first trip to Hawaii faded with the fear of traveling alone. My husband, on a ministry trip to Japan, would meet me in Honolulu. I would have to conquer the intimidating Los Angeles International Airport by myself. Just the thought sent nervous tingles down my spine.

The night before my flight, I settled the kids with friends and checked into a hotel close to the airport. Anxious and restless, the next morning I drove my car to the long-term parking area and found the shuttle that would take me to that daunting airport. The first one in the empty vehicle, I found a seat close to the front. To calm my jitters, I took a deep breath and glanced around.

A sign posted at the front snagged my attention. "Your driver today is JESUS." My gaze froze on the words, and the butterflies in my stomach suddenly stopped flittering. *Jesus!*

It was as if the Lord had reached down and written His name Himself, reminding me that I was not traveling alone, after all. He was at the wheel, and I had nothing to fear, not even LAX.

When the driver finally arrived, and the shuttle filled with people, we made the short trek to the airport. Before I stepped out of the bus, I peeked at the driver's nametag and had to smile. As I suspected, the sign up front was there just for me. The driver's name was JOSE!

> . . . Do not be afraid . . . for the Lord your God goes with you . . .
>
> —DEUTERONOMY 31:6

Thought . . . When you stop and think about it, do you really have anything to fear? God promises always to be with you and to prepare the way before you. What more reassurance do you need?

Your Fishing Net

BY JEAN FLEMING

The way from God to a human heart is through a human heart.

—SAMUEL DICKEY GORDON

I asked God to make our family a chain of the faithful until Christ comes again. I pray that my children will all love God and walk faithfully with Him. I pray for their children, and their children's children—that all would be ardent in their devotion to Christ and fruitful in touching lives for Him.

I've decided that a chain doesn't portray the idea well. A fishing net is much better! Chains bind people, but nets catch people, and Jesus said He would make us fishers of men. Imagine your family's net starting with you and your husband—or with your parents or grandparents if they were followers of Christ—and enlarging as you add children and grandchildren. Picture countless people rescued by Christ through your family net.

Mothering can seem an isolated occupation unrelated to anything beyond the immediate needs of the family, but there is no more natural way for a mother to influence her world for Christ than through her own children. The implications of this are awesome. Time devoted to our children should not be seen as marking time, but as an investment in one of the greatest ministry opportunities. Although our children should not be the total focus, if we neglect them to pursue other ministries we will one day find we lacked a Biblical vision of mothering.

"Come, follow me," Jesus said, "and I will make you fishers of men."

—MATTHEW 4:19

Thought . . . How can you influence others for Christ? Train your children in God's ways. Rarely inhibited, children easily share the Gospel with their friends, teachers, and strangers. When you reach one child, you automatically reach countless others, as well.

Stop, Look, and Listen

BY DELORES ELAINE BIUS

The obscure we see eventually. The completely apparent takes longer.

—EDWARD R. MURROW

A friend recently gave me new insight into the marvelous delights that I had been missing right in my own home. Marge, a blind friend who visits my home frequently, remarked, "Something is missing." I could see her turning her head, listening for something.

"What do you hear, Marge?" I asked.

"It's not what I hear. It's what I do *not* hear," she explained. Then she pointed out, "Now I know what it is. The wind is blowing outside, and yet your wind chimes by the front door are not singing their usual melody."

Upon examining them, I discovered that the clapper that causes the music had fallen off. Looking around on the porch, I found it. Soon I had reattached it and the chimes played again.

"Oh, that is much better!" Marge announced delightedly. "It just didn't seem like your house without those chimes."

Later, while I was describing the flowers in my flower beds to Marge, she asked if she could touch the petunias. When I guided her hand to them, she exclaimed, "Oh, feel how soft they are—just like velvet!"

My friend's observations reminded me to take time to notice life with all my senses. I decided to stop, look, and listen, and then thank God for His blessings, great and small in every season!

Ears that hear and eyes that see—the Lord has made them both.

—PROVERBS 20:12

Thought . . . Does your life seem dull and uneventful? Perhaps you just have not taken the time to notice the beauty and blessings all around you. Read Karen O'Connor's *Basket of Blessings* as a springboard for launching your own observations.

Singer for the Lord

BY MARIE ASNER

Music is the universal language of mankind.

—HENRY WADSWORTH LONGFELLOW

I was a piano-organ major in college. Singing was something I enjoyed, but for which I did not have time. Years passed. Handel's *Messiah* was presented every Christmas by a select chorus for which auditions and subsequent rigorous rehearsals were held. Gathering courage, I auditioned. The regular accompanist was absent and the substitute so bad that she made even *me* sound good. I passed! I followed the conductor's recommendations for practicing vocalises and sang all day, every day—but always in private.

The day came for the performance which was held on the stage of an elegantly restored opera house. Moments before the processional, I was in my place in the fourth row behind a tall soprano. Then it was announced: there was an open spot in the coveted front row.

The sopranos preened themselves, while I slouched behind them. I felt a jab in the ribs and promptly stood straight to find myself staring into the face of the conductor who said, "You! Come and take the front row place." All eyes turned on me, as I cautiously stepped down and assumed my position.

I was in a dream-world as we processed onto the stage and I could see my husband's startled face. His wife—the piano player—in the front row? I sang for all I was worth. At the end of the performance I knew that God truly makes dreams come true. It was the beginning of a new season in music—singer for the Lord.

God's voice thunders in marvelous ways; He does great things beyond our understanding.

—JOB 37:5

Thought . . . Is there something you have always wanted to do, but never had the courage to try? This could be the very desire God has inscribed on your heart. Keep doing His will and He will surprise you with a chance to fulfill your dream.

Designed for Glory

BY RUTHIE ARNOLD

Open my eyes that I may see glimpses of truth Thou hast for me.

—CLARA H. SCOTT

At last! A gorgeous Sunday afternoon, and I lazily browsed through the editorial page. But when I came to one particular sentence, I sat upright and scrambled for a pen to underline, "C.S. Lewis was led to Christianity not by logic . . . but by a sense that the everydayness of life is permeated by glory."

Yes! I thought, *That's it!* But why was I so aware of it?

Though I have journaled most of my thirty-year adventure with God, in life's autumn season, I've changed my procedure to help me be much more aware of Jesus' presence. During my morning time of prayer and song, I journal, and in the margin by the first entry, I write both the date and time of day. Then throughout the day, I keep that day's writing handy.

As the day progresses, Christ brings to mind a Scripture, hymn, sentence in a book, friend's call, or answer to anguished prayer—some occurrence—that indicates His awareness of what happened in my morning devotional. Quickly, I jot down the time and the occurrence to help me remember. There is often a remarkable connectedness that confirms He hears my prayer, delights in my song, and is working on me, in me, with me, and for me.

There is much more going on around us than we know—a kingdom filled with activity that only God's Spirit gives us eyes to see. Truly, "the everydayness of life is permeated with glory."

> . . . no one can see the kingdom of God unless he is born again.
>
> —JOHN 3:3B

Thought . . . How can you experience God's glory in everyday life? Seek His presence, asking Him to reveal Himself to you. Then expect Him to "come" and keep a watchful eye. Before long, you will experience the sacred intersecting the secular at every turn.

What I Put in My Raincoat Pocket

BY LUCI SHAW

The only imperative that nature utters is look, listen, attend.

—C.S. LEWIS

It was late autumn in Vancouver.

I left a friend's house after a very early-morning Great Books discussion group and moved along the walk toward my car. Under my feet the concrete sidewalk felt mushy. Looking down, I realized that it was so thickly carpeted with wide, yellow chestnut leaves that the pavement was completely covered. The parent chestnut tree loomed above, muddy gold in the early gray of the rain-filled dawn. A long day of reading, tutorials, and teaching lay before me. I was already tired. It was cold. I shivered.

Then, I felt as much as heard a faint plop behind me. As I turned and looked, the green, spiny husk of the chestnut that had just thudded on the leaves split open, and the glossy, brown nucellus rolled toward me, as if heaven had not only dropped me a gift but had unwrapped it.

I love chestnuts, the silk feel of them, their pregnant weight, their uneven roundness, their satin shine. This one seemed to gleam with potential life at a time of year when everything was dying or rotting or going to sleep. I picked up the small present and put it in my raincoat pocket. My day had been renewed.

In time my chestnut lost some of its plump gloss, but it stayed in my pocket all winter. Every time I fingered it I was warmed by the thought of its Giver and the timing of the gift.

Every good and perfect gift is from above, coming down from the Father . . .

—JAMES 1:17

Thought . . . Are you enduring a season of barrenness? In times of loss, when you are undistracted by worldly pursuits, God catches your undivided attention. Then you are ready to receive His most delightful, unexpected gift of renewal.

Childhood

# A Child's Cry

BY SHIRLEY DOBSON

God is not in need of anything, but all things are in need of Him.

—MARCIANUS ARISTIDES

I was the daughter of a confirmed alcoholic. I could never ask a friend to spend the night for fear my father would return in a drunken stupor. He would stumble home, belligerent and foulmouthed. We would be awakened by his shouting and hide to avoid his wrath.

It was through the wisdom of my mother that I survived emotional pressures of those years. She is a strong woman, and marshaled all her resources to hold our family together. Since Dad spent his paycheck at the bar, Mother went to work to support the family.

Most importantly, mom convinced my brother and me that she loved us. She had the wisdom to know she needed help in raising two kids, and turned to a local evangelical church.

In that little neighborhood church I was introduced to Jesus, and invited Him into my heart and life. He became my special friend, and I've never been the same.

As I look back on painful experiences of childhood, I am overwhelmed with gratitude to God. He heard the desperate cries of a ten-year-old who could offer nothing in return. I had no status, no special abilities, no money to contribute. My father was not a physician or lawyer. Yet the Creator of the universe entered my little room and communed with me about the difficulties I was experiencing. It was awesome to realize that He loved me just as I was, and my pain became His pain.

> In my distress I called to the Lord; I cried to my God for help. From His temple He heard my voice; my cry came before Him, into His ears.
>
> —PSALM 18:6

Thought . . . Does your childhood haunt you? Cry out to God for relief from the pain. God allowed your past to strengthen your present. Receive His healing and use it to help others.

Linda's Gift

BY DONNA MESLER NORMAN

It is the habit of making sacrifices in small things that enables us for making them in great, when it is asked of us.

—ANTHONY W. THOROLD

Colorful Easter baskets rekindled a bittersweet remembrance transporting me to a long-ago Saturday, ripe with laughter and sprinkled with bursts of reds, greens, and yellows—the ritual of Easter eggs!

Our kitchen tingled with the pungent aroma of vinegar and boiling water. Mom dashed from stove to table, pouring the bubbly liquid into melmac cups, where we mixed and measured magical potions dripping from vials of food dye. As we slowly dipped and swirled, delicate white egg shells transformed into rainbow array, leaving blotchy smears on sticky fingers. Triumphantly, we printed our names on each egg. A creative showcase, indeed!

In the corner, my little sister's eggs were perched in royal splendor—one egg for each of us, and one aglow with the cross of Jesus.

However, as she glanced around our work table, her crestfallen eyes told yet another Easter story. She had given all her eggs to us, and we had none for her. No egg bore her name. I felt my sister's heartbreak, even as tear-stained smiles transcended her sadness. Her gift of love was all that mattered.

Forty Easter celebrations have since passed. For many years, a porcelain egg has proudly adorned her reading study: *Linda*. A simple token from her now—wiser sister who will never forget her priceless gift, an illustration of God's creed for all seasons . . . serve one another in love.

> Serve one another in love. The entire law is summed up in a single command: Love your neighbor as yourself.
> —GALATIANS 5:13B-14

Thought . . . Have you ever given sacrificially, receiving nothing in return? Often, even years later, your generosity will be reciprocated. But if it isn't, remember, that you already possess the *greatest* gift, given at considerable sacrifice—Jesus, Himself!

Beautiful Feet

BY JEWELL JOHNSON

Preach the Gospel at all times. If necessary use words.

—SAINT FRANCIS OF ASSISI

I have never considered feet an attractive part of the human anatomy because I didn't like the size of mine; they are big!

It was embarrassing to have the biggest feet of all the eighth-grade girls. Looking in the mirror during that difficult season, I decided, *My nose is cute, my brown eyes are okay, but my feet—ugh!* My self-conscious attitude toward my feet persisted into adulthood.

One day that changed. My friend Helen and I were giving out Gospel literature door-to-door with an evangelism team.

"We're from the church down the street," I explained to the young man who opened the door. Handing him the literature I commented, "We'd like to invite you to attend Sunday services."

He leafed through the Gospel of John, then looked up, his blue eyes filled with gratitude. "This is really something! No one has ever invited me to a church before. Thanks—thanks a lot!"

As Helen and I walked away from the door, I felt a lightness in my step. Looking down, I saw my feet. They were the same size as before, but I was beginning to see them in a different light.

My feet are important—not the size or shape of them, but where they go. The Bible says, "How beautiful are the feet of those who bring good news (Romans 10:15)!" That day I knew that my feet qualified to be called beautiful—even though they were a size ten!

. . . you will be my witnesses . . . to the ends of the earth.

—ACTS 1:8

Thought . . . Do you have beautiful feet? No pedicure in the world can compare with making your feet beautiful by sending them on a mission to spread the Gospel of Christ! *Feet, start walking!*

Recollections and Roses

BY CHERI FULLER

I expect to pass through life but once. If, therefore, there be any
kindness that I can show, or any good thing I can do to any fellow
being, let me do it now, and not defer or neglect it, as I shall not
pass this way again.

—STEPHEN GRELLET

The six of us children sat around mother in the long black
limousine. Dressed in our Sunday best, cheeks streaked with
tears, we watched as the procession of cars began its slow journey from the Baptist church to Restland Cemetery, where Papa
would be buried. Eleven years old, I was stunned by our loss,
and felt as if my world had fallen apart.

Yet others bustled by, hurrying to luncheon and shopping dates
in the September sunshine. Cars loaded with businessmen, mothers, and laughing children sped down Northwest Highway. They
didn't even take time to glance at our procession. I felt a heavy
loneliness sink to a deep place inside as we rode in silence.

As we turned down a country road toward Restland, we came
by a field. Between short rows of corn was a farmer in faded
overalls, hoeing with intensity and vigor. When he saw our limousine, he stopped, leaned on his hoe, took off his straw hat,
and bowed his head in prayer. I took a deep breath and sighed.

Someone cared. The respect and compassion he showed in
that simple gesture touched and lifted my heart, giving me courage to get through the day.

The memory of that farmer standing in the field lingers like
the sweet scent of the yellow roses with which we covered Papa's
grave that day, forty years ago. Whenever I think of the farmer's
concern, I renew my determination to stop my busyness and be
a caring person for someone else—even a stranger.

Therefore, as God's chosen people, holy and dearly loved,
clothe yourselves with compassion, kindness, humility,
gentleness and patience.

—COLOSSIANS 3:12

Thought . . . Do you treat strangers with compassion?
Yours may be the only kindness someone will experience for many seasons to come.

A Glimpse of My Father

BY KACY BARNETT-GRAMCKOW

Whom might I follow? Who could show me a life worth having, a pattern worth tracing?

—JAMES ROBISON

I started school on a summery, tropical island in the Pacific. The main source of light for my class was the sunlight, itself, streaming through wooden slat windows and the open door of the classroom. I learned my A-B-Cs and read my first book in the light of that doorway.

But my most vivid memory is of the day when all the light vanished from the entranceway in an instant, without warning. My classmates and I looked up, startled.

My father was standing in the doorway, his white naval uniform perfectly pressed and gleaming from the crown of his hat to the tops of his shoes. His resonant voice filled our small classroom as he said, "I've come to take Kacy home."

Then he smiled at me with his wonderful "Dad" smile. I could hear my classmates whispering to each other in amazement, "Wow! Look at her father . . . he's so tall!"

I took my father's hand and almost floated out of the classroom. My dad was the tallest, most awesome dad in the whole world, and he had come to take me home with him. Even now, that memory makes me smile.

I thank God for giving me an earthly father who showed me how to consider my Heavenly Father: He is awesome, from the crown of His head, to His feet. And one day, He will smile at me and say, "I've come to take you home . . . for all seasons, eternally."

> I looked, and there before me was a white cloud, and seated on the cloud was One "like a son of man" with a crown of gold on His head . . .
>
> —REVELATION 14:14

Thought . . . Did your earthly father portray an accurate picture of your Heavenly Father? If not, ask God to give you a clear "picture" of Him in His Word. He can more than compensate for any deficiencies your own dad may have had.

We All Need a Little Applause

BY LINDA J. GILDEN

There are high spots in all of our lives and most of them have come about through encouragement from someone else. I don't care how great, how famous or successful a man or woman may be, each hungers for applause.

—GEORGE M. ADAMS

Yesterday I pulled up to a four-way stop. As usual, I looked over to the other cars waiting at the intersection.

I noticed a red Suburban sitting at the corner. The lady at the wheel was clapping excitedly, nodding her head and smiling into the mirror. Once I got closer, I saw the toddler in the back seat, also smiling and laughing. There was no clue as to exactly what the accomplishment was, but it was obviously cause for celebration.

My thoughts returned to the days when I had toddlers in the back seat everywhere I went. Many times I looked into the rearview mirror just to see a child point to her nose on demand, retrieve a pacifier, play pat-a-cake, or correctly identify a dog or cat or light—all definitely appropriate occasions for applause.

From the time my memory bank begins, I remember having my own personal cheering section. Whether I learned to share a toy, ride a bike, climb a tree, drive a car . . . Mom and Dad were there, applauding. And their applause encouraged me to set my goals a little higher each time.

No matter what our season in life, we all need a little applause every now and then. And especially when we encourage little ones as Jesus did, we can even hear His applause from heaven!

Therefore encourage one another and build each other up, just as in fact you are doing.

—I THESSALONIANS 5:11

Thought . . . Are you generous with your applause? Everyday, try to pay one compliment to each and every person you meet. Your encouragement may literally change their lives.

Fruit of Honesty

BY KAREN DYE

A guileless mind is a great treasure; it is worth any price.

—A.W. TOZER

One evening, my twelve-year-old daughter, Kelly, approached me timidly, visibly upset. "Mom, I've been reading my *Brio Magazine* and every article has been convicting me of something. Last quarter at school, I signed your name on a form that I forgot to have you sign."

My heart sank as my mind raced through scenarios of consequences for Kelly. I quickly composed myself and then told her that she would have to confess to her Dad and her teacher. Kelly began to sob out of control and screamed, "I'd rather die!"

"Honey," I comforted her, "freedom only comes when we confess to God and to others involved."

After telling her Dad, he assured her, "That took a lot of strength to confess."

Even though that evening was very painful for us all, the situation allowed us to talk about how pain and suffering can build character within us.

Two days later, Kelly, Dad, and Mr. Langley met. Her teacher said that she was a very special person for coming forward and that he respected her for it. But the best part came the very next month. Kelly's middle school had a Student of the Month Award and Kelly received an award from Mr. Langley, who said, "Kelly is one of the most honest students I have ever taught."

I know that Kelly has matured in her faith because of this. I'm so thankful that God even uses unhappy incidents of failure to contribute to our season of growth.

If we confess our sins, He is faithful and just and will forgive us our sins and purify us from all unrighteousness.

—I JOHN 1:9

Thought . . . In this season of difficulty, are you *wasting* your suffering? Obey God in the midst of it and ask Him to teach you eternal truths that will make you a better person.

Out of the Mouths . . .

BY DORIS SMALLING

Children must be valued as our most priceless possession.

—JAMES C. DOBSON

"Mom, why do people sing in choirs?" five-year-old Marcia asked as we drove to the final rehearsal before the Christmas program.

"Because we want Jesus to know that we love Him and we want our friends to hear us praise Him."

"Oh, okay. I'm going to lead the kids onto the stage, then I'm going to sing a special song."

She continued chattering. I listened, thrilled that my children enjoyed church activities. Rehearsal went well and ended early.

Sunday evening's program opened with the traditional manger scene. Because Marcia had led the youngsters onto the stage, she was the last to leave. Stopping at the microphone, she curtsied demurely in her red bouffant Christmas skirt and then began to sing, "What a Friend We Have in Jesus."

I gasped. The choir director looked stunned. Then she quickly nodded to the pianist, who immediately began accompanying Marcia. She joyfully sang three verses in perfect pitch, missing neither word nor note. She finished and curtsied again.

I looked at my program, mortified. Marcia's *encore* was not listed. The director announced to the delighted audience, "You've just received an unscheduled bonus!"

"Why," I questioned Marcia almost angrily after the program, "did you sing by yourself?"

She appeared puzzled. "But, Mom, I'm not in a choir and I wanted Jesus to know I love Him and for my friends to hear me praise Him. So I sang His favorite song and mine." After hearing Marcia's innocent explanation, it became my favorite song, too!

Even a child is known by his actions, by whether his conduct is pure and right.

—PROVERBS 20:11

Thought . . . Are you easily embarrassed by your child's innocent spontaneity? With the heart of Christ, delight in your child. Be grateful that she has escaped the world's influence.

Heaven's Gain

BY FERN AYERS MORRISSEY

Earth has no sorrow that heaven cannot heal.

—THOMAS MOORE

We were poor, but determined to provide a fine funeral. When my little friend, Marilyn, her older sister, Norma, and I found the dead bird, we were glad for God's tiny, tragic gift—His sky's small loss was our great gain!

After Marilyn's mom donated a matchbox for the coffin, we girl undertakers searched the sidewalks for cigarette wrappers, prizing their aluminum foil linings like silver. Pressing this luster around the matchbox, we lined it with cotton and laid our bird to rest.

In the backyard we dug a shallow hole among sunny marigolds, entombed our shiny coffin, and adorned the grave with petunias and a cross of twigs. Norma opened the service with prayer, Marilyn and I followed with Bible verses, then a hymn.

Suddenly, some of our block's bad boys burst into the yard, desecrated the grave, destroyed our bird, and laughed. Why did God let this happen?

Seven years later I attended another funeral and stood beside another small coffin. My dear friend Marilyn, only thirteen, died suddenly from complications of rheumatic fever. Swift as the fall of a bird from the sky, Marilyn's life was abruptly gone. Norma and I embraced beside her grave and wondered why.

Many seasons have passed since then, and I no longer ask God *why* but praise Him *because*—because He values every sparrow who falls and because our Marilyn's loss is Heaven's great gain.

Do not let your hearts be troubled. Trust in God; trust also in Me. In My Father's house are many rooms . . . I am going there to prepare a place for you.

—JOHN 14:1-2

Thought . . . Do you grieve the loss of a child? Yours is a devastating pain that no one truly understands . . . except God, because He sacrificed His only beloved Son. He loved your child and you so much that through Jesus' crucifixion He provided a way for you both to spend eternity with Him.

Love-Talking

BY EVELYN W. DAVISON

If your work is not going to communicate, what good is it?

—LAURA J. HOBSON

"*Love*-Talking" is one of my favorite things to do, although it has not always been easy. I have struggled all my life with a speech impediment. Stuttering and stammering made life as a child difficult.

My parents invested in speech training to help me overcome this obstacle. It paid off when, at nine, I became a popular "record jockey" for our family-owned hillbilly radio station. I learned early to turn the knobs and pull the levers.

In those days, most people in town did not have telephones. They would come by during the week and drop their requests into a milk jug on the porch. I acquired some pretty funny nicknames from my musical dedications on my Saturday shows. Most importantly, I gained the confidence to speak up and reach out to people, despite my physical difficulty.

That early training reminds me often that having confidence is critical to being able to make life joyful for others. Today, although I still have a speech impediment, I'm able to keep "Love-Talking" on my long-running Christian radio talk-show and television program which bring help, hope, humor, and happiness to others.

Life in America has changed since those early radio days. People don't leave notes in milk bottles. They phone, fax, and e-mail questions, instead.

But some things never change. God is still building my confidence and completing that work He began in me as a young radio star. And people will always need to be communicated to *in love* in any season!

> . . . being confident of this, that He Who began a good work in you will carry it on to completion until the day of Christ Jesus.
>
> —PHILIPPIANS 1:6

Thought . . . Do feelings of inadequacy from your childhood plague you? When your confidence is *in God* and not in yourself, you can overcome and achieve anything *He* sets your mind to do!

Beautiful in Jesus' Eyes

BY MARILYN HEAVILIN

Beauty is in the eye of the beholder.

—ANONYMOUS

I was reading on emotional healing and asked God to show me areas in my past not resolved. God brought a familiar child-hood scene to mind.

I was three. While our house had some nice features such as beautiful hardwood floors, which my mom waxed frequently, there was no indoor plumbing. The kitchen was equipped with a slop bucket. The mirrored medicine chest was mounted on the wall above the bucket. While Mom was gone, I decided to get cleaned up so I could look pretty when Mommy came home. I placed my tiny feet on the rim of the bucket so I could stand high enough to look into the mirror.

I looked and said, "You're pretty." I lost my balance, tipping over the bucket, causing its contents to pour onto the freshly waxed floors. Although my gentle dad usually did not react rashly, watching that dirty water run over those beautiful floors caused him to suddenly pick me up, swing me back and forth, and mop the floor with the lower portion of my body.

I grew up feeling sorry for Dad, but never considered my feelings. This time God allowed me to see His perspective. The little three-year-old was humiliated, and felt ashamed and unat-tractive. Since that time I have had difficulty believing I am at-tractive. As God walked me through that event, He allowed me to see Jesus pick me up, wipe me off, brush my hair, look me in the eye, and say, "You are pretty."

Those who look to Him are radiant; their faces are never covered with shame.

—PSALM 34:5

Thought . . . Are you attractive? Look into Jesus' eyes. You are absolutely beautiful to Him. He let you know just *how* beautiful by giving His life for yours.

The Nicest People in the World

BY BARBARA CURTIS

At the moment of death, we will not be judged by the amount of work we have done but by the weight of love we have put into our work.

—MOTHER TERESA

One dark winter night I piled my sons into the car to make collections for their newspaper routes.

As we stopped in front of the first house on Ben's route, he looked out the window. A big smile spread over his face.

"The nicest people in the world," he said before stepping out into the cold. With the engine off, his brothers and I blew on our hands to keep them warm. Ben came back with his dimples flashing, stuffing his earnings into his pocket.

Ben's next customer lived four houses away. As I turned off the engine, Ben said, beaming, "The nicest people in the world!"

"I thought the nicest people in the world lived in the first house?" I questioned.

"Yeah, but these people are, too," Ben said, sincere as sunshine. Another big smile, another big tip.

We replayed this scene again and again. Soon Ben's brothers and I forgot the cold as we caught Ben's infectious love for his little piece of the labor that, after all, makes our world go 'round. Soon we were all chanting, "The nicest people in the world," in front of each customer's house.

Later I marveled at the vivid lesson God gave me through my son. Ben's selflessness—forgetting the cold and focusing on the people he served, instead—generated a warmth which kept us all aglow that winter season.

Oh, Lord, how I hope that I can be so enthusiastic about whatever you give me to do! I thought.

Serve wholeheartedly, as if you were serving the Lord, not men . . .

—EPHESIANS 6:7

Thought . . . Has your enthusiasm waned? Pausing to remember that God has blessed you with salvation and eternal life is enough to resurrect your passion and gratitude.

Leans against the Phone

BY ELAINE CUNNINGHAM

Prayer is the most important thing in my life. If I should neglect prayer for a single day, I should lose a great deal of the fire of faith.

—MARTIN LUTHER

My four-year-old daughter, Ruth, and five-year-old son, John, sat on either side of me in the front pew of our little church. Their daddy, the pastor, stood behind the pulpit leading his congregation in singing *Onward Christian Soldiers*.

Suddenly, the piping voice of little Ruth caught my attention. "Christ, the royal Master, leans against the phone," she sang, in place of "leads against the foe." Picturing Christ leaning against the phone was as natural to her as seeing her parents leaning on the phone as they listened and counseled.

Isn't that a true picture of Christ? He "leans against the phone," so to speak, eagerly waiting to hear from us—ready to forgive and cleanse—ready to take the wayward one as His child—ready to give guidance and direction for every season of life.

> The Lord is near to all who call on Him, to all who call on Him in truth.
>
> —PSALM 145:18

Thought . . . Is Jesus your best friend? In John 15:14, Jesus calls you His friend. While always reverencing Him, approach Him in the *personal, intimate* way that He desires. Your love for Him will know no bounds.

My Six-Year-Old Teacher

BY JUNE L. VARNUM

The reasonable thing is to learn from those who can teach.

—SOPHOCLES

I worried about how I would amuse Bethany during her five-hour visit. We were friends, but I wasn't the best model of fun; most of my days seemed frantic. I seldom made time just to sit and enjoy God's world.

Bethany and I decided to make Pilgrim Bread. Bethany sifted, measured, and helped to knead the dough. We set it in a warm place to rise. Hungry from working, we stopped for a picnic lunch on the back yard deck.

We set out sandwiches, chips, glasses of cold water—a gourmet lunch! I had pulled over my garden chair, but Bethany patted the blanket beside her. "Sit here, June."

For a while, we munched in silence. Then my young friend stretched out on her back to watch the clouds. Firmly patting the blanket beside her, I knew that I was to do the same. We watched in amazement as giant ships sailed past. A huge bear and a horse ambled along, while a unicorn sedately followed. I stretched luxuriously, then hesitantly rose. Remembering the bread, I turned to Bethany. "We need to check the oven."

But I paused one minute longer to gaze at the mountains, tall pine trees, butterflies, birds, blue sky, and cloud-beings—exquisite adornments of God's creation. As Bethany's small hand reached up for mine, the breeze seemed to whisper, "Be still and know that I am God."

I held her hand tightly and whispered, in return, "Thank you, Lord, for this little teacher."

. . . and a little child will lead them.

—ISAIAH 11:6

Thought . . . Do you take time to appreciate life through the eyes of a child? If you did, you would be in a continual state of wonderment.

A Lesson in Forgiveness

BY JOAN CLAYTON

Pride is a high price to pay for unforgiveness.

—ANONYMOUS

*B*etty was having a bad day. The other children complained as they kept reporting instances of insults and mistreatment from her.

I took Betty aside and tried to reason with her. She vehemently denied any wrongdoing. When Bobby reported that he had been pinched by Betty, and the redness of his arm testified to the fact, I asked her to stay in at recess so that we could talk. She remained in her seat and worked on her math. Bobby wanted to finish his math and asked if he might stay, too.

They both brought their papers to me at about the same time. I checked them and looked into Betty's deep blue eyes. "Betty, do you have something to say?" Betty quickly looked at Bobby and burst into sobs. "I'm so sorry. I don't know why I did that! I really wish I wouldn't do things like that." Bobby, with his little red arm outstretched, whispered with a quivering chin and teary eyes, "That's okay."

It was over . . . complete forgiveness—never to be remembered again. It was just that simple. Other infractions of the rules would occur, but they would be handled then. This particular incident was closed forever.

I resolved that day to *choose* to forgive. I resolved to always "be a child" in loving and forgiving. And I also learned to look within myself for any offense. I'm so thankful that my job allows me to be with children because "of such is the kingdom of heaven."

Forgive us our debts, as we also have forgiven our debtors.
—MATTHEW 6:12

Thought . . . Is there someone whom you need to forgive? Ask God to give you the innocence of a child's heart that both forgives and forgets. With a free conscience, you'll enjoy a season of heaven on earth.

Thanks for Cheese

BY EUNICE ANN BADGLEY

Thank you, God, for little things that often come our way—the things we take for granted, but don't mention when we pray.

—HELEN STEINER RICE

*S*ome days bring enough stress and problems that I have to struggle to find things for which to be thankful. Of course, blessings are always there in abundance, but I allow troubles to obscure them. It is then that I often remember the words, "Thank You for cheese."

I taught first- and second-grade children in Sunday School for many years and heard a lot of stories from their lives. Most children were eager to share what had taken place during the week with brothers, sisters, parents, pets, and friends.

These beginning readers were also eager to discuss their Scripture verses and to engage in lesson-related activities and prayer. Being sensitive to the few shy children's needs, I never called on a child to pray, but always asked if anyone *wanted* to pray.

Jason was always ready. On that particular Sunday, he prayed for his family, pets, friends, school mates, teachers, and the sick people he knew. After closing with "Amen," he added, "P.S. Lord, thank You for cheese."

I have remembered his sincere prayer for many years. I don't know if he were especially fond of cheese or whether it was just an afterthought, but it has helped me remember through many seasons to be thankful for little things.

And be thankful.

—COLOSSIANS 3:15B

Thought . . . Are your problems overwhelming you? Thank God for the little blessings all around you. They will soon add up, totaling far more than the number of your difficulties.

I'm Here, Lord!

BY VALERIE HOWE

The time is past when parents can give their children a pleasant surface-coating of religion. Our children are either going to be filled with Jesus and excited about Him, or filled with sin and excited about it. All that we can bring our children will be worthless unless we can bring them Jesus.

—LARRY CHRISTENSON

$\mathcal{I}$n all my life there is nothing more important to me than to see my children come to know Jesus. I pray for it daily, cry for it passionately, imagine it with great delight, and when it happens, I celebrate with the angels in heaven.

One December afternoon in the Wal-Mart parking lot, five-year-old Timothy prayed for Jesus to take his sins away, believing Jesus died and rose again for him. He then asked Jesus to lead his life.

I fretted some over the decision he had made in such a youthful season and asked God to assure me that he was truly saved.

One Sunday as I stood by him singing, *When the Roll Is Called Up Yonder*, I asked Timothy if he knew what that song meant. He told me he did not, so I asked, "What do you do when your teacher calls your name at school?" "Raise my hand and say, 'Here,'" he replied. "Yes," I said, "and the Bible says that when Jesus comes again, the Book of Life will be opened and the roll will be called. Everyone who has asked Jesus into his life will have his name written there."

Then I asked, "What will you say on that day, Timothy?" He answered, smiling from ear to ear and literally waving his hand in the air, "I'm going to say 'here,' Mom!"

In that moment, as we both joyfully continued to sing, I knew that I was standing next to my little brother in Christ. Hallelujah!

> . . . I tell you the truth, unless you change and become like little children, you will never enter the kingdom of heaven.
> —MATTHEW 18:3

Thought . . . Do you think your child is too young to be saved? Jesus says that anyone who will not receive God's kingdom as a little child, will never enter it. Children have the beautiful capacity simply to believe.

The Happies!

BY LINDA EVANS SHEPHERD

There is no duty we so much underrate as the duty of being happy.
By being happy, we sow anonymous benefits from the world.

—ROBERT LOUIS STEVENSON

Sometimes, when happiness comes my way, I'm too preoccupied to notice. One day, my three-year-old son, Jimmy, and I ran some errands. I let him take his red and yellow tape player into the print shop to entertain himself while I ran off some photocopies. Standing next to the purring copy machine, I hadn't realized how loudly Jimmy's *Sesame Street* sing-along tape was blaring. Suddenly, Jimmy turned up the volume even higher and jumped up from the floor, "Let's dance!" he shouted.

My eyes widened as I watched Jimmy gyrate, beckoning me to join his fun.

"Mommy's busy right now," I murmured. I turned my head to sneak a peak at the print shop staff. Were they watching the show? My mouth fell open. All the workers, owner included, were standing at their desks doing the twist to Jimmy's music!

I laughed at all the happiness around me. This time, I couldn't ignore Jimmy's glee.

Later, I thought of a quote from poet Elizabeth Barrett Browning: "Earth's crammed with heaven." Miss Browning was right. Despite our trial seasons, happiness can be found all around us, but we must take the time to notice and enjoy it.

> Let them praise His name with dancing and make music to Him . . .
>
> —PSALM 149:3

Thought . . . When is the last time you just plain *had fun?* If you no longer know the meaning of the word, spend time with a child and follow her lead. Kick up your dancing feet! (But take off your high heels first.)

Faith of a Child

BY SANDI GORDON

The faith that stands on authority is not faith.

—RALPH WALDO EMERSON

*O*ne evening following our prayer, my seven-year-old daughter, Gina, began pondering about Heaven and God. Gina said that she expected there to be many rooms in Heaven and a small church where "Jesus will give all the sermons." Gina's older sister jumped into the conversation saying that she had heard that Jesus would return in the year 2000.

This led to a discussion as to how the girls would know Jesus if He came. Gina said, "I think that Jesus wears a long white robe, has long hair, and wears a cross necklace. If someone said he were Jesus but didn't look anything like that, I wouldn't believe him." Gina paused, and then added, "He doesn't have to look exactly like that . . . except for the necklace! I know Jesus will have a cross necklace." She smiled with confidence.

When I consider the precious qualities of a child, it is no wonder that Jesus instructed us to become like children. They live in a world in which Santa Claus can make millions of deliveries in one night, the Tooth Fairy knows the value of a tooth from one house to the next, and purple dinosaurs can talk.

Thus, their faith in a God Who cannot be seen, and Who knows the number of hairs on each head, is not the struggle for children that it is for many adults. Children readily accept the mystery of God. I pray that one day I will have the unwavering faith of my children.

And whoever welcomes a little child like this in my name welcomes me.

—MATTHEW 18:5

Thought . . . Do you have the faith of a child? It would help to think like one. Why not spend some time with children, talking on *their* level. Their innocence and wonderment about life is bound to rub off on you.

The Gift

BY RAYEANN LONGWELL

We get in return exactly what we give. It all comes back. Incredible echoes mirror our actions to an emphatic degree, sometimes in greater measure than we give.

—CHARLES R. SWINDOLL

I was ten and attending summer camp. My "team" had just found a large treasure chest. As it was opened, children began to push, shove, and pinch to get near the front. I stood near the back, patiently waiting for my turn. When I finally reached the front, the chest was nearly empty. I was searching for a rabbit's foot, the most coveted prize of that time. But they were all gone.

My mother was a counselor that year and I ran to her, crying. Through my tears, I tried to explain that it wasn't so much that I didn't get what I wanted that mattered, but I wanted to know why I always got hurt whenever I tried to be nice.

Comforting me, my mother took me outside to pray. She began by thanking God for a child with such a tender heart, then asked Him to bless me in a special way for doing what was right. As we turned to go back inside, I saw a rabbit's foot lying on the ground which hadn't been there before. It was double the size of all the others and it was a brilliant green, unlike any color I had ever seen. Shocked, my mother stood motionlessly. She couldn't believe her eyes. Yet we both knew that God had placed it there just for me!

> Delight yourself in the Lord and He will give you the desires of your heart.
>
> —PSALM 37:4

Thought . . . What disappointment is causing you pain? Surrender it to God. He will often give you something far greater than what you had desired. But most of all, He will give you *Himself*!

He Holds My Hand

BY MURIEL LARSON

Remember never to say that you are alone; for you are not alone, but God is within.

—EPICTETUS

One day, when I was about ten years old, I was having such a good time playing at a friend's house that I didn't realize it was growing dark outside. Suddenly, I noticed a mouth-watering aroma coming from the kitchen. Paula's mother was making supper.

Glancing out the window, I exclaimed, "Oh, I'd better go home now!" Paula's younger brother often gave us a bad time. Now he taunted, "You'd better watch out for that scraggly-looking guy I saw yesterday by the railroad tracks!"

Those tracks were just a block from Paula's house, and I would have to cross them. As I set off for home, my heart began beating rapidly. Seeing dark shadows of trees falling across the road, I hastened my steps.

Then I remembered something my Sunday School teacher had told me—that Jesus was with me wherever I went. Reaching out my hand, I imagined that Jesus was holding it in His. The fear disappeared. I felt safe because Jesus was with me!

Through years of experience, I have learned that this is true no matter how old I get. I have had many occasions to feel fearful and anxious. But when I look up and pray and trust in His presence and love, I feel just as safe as I did that day when I was ten years old!

> . . . And surely I am with you always, to the very end of the age.
>
> —MATTHEW 28:20

Thought . . . How can you overcome fear in any situation?—by having the faith of a child who reaches out for God's hand and trusts that He will take it. He won't let you fall.

Growth

You Are an Overcomer

BY LIZ CURTIS HIGGS

My life is in the hands of a fool who makes me lose my temper.

—JOSPEH HUNTER

*M*ost of the time I live like an overwhelmer rather than over-comer. With a busy schedule and many demands, I run around like the proverbial headless chicken about to collapse. When my stress builds I get in big trouble.

One afternoon, with a plane to catch and too much to do, I tore into the kitchen and knocked over the cat's milk dish. I launched it with my toe and milk went all over my freshly mopped floor.

I now had warm milk all over my nice new shoes.

I was not happy or feeling like an overcomer. At the top of my lungs, I shouted, "That ?@#$%%! will have to go somewhere else!"

At that exact moment, the door to our bathroom began to swing open, and our house painter appeared, wide-eyed and fear-stricken.

Beet red, I stammered, "*Oh!* No, no, not you! *You* are welcome to go . . . anywhere you like. I was talking to the cat dish."

The what?

"Sure, ma'am," he said, as he bolted for the back door and certain safety.

I slumped into a chair, embarrassed and laughing at my fool-ishness, yet deeply ashamed by my lack of control. Why *can't I overcome, Lord? Why do I succumb to old habits? Why don't I "Let go and let God"?*

Wretched woman that I certainly am. Who will get me out of this mess? The Overcomer: my Lord Who forgives me when I fail yet persuades me to press on and be an overcomer like He is.

In this world you will have trouble. But take heart! I have overcome the world.

—JOHN 16:33B

Thought . . . Have you failed? Jesus doesn't condemn you, He forgives you. Your failures need never stop you from trying again in His strength.

This New Day

BY SYLVIA DUNCAN

New every morning is the love our wakening and uprising prove.

—JOHN KEBLE

I reread some of my journals as I stored them away to make space in a desk drawer. What had I learned from those careful entries? Had I always followed my own advice?

Here was a day when I had eaten half a box of chocolates. This was the year when I bought a membership at the Y.W.C.A. and did not swim once. Here was a mini-journal from an unexpected journey abroad when my brother had died. Oh, here were entries that led to my taking early retirement from my job.

It intrigued me to see the patterns, the struggles, the searches for a *new me*. At least, I thought, keeping accounts had kept me in balance on a daily basis.

What about today, now, this very moment God had given me?

Crows flew by, cawing noisily at the sight of the bread I had put out for them under a tree. Lex, the huge chocolate Labrador Retriever, put his graying muzzle on my lap for a biscuit. There was a gift to wrap, a call to make to a shut-in, a piece of new music to sing.

I would be aware, ready to do my best. Maybe I would not always be able to do what I knew was the right thing, but I would try. Having just read my journals helped me determine that I would act upon what God had given me to do. After all, I had *this new day*.

Do not merely listen to the Word, and so deceive yourselves. Do what it says.

—JAMES 1:22

Thought . . . Are you wasting today by regretting yesterday and dreading tomorrow? Today is reality. It is what you have been given to enjoy as a precious gift. Savor it.

A Fat Soul

BY JEWELL JOHNSON

God has given us two hands—one to receive with and the other to give with. We are not cisterns made for hoarding; we are channels made for sharing.

—BILLY GRAHAM

One summer day I came from our garden, my arms loaded with freshly-picked sweet corn and tomatoes. Under a willow tree, I settled into a lawn chair to husk corn for my family's noon meal.

"What a day!" I exclaimed. A yellow butterfly flitted nearby. I brushed it aside and began pulling the silk from an ear of corn.

A Bible verse flashed into my thoughts. "The liberal soul shall be made fat (Proverbs 11:25)." *Where did that come from?* I hadn't thought of that Scripture for a long time.

Glancing at my watch, I noticed it was soon time to start lunch. The thought returned. *What . . . again? Why does this verse keep coming back? The liberal soul,* I pondered. *Lord, what are you trying to tell me? I get it! Garden produce!*

I filled a grocery bag with corn and tomatoes. Calling our son, I instructed him to deliver the produce to a family who didn't have a garden. In the kitchen I smiled as I dropped corn into boiling water. *A fat soul! You thought my soul needed some fattening up, did you, Lord? You're right. This full-to-the-brim feeling that comes from sharing—this contentment I'm feeling is definitely a fat-soul feeling—and what I needed to make a good day even better!*

Give, and it will be given to you . . .

—LUKE 6:38A

Thought . . . Do you have a "fat soul"? Paradoxically, the more you give of your time, talents, and possessions, the more blessings will be yours. The Bible teaches that it is more blessed to give than to receive.

Baby Jesus and Humpty Dumpty

BY ELIZABETH WILT

Don't sweat the small stuff.

—RICHARD CARLSON

*O*n her first Christmas, my daughter broke baby Jesus! Though she knew she was only allowed to "look," barely tall enough to reach the manger, she took the tiny ceramic baby and swaddled Him in a washcloth. He was just the perfect size for her to hold.

Then the unthinkable happened. She accidentally dropped Him on the tile. His head broke off. She cried. I cried.

This was the one Christmas decoration for which I had splurged. I treasured it. But as I looked into her teary eyes, I knew that she was sorry. She wanted me to make it better. Thankfully, unlike Humpty Dumpty who was unable to be reassembled despite help from all the king's horses and men, Mommy and Mr. Elmer were able to glue baby Jesus back together again. It wasn't such a big tragedy, after all.

Years from now, this once traumatic experience will have become a priceless, painless memory. Our Jesus now has been personalized by my daughter's loving hands.

I wonder how often I "lose my head and come unglued" over little things? . . . a gouge in the woodwork, ketchup on the car seat, syrup on a suit? Sometimes mishaps are a result of disobedience, and sometimes not.

But, as my daughter discovered that day with baby Jesus, brokenness can be mended. Like children, we can take the broken shards of our lives and place them into Jesus' hands. Through His love, grace, and forgiveness He will make us whole again.

. . . He has sent me to bind up the brokenhearted . . .

—ISAIAH 61:1

Thought . . . Is your life broken? Surrender all pain to Jesus. As He works *everything* together for good, He will reassemble the pieces into a completed puzzle. With Jesus designing your life, it will make sense again.

Spring Cleaning

BY CASSANDRA WOODS

Spring cleaning should begin with the head and end with the heart.

—ANONYMOUS

As a child I can remember helping my mother spring-clean at my great-grandmother's home. We called her Big Mama. Despite her petite size, she had a big, generous heart.

Having lived a long life, she also had a big capacity for accumulating a lot of things. It was our job to get rid of some of the clutter.

I was eager to help, but quickly got a little frustrated. It didn't take me long to realize that Big Mama wasn't planning on getting rid of *anything*. However small or insignificant the trinket, she was never quite ready to part with it. It didn't matter if she hadn't laid eyes on it in ten years.

Although it has been many years since I helped Big Mama, and she has since passed away, that memory lingers vividly. I am continuously involved with seasons of spring cleaning, too—and not just in sprucing up my house.

I regularly use my Bible as my cleaning aid. Obeying it enables me to rid the clutter from my heart—sweep away the cobwebs of unforgiveness—wipe off the dust of pride—wash the windows of my soul, my eyes, that have turned green with envy.

Sometimes I'm not quite ready to part with something God wants to remove. But when I let Him have His way, the cleaning process is worth it. He assures me that the result will be a pure heart. Then the only thing I will accumulate in my heart is His peace.

Create in me a pure heart, O God, and renew a steadfast spirit within me.

—PSALM 51:10

Thought . . . Does your heart need a little spring-cleaning? The project is always too much for one person to handle. Ask God to help you complete the task by making a clean sweep of your sins. Then you will be able to love Him with all your heart.

The Eyes of the Heart

BY LUCI SWINDOLL

Compassion involves us in deep consciousness of our solidarity with all people rather than our distinction from them.

—DON POSTEMA

The filthy station wagon pulled into the car wash, loaded with kids and a driver who looked as if he hadn't shaved in weeks. With his hair tousled and a cigarette hanging out of the right side of his mouth, he was wearing clothes he probably had slept in. All eyes turned toward him.

He opened the back of the wagon. One by one he hugged and kissed each child, whom he gently lowered to the ground. Then they romped with their father to their little hearts' content.

"Oh, Daddy, play with us. Daddy, throw me the ball. Look, Daddy, look at this . . . watch!"

Slowly, lovingly, deliberately, this disheveled man gave attention to all six children, playing, talking, laughing, discovering . . . they had a wonderful time. I sat, astonished and ashamed for thinking the guy was a creep.

How quickly we judge another's outward appearance. We look at another's car, manners, music, posture, or facial characteristics . . . judging all the while.

Not only do we have no right to pass judgment, but we also have no way to see what's inside that person.

Who cares if the guy at the car wash was the opposite of my view of a proper dad? All those kids cared about was the attention he gave them. He listened. He played. He loved them.

When I don't put judgmental demands on others, I'm happiest because I know I'm doing what is right. When nobody puts demands on me, it frees me to be who I really am—a slob, clothed in Christ's righteousness.

Stop judging by mere appearances, and make a right judgement.

—JOHN 7:24

Thought . . . Do you make snap judgments about a woman's mothering based on her appearance or behavior? Does she show her children love, tenderness, and devotion? God looks at her heart.

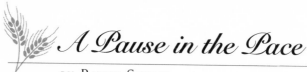

A Pause in the Pace

BY PATTY STUMP

The nicest thing we can do for our Heavenly Father, is to be kind to one of His children.

—Saint Teresa of Avila

Life in our home seems to exist in constant motion—usually "fast forward." Amidst the hustle and bustle, I tend to become stricken with what I refer to as *Marthitis*: scattered thoughts, shortened memory, a hardened heart, callous emotions, an uncontrollable tongue, fidgeting fingers, decreased stamina, and ingrown eyeballs!! Like Martha in Luke 10, I can become absorbed in my agenda, failing to prioritize.

Marthitis took root one evening as my agenda loomed before me. I was distracted with getting our children to bed. Preoccupied with the desire to attend to what I considered to be more important matters, I impatiently snapped at my daughter, insensitive to the impact that my words had on her.

In such moments, I'm often unwavering in pursuit of my agenda, yet this particular evening I caught a glimpse of my compulsion and chose to pause my pace. I asked Elisabeth to forgive my harsh words and sit beside me for a few moments before going to bed. Settling onto our sofa, she leaned against my side, sharing highlights from her day. As I listened, I realized that my agenda almost had crowded out the best moments of my day—the moments invested in hearing the heart of my daughter.

Juggling the daily demands of life is an ongoing challenge for me; the urgent easily crowds out the important. Yet, when I pause my pace and adjust my priorities, I'm able to identify and embrace life's subtle delights that God has placed right in my midst!

"Martha, Martha," the Lord answered, "you are worried and upset about many things . . ."

—Luke 10:41

Thought . . . Are you suffering from *Marthitis*, upset and worried about many things? Jesus tells us, through His comments about Martha's sister, Mary, that only *one* thing is needed . . . to "sit at His feet" and listen.

Just Little Things

BY MARGARET PRIMROSE

The unexamined life is not worth living.

—PLATO

The stitches in the fabric on the bobbin side of the sewing machine were much too loose. I checked to make sure that the needle was threaded properly. It was. I adjusted the tension. That made no difference. Then I changed the needle to one for lighter weight fabric. When that did not work, my frustration grew.

One of my bobbins was slightly bent, but it proved not to be in the machine. At last I discovered a wad of lint that had collected between the needle and the bobbin. The thread could not feed upward as it should. All it took to solve the problem was to brush out the lint. How small and insignificant it seemed compared to the size and weight of the sewing machine!

That incident reminded me that buried inside me, where I had all but forgotten them, some little things were building up that could hinder my Christian life. Exposed to friends, my faults seemed to be more fluff than substance to some of them. Nevertheless, I resolved to let the Holy Spirit keep the "lint" out of my actions, so that, uninhibited, He can stitch into my life His beautiful design.

A little folly outweighs wisdom . . .

—ECCLESIASTES 10:1

Thought . . . Do you tend to differentiate between "big" and "little" sins? Little sins often grow into big strongholds. *Any* sin, left unconfessed, impedes your fellowship with God and others. Sin, any sin, isn't worth the pain it brings.

Little Things

BY LUCINDA J. ROLLINGS

You can dodge an elephant, but not a fly.

—ANONYMOUS

I wondered if it were okay to peel off a used, but uncanceled stamp and glue it onto another piece of mail? I had never thought much about it being dishonest. After all, wasn't recycling considered a virtue?

Once I had sent an envelope with a new stamp that I had cut from a letter I had decided not to send. It was returned from the post office with a note stating that it was a used stamp. I wanted to immediately march there and nicely say that they owed me thirty-two cents! But then I retrieved an uncanceled stamp on a letter delivered to me. So I soaked it off and reused it. *Now we're even*, I rationalized.

But something pricked at me. I was shocked at how guilty I felt about that thirty-two-cent stamp and asked God to forgive me.

The next envelopes I received with uncanceled stamps, I reluctantly threw away. Six dimes and four pennies jingled from the bottom of my wastebasket. Later, on two 9 x 12 envelopes, $2.24 in uncanceled stamps glared enticingly at me! I stuffed the envelopes in my cabinet to reuse as file folders.

I could still hear the jingling! Every uncanceled stamp that I receive is a loving reminder that to be like Christ means to be honest, even in the little things, even as little as thirty-two cents. (I think I'll turn on the stereo to drown out the jingling!)

> . . . Don't you know that a little yeast works through the whole batch of dough? Get rid of the old yeast that you may be a new batch without yeast . . .
>
> —I CORINTHIANS 5:6-7

Thought . . . Is there a seemingly innocent little "habit" in which you engage? The next time you're about to repeat it, ask yourself, *What would Jesus do?* Then decide if you can do it again.

Look Inside

BY DORIS SCHUCHARD

Love is a great beautifier.

—LOUISA MAY ALCOTT

I had to smile as I scanned the real estate ads in search of a new house. Pictures of homes that had clearly witnessed two world wars were now proclaimed to "look great for their age." An old house seems like a bargain when it is advertised as a "perfectly-priced peach." Even a home with peeling paint and broken windows is transformed when "your imagination perks this right up."

But maybe I didn't see the inside story . . . grandparents passing down family traditions in a century-old house . . . a couple who may have spent their hard-earned money on others instead of a bigger and better dwelling . . . or a young family's house with holes in the windows, resulting from a game of catch . . . and smudges on the walls from little hands, belonging to children who brought their parents joy.

It is hard to focus on inner beauty when the world around us glamorizes fame and riches. I have a friend whose favorite dress is a bunched-up sweatshirt and sweatpants and whose apple-shaped body, with its well-worn wrinkles, has never appeared on a magazine cover. And yet, her seasoned character shines as she cares for a dying husband, bakes coffeecake for a neighbor who moved, or prays for a young woman and her unborn child.

God's beauty contest doesn't require flawless skin and a trim physique, but goes deeper to the loveliness of a caring heart. Give me *your* eyes, Lord, to look past the superficial and into the eternal.

Your beauty . . . should be that of your inner self, the unfading beauty of a gentle and quiet spirit . . .
—I PETER 3:3–4

Thought . . . Do you ignore a woman's scruffy "surface," preferring her genuinely beautiful character? Or do you avoid someone with gorgeous clothes and just-so make-up because you don't measure up? She may be using her *polish* to hide her *pain*. Determine to look below the surface and love all God's women.

Don't Let Me Forget

BY BETTY CHAPMAN PLUDE

Patience is bitter, but its fruit is sweet.

—JO PETTY

My curiosity was aroused. *Why,* I thought, *does that cheerful lady wear a headband? That style left with the "Hippy" era!*

After three years of observing this happy lady rushing around our conference, obviously one of the organizers, I continued to wonder.

This year the "headband lady" was the director of the conference. The last day she gave the farewell talk. The closing address was always dynamic, so I knew to expect something incredibly touching.

She began by saying, "Many of you, I am sure, have wondered why I wear this headband." I perked up and listened as she continued to explain. In a past season, she had been a "Hippy" and had taken drugs.

When she became a Christian, she relinquished her former lifestyle and began to minister to those who were now in the same trap. Surprisingly, she became critical and impatient. In amazement, she recognized that in forgetting her own struggle to change, ugly intolerance had crept in. The outdated headband adorning her forehead was to remind her from where she came. Her exuberance stemmed from her thankfulness and love for God.

Her words checked me and demonstrated a wonderful attitude that I will never forget. I pray that I will feel God's nudge whenever I begin to lose sight of my past.

And we urge you, brothers, warn those who are idle, encourage the timid, help the weak, be patient with everyone.

—I THESSALONIANS 5:14

Thought . . . In your "zeal" to serve the Lord, do you judge others? We are all *sinners.* If you never lose sight of that, you will have a "common ground" and compassion with which to reach others for Christ.

Fitting In

BY DEBORAH SILLAS NELL

I am only one; but still I am one. I cannot do everything, but still I can do something; I will not refuse to do this something I can do.

—HELEN KELLER

"There, Dad, I think that piece goes there," said my daughter, Sophia, pointing to a hole in the jigsaw puzzle.

Craig picked up the piece and tried to make it fit into the space, turning it in various directions. He even tried pressing and ever so gently pushing it into place.

"No, Sophia, this does not fit." "Ohhh," sighed my daughter, disappointed. "Every piece fits into its own special place. If we force one piece into the wrong spot, the puzzle won't be what it's supposed to be," I explained.

This was my daughter's first 500-piece jigsaw puzzle and she was eager to complete it.

A few nights later, only three pieces left to be inserted, we discovered that they were missing. We searched every inch of our apartment, to no avail.

What a shame, I thought. *The puzzle is not complete without those three pieces. All that work for nothing!* I had never before realized the importance of each individual puzzle piece. It didn't matter if all the other pieces were in place. If one were missing, the puzzle was flawed.

We did eventually find those pieces. When we did, I realized how important each of us is to the body of Christ. We're like those puzzle pieces. As Christians, each of us uniquely fits into God's puzzle, Christ's body. No one can take another's place. And if one is missing, His body is incomplete.

Just as each of us has one body with many members, and these members do not all have the same function, so in Christ we who are many form one body, and each member belongs to all the others.

—ROMANS 12:4–5

Thought . . . Are you a pillar or a pew-sitter? If you do more than your share of ministry in the Church, you prevent someone from doing hers. If you do nothing, Christ's body is incomplete.

Your Day Is Coming

BY RITA J. MAGGART

God said that He will exalt you in due time, but remember, He is referring to His time and not yours!

—A.W. TOZER

*A*s a young girl watching my older sister go on dates, ride in cars with friends, wear makeup, and go to ball games, the words "Your day is coming" did little to stave off that old green-eyed monster of jealousy.

Life's not fair, I thought, as my mother tried to comfort me. Once I even accused my mother of loving my sister more than me because she let her be born first! Mother just looked at me lovingly and reminded, "Your day is coming." Waiting to turn sixteen in the turbulent 1960s was not easy.

And some twenty years later, another test of my patience presented itself when I became the mother of three young sons who participated in almost every sport imaginable. Again, I was waiting—waiting on the sidelines, beside swimming pools, at hockey rinks, and in gyms. Yet, along the way, I did become a pretty good photographer and had the opportunity to read many books.

Waiting seasons can be productive when they are used for preparation. I look back at all the time I have been getting ready for my day to come and realize that the joyride has actually been in learning new skills, building relationships, educating myself, embracing patience, and, most importantly, in getting to know Christ. Mother said, "Your day is coming." But Jesus says, "Your day is here. Spend it with me."

You need to persevere so that when you have done the will of God, you will receive what He has promised.

—HEBREWS 10:36

Thought . . . Do you find *waiting* hard? In reality, waiting is really *living*. Make the most of it and enjoy where you are on the way to where you are going!

Ah, Sweet Repose

BY THELMA WELLS

God wants to lead you into His purposes.

—DR. GEORGE O. WOOD

*F*or years I felt anxious, unable to determine what my mission in life should be.

It wasn't that I hadn't set goals. It's that I didn't know how to set my sights on God and let Him lead me.

My business was at an all-time low and we had a mound of bills. I heard Dr. Charles Stanley teach on anxiety. He said the only way to get rid of anxiety was to humble yourself before the Lord and cast your cares on Him.

I was broken. I lay sobbing on the floor praying, "Lord, I give my body, mind, soul, career, and family to you. Teach me your will."

Later, I woke up and discovered I was still on the floor. I had been in a deep, restful sleep. It must have been what the Bible calls "sweet sleep" because I awakened singing. That was a turning point.

A couple years later I was in a gathering with established businesswomen. One said, "Let's share our goals for next year."

It was my turn. "I don't have any goals." The group looked puzzled. *No goals? How can she be successful?*

"I used to set goals, but I've decided that wherever God leads me, I'll follow."

It's true that goals help us to be disciplined. Goals in and of themselves aren't bad. But setting goals had led me into a perplexing and fretful place I didn't want to go back to. First I needed to humbly go before God and give Him my concerns. Then He will provide me with direction.

Many are the plans in a man's heart, but it is the Lord's purpose that prevails.

—PROVERBS 19:21

Thought . . . Are all your actions strictly goal-driven? Make your foremost goal to know God. Then it will be easy to follow His directions.

Joy on a Roller Coaster?

BY SHERYL PATTERSON

For every minute you are angry you lose sixty seconds of happiness.

—RALPH WALDO EMERSON

*H*eat waves radiated from the asphalt and the blistering sun beat down upon me. I pushed on, going from ride to ride, in an "amusement park." "Amusing" at this point it was not! My children ran around screaming and playing. Where did they get all their energy?

With peak crowds and lines sprawling like a giant octopus, I followed the traffic flow, only to inflict my body with more tortures in what people called an awesome, incredible, cool ride. The contraption slung me back and forth horizontally, while viciously flipping me upside down, then crashing to a halt. My challenge was not so much to survive and "tell about it," as it was to keep my lunch down and pray that everyone else did, too! I felt like a large bottle of *Elmer's Glue* when the little boy ahead of me dropped his melted ice cream bar on my foot, and it ran down through my sandal straps and between my toes. This season of motherhood was also melting from joy to anger—fast!

Life can leave us feeling as if we are continually on a roller coaster, our emotions in constant flux—climbing high one minute, then instantaneously plummeting the next.

In that stressful, overheated day, after I began to pray, I quickly felt the Holy Spirit stir in me the fruit of joy as I entered into my children's delight. How comforting it is to know that because of Christ's death and resurrection, no season of my life is slow or boring. Life with Jesus is far more exciting than any amusement "joy ride" that man can invent. It is a life filled with *His* joy—and that is absolutely awesome!

You have filled my heart with greater joy . . .

—PSALM 4:7

Thought . . . Are your emotions dictated by your circumstances, which continuously fluctuate up and down? Jesus remains the same yesterday, today, and tomorrow. And He promises you His full joy, despite your situation.

Preparation Is Everything

BY ARMENÉ HUMBER

Nothing is for nothing in the kingdom of God.

—BARBARA CARR

A job seeker's class was the last place I expected to be at this stage of my life. But here I was, by necessity not choice, with thirty women in the "midlife" season, trying to transform myself from homemaker to career woman. The career counselor called it "transitioning." I called it terror.

A battery of tests had determined my goal: medical sales. But I wondered, hopelessly, how I could get a sales job when all I could put on my résumé was outdated nursing experience and twenty-odd years of PTA fundraising, room-mothering, and a little church leadership. I treasured those years of mothering and volunteer work, but my absence from the marketplace had not equipped me for a career, especially one in sales.

Somewhat embarrassed, I slid my list of accomplishments across the desk to the résumé counselor and waited to hear that I was wasting my time. Instead, she smiled brightly, "You have accumulated some great sales skills!" I leaned closer to be sure that she had the right list. "Think about it," she encouraged. "Weren't you *selling* when you convinced donors to contribute to the school fundraiser or persuaded women to attend your church retreat? You have developed strong verbal persuasive skills that are perfect for sales!"

I was amazed at the competent woman I now saw in my finished résumé. Maybe I wasn't lacking after all! I may not have earned a penny during those twenty years, but while I was busy with the PTA, God had been busy preparing me for a career.

And God is able to make all grace abound to you, so that in all things at all times, having all that you need, you will abound in every good work.

— II CORINTHIANS 9:8

Thought . . . Are you making a ministry change—whether in the Church or workplace? All of life is a preparation for ministry. List all your cumulative skills and find the common thread that God has woven through them to pull you in a new direction.

The Cheerful Giver

BY BECKY TIRABASSI

Giving is a joy if we do it in the right spirit. It all depends on whether we think of it as "What can I spare?" or as "What can I share?"

—ESTHER YORK BARKHOLDER

One Christmas, my prayers focused on giving *cheerfully*. I was inclined to give out of duty. But the Word of God caused me to examine my motives.

I purposed to change. An opportunity arose for me to act.

We put our house for sale after I developed the desire to become a cheerful giver. At the same time a Jamaican missionary wanted desperately to attend the *Billy Graham Evangelists' Conference* in Europe. He did not have money and did not know anyone who could help except for me, because I had been his group leader in *Youth For Christ*.

When my friend boldly asked me for five hundred dollars (which I did not have), it appeared God prodded him to call me, providing me an opportunity to give willingly and obey. I believed we would sell our house by the time he needed the money. I told my friend I would send him ten percent of the earnings in time for him to attend.

At that point I got down on my knees and asked God if He would quickly sell our house. I told Him we would give ten percent of our earnings to our friend. It was exactly ten percent of our profit that I sent in the nick of time for our friend to attend the conference! That experience was a turning point in trusting God. I was stretched to believe I could be a cheerful giver and that God would help me in the process.

Jesus answered, "If you want to be perfect, go, sell your possessions and give to the poor, and you will have treasure in heaven."

—MATTHEW 19:21

Thought . . . Do you find it easy to give? If not, consider all the blessings God has given you and that He owns everything anyway. Can you share *His* bounty with others?

144

Singleness

Mr. Right

BY MARY WHELCHEL

When peace, like a river attendeth my way, when sorrows like sea billows roll—Whatever my lot, Thou hast taught me to say, it is well, it is well with my soul.

—HORATIO G. SPAFFORD

After eleven years of marriage, I got divorced. Nothing could have been farther from my plans or Christian beliefs. Thrust overnight into a world for which I was unprepared, I was insecure and felt pressured to succeed as career woman and mother. I felt proving I was okay meant finding a man.

I knew God hated divorce and thought He would punish me with being single forever. Determined not to allow that, for ten years I pursued one main goal: finding the perfect man to marry. Because I thought this relationship would bring me happiness, my relationship with the Lord took a back seat as I "blended into" my new world. People would have been surprised to know I was a committed Christian.

My life was an emotional roller coaster: I flew high when a relationship was good, but when it soured, I pursued job promotions, bought clothes—anything to fill my void.

Finally one night after ending an especially promising relationship, for the first time in ten years I began reading my Bible. In a desperate prayer of relinquishment and commitment I said, "Lord, I'll do anything you want, only give me peace. I'll even be single forever."

When I released clenched fists, peace like a river flooded my soul immediately. Although for the past eighteen years I've remained single, I've found the perfect Man in my life. His name is Jesus and He is all and more than I ever wanted in an earthly man. He's my Mr. Right!

You will keep in perfect peace him whose mind is steadfast, because he trusts in you.

—ISAIAH 26:3

Thought . . . Do you long for a husband? No man, no matter how godly, will ever meet your needs like Jesus. Find complete satisfaction and identity in Him.

The Assignment

BY KAREN RILEY

One of the reasons why it needs no special education to be a Christian is that Christianity is an education itself.

—C.S. LEWIS

*M*artha was my deaconess "assignment," my requirement to visit the sick and elderly in our church. I dreaded the thought of visiting this ninety-year-old woman. To me, a woman in her mid-thirties, these visits seemed daunting. How could I relate? I worked full-time and was extremely busy with my career.

Yet somehow I found the courage to see Martha. Over the years I was to eventually visit with her, I discovered that Martha had more to teach me than she needed my comfort. I learned that she had been single all her life, so she, too, had worked full-time. And, although she *retired* the year I was born, she understood the struggles of balancing work and home.

Martha dedicated her life to serving Christ and others, and when the rough roads came in her life, she clung to the knowledge that Jesus held her in His precious hand. By showing me her humble surroundings, she taught me that material possessions have little value and God honors a thankful heart.

Martha did not have much money, and although she had not been able to attend church for several years, Martha would often hand me a small green envelope and end our visits by saying, "Would you please take my offering and place it in the plate when it goes by?"

God gave me priceless life-lessons through the life of a woman who had lived through many more seasons than I. My "assignment" turned out to be *me*.

Teach us to number our days aright, that we may gain a heart of wisdom.

—PSALM 90:12

Thought . . . Do you cultivate women friends of all ages? Not only can you learn valuable spiritual lessons from mature women, but you, in turn, can pass them along to women who are younger than you.

Never Alone

BY VESTA-NADINE SEVERS

Millions of spiritual creatures walk the earth unseen, both when we sleep and when we wake.

—JOHN MILTON

I had spent an hour in the lawyer's office discussing my up-coming divorce. The decision had not been easy; it was fraught with emotion, tears, and anguish about my five children who needed protection from constant verbal abuse. Professionals said that I must stand between their father and them. Now was time for other action.

It was a clear, crisp fall morning, and the sun shone brightly when I left the parking lot after the visit with the lawyer. I really wasn't thinking of anything special, just glad to get the hurdle behind me. As I entered the freeway, I suddenly began singing *Never Alone*: " I've heard the voice of my Savior, telling me still to fight on. He promised never to leave me, never to leave me alone."

There appeared a brilliant large oval light beside the car and I felt a holy presence. I believed it to be an angel. But I was driving rather quickly around a curve, so I didn't dare look for fear I might loose control of the car.

The presence not only calmed me, but confirmed the words of the song that God would never leave me through the difficult days and years ahead.

The memory of the angel's presence and the song have strengthened me repeatedly during the child-raising season. God provided many things for us and has never left me alone.

The Lord is close to the brokenhearted and saves those who are crushed in spirit.

—PSALM 34:18

Thought . . . Since your divorce, do you wonder how you will manage without your husband? Because He never leaves you alone, God will provide for all your needs—and for those of your children.

After the Storm Comes the Rainbow

BY INA C. STRAIN

In Christ we are relaxed and at peace in the midst of the confusions, bewilderments, and perplexities of this life. The storm rages, but our hearts are at rest. We have found peace—at last!

—BILLY GRAHAM

Sometimes I sit and think. Sometimes I just sit! Such was the case as I sat curled up in the corner of my couch. I was at peace with myself and my world, until I glanced down at my hand. I couldn't believe my eyes. The diamond in my engagement ring was missing! I had worn that ring for nearly fifty years. My husband had just recently died and now the token of our love was gone, too.

I searched everywhere, but didn't find the diamond. I was devastated. A "storm" had broken over my head, an emotional deluge that overwhelmed me. I called several of my friends, asking them to pray that God would "still the storm" and give me peace. He did! I went to bed and, amazingly, was able to sleep.

Ten days later while waiting for my cleaning lady to come, I opened the louvered door of my closet. Noticing that my shoes were in disarray, I sat down on the floor to rearrange them. Still sitting on the floor, I saw three tiny specks of lint on the carpet. I picked up the first, reached for the second, and "Oh, Glory Be," it was my diamond! It had been buried, face down, in the mat of the carpet with only a tiny bit showing. I picked it up and it shone like a rainbow.

Coincidence? Happenstance? Impossible! It was God's divine intervention. He gave me my very own miracle. But the greater miracle was the peace that God had already given the night I had lost my diamond, the night He calmed my storm.

He stilled the storm to a whisper; the waves of the sea were hushed.

—PSALM 107:29

Thought . . . Are you being tossed about in an especially stormy season? Ask for the Prince of Peace to calm the waves. If He doesn't, ask Him to get in the boat with you. The storm will no longer matter—only His presence and peace in the midst of it.

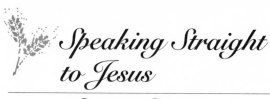

Speaking Straight to Jesus

BY ROSALIND RINKER

Prayer is nought but a rising desire of the heart into God by withdrawing of the heart from all earthly thoughts.

—WALTER HYLTON

On a snowy night, I had a difficult choice to make for a girl of fifteen. There was a party at one house and a prayer meeting at another. I chose the prayer meeting.

I couldn't spot a person my age. My first thought was to get out, but hadn't I made my choice?

I stayed. Sometimes I felt I was an onlooker. How did they know when to pray? My heart beat faster. Should I pray when I was the only teenager?

While I was struggling, an older lady began to pray.

I said to myself, she can't speak English! No one can understand. I listened some more.

I withheld judgment. Suddenly I felt my heart being held in God's hand. The old German lady was crying! She wasn't ashamed. She was speaking to Him. Not to us. He was there. I knew it.

I would pray aloud and speak straight to Him. I would not be afraid and not care if my words got tangled. I would forget people and think about Him.

"Dear Lord Jesus . . ." I heard myself praying aloud for the first time. I did cry and my words did get tangled, but it was all right. I had spoken to Him. He was there.

As the snow crunched under my feet that cold winter night on my way home, my heart was warm with the freshness of talking with Jesus Christ. I had met Him.

He loved me and I loved Him, and the world was new, and I was young and life was good.

After they prayed, the place where they were meeting was shaken . . . All the believers were one in heart and mind.

—ACTS 4:31–32

Thought . . . Do you struggle with prayer? Think of it as simply a conversation between two people who love each other and you will never run out of things to say to God. You will also pause often to listen.

Such a Simple Revelation

BY JAN NATIONS

He who has not Christmas in his heart will never find it under a tree.

—ROY L. SMITH

*E*ach day had blended into the next in my quest for survival after an unexpected divorce. Now the most difficult time of the year was rapidly approaching—the holiday season.

As I prepared to leave the office on Friday before Christmas, the owner of the company handed me a ticket to an event that he was unable to attend. "Here, Jan, I'd like you to represent me at this gala tonight." In my current state of numbness, I didn't realize that he was actually sending me there to help me avoid one more lonely evening.

Thinking I was obligated to attend, I forced myself to drive downtown, parking my car a few blocks from the building where the festivities would occur. I found myself virtually alone on the city sidewalk that giant snowflakes had shrouded in a blanket of white.

Wondering how I would be able to appear happy to the crowd of people inside, I slowed my steps and looked upward to a streetlight which magnified the drifting snowflakes. Staring into the beauty of each unique flake, I was momentarily mesmerized. Filled with the intensity of God's presence, it was as though I heard the words, "The gift of the Christ Child is for single people, too." Stunned by such a simple, yet profound revelation, my heart quickened with joy at the realization that the miracle of Christmas truly is for everyone.

> For to us a Child is born, to us a Son is given, and the government will be on His shoulders. And He will be called Wonderful Counselor, Mighty God, Everlasting Father, Prince of Peace."
>
> —ISAIAH 9:6

Thought . . . Are the holidays difficult for you because you live alone? Concentrate on the meaning of Christmas, letting the Christ child be "born in you." Feel His presence and know that you are never alone.

Life after Divorce

BY MARTICIA BURNS MCKINNEY

Be not afraid of life. Believe that life is worth living, And your belief will help create the fact.

—WILLIAM JAMES

Several years ago my son, Will, talked me into taking a trip out West. Common sense would have told me that we could not afford this trip, but I had just been through a divorce and I was not thinking like a rational adult. I was thinking like a woman who had lost her faith. For two years I had been praying for my marriage to be restored. When that didn't happen, all I wanted to do was run away from the past, the painful memories, and God. I felt certain my life was over.

Even though I had a gnawing suspicion that only a crazy woman would drive all over the West alone with an eleven-year-old, Will's enthusiasm was infectious. And every time I thought about the trip, I felt something I hadn't felt for two years—excitement!

When we finally arrived out West, we were overwhelmed by the beauty of brilliant blue skies, water-colored deserts, and craggy canyons. But the memory I cherish the most was of Touloume Meadows, a vast flowered field dotted with sparking puddles. As I stood there breathing the fragrant air, I sensed God's presence and His love for me. I realized that I had so much to live for, starting with my son.

Will is grown now and, recently, he sent me a postcard from Touloume Meadows. "Remember this place, Mom?" he wrote. Remember? How could I forget? That wasn't just a beautiful place that I visited once, it was where God taught me that life's seasons continue after divorce.

For your Maker is your husband—the Lord Almighty is His name—the Holy One of Israel is your Redeemer . . .
—ISAIAH 54:5

Thought . . . Have you gone through a divorce? . . . are you about to? Though you experience great pain in being irrevocably separated from your husband, you will never be abandoned. God, Himself, will be your husband.

A Lesson in Obedience

BY JAN NATIONS

Beware of succumbing to failure as inevitable; make it the stepping-stone to success.

—OSWALD CHAMBERS

Three years after an abrupt end to my thirty-two-year marriage, I was vacuuming one day and felt my mind being flooded with thoughts about how the pain of it all could have been lessened. Grabbing a pen and pad, I hastily jotted down the healing insights. Once I had written them down, I thought I could file those notes and forget them.

Surprise! Not being able to shake the feeling that I was supposed to *do* something with these words, I finally decided that they resembled greeting card verses. The only artist I knew was my former husband, whom I promptly called (for the first time since the divorce) and asked if he would like to design original watercolor artwork. He not only agreed, but also paid for the printing!

The message of the cards is to encourage protecting the children, maintaining dignity, and conducting oneself in a way that can always be looked upon later without shame.

The local newspaper featured an article about how a divorced couple could work together to help heal other families through similar seasons of pain. Many radio and television interviews resulted.

People told me that they had received hope from realizing that God could help them forgive and transform their pain into joy.

I was reminded that God is able . . . all He needs is our obedience!

Bear with each other and forgive whatever grievances you may have against one another. Forgive as the Lord forgave you.

—COLOSSIANS 3:13

Thought . . . Do you feel bitterness since your divorce? While you must forgive, sometimes relationships are severed completely. However, if you think that God wishes you to maintain some form of contact, rely on Him to show you what it is.

Sharecropper's Daughter

BY DR. KATHRYN PRESLEY

Happiness, I have discovered, is nearly always a rebound from hard work.

—DAVID GRAYSON

*M*iss Lasater taught children in the "little room" of our two-roomed country school during the Depression, and her "sweet fragrance" and encouragement called me to teach. Our "share-cropper" family carried water from wells a half mile away, and worked all day in the cotton fields. Getting a good education seemed like a dream, but Miss Lasater showed me possibilities.

It took decades to work my way through college, but I never stopped dreaming of being a teacher. My public school teaching career was filled with chaos: violence, drugs, despair. Graduate school was interrupted by family tragedies. I learned to do everything through Christ Who gave me strength.

Yet the coveted Ph.D. came just forty-one years after I graduated from high school. Prestigious positions went to much younger neophytes, so I took a position on a small campus. Many of my students are older; most are minorities from impoverished backgrounds, the first of their families to attend college. Who could understand their struggles better than I? As they grapple with standard English, I tell them my family "seen" things others saw, and "heerd" things others only heard. We watched smoke drift up our "chimley" and checked books from the local "liberry."

God truly had a sense of humor when He made ME an English teacher, but I have a sure solution for poverty. It's a personal, vital relationship with our Creator, hard work, and as much education as the mind can absorb. Then "dare to dream" and never, never give up!

No discipline seems pleasant at the time, but painful. Later on, however, it produces a harvest of righteousness and peace for those who have been trained by it.
—HEBREWS 12:11

Thought . . . What teachers, whether in school or Sunday School, helped influence you positively and changed your life forever? If there is still an opportunity to thank them, write a special letter of appreciation.

God's Red Pacer

BY KAREN KOSMAN

A laugh, to be joyous, must flow from a joyous heart, for without kindness there can be no true joy.

—THOMAS CARLYLE

*B*ecause I was a single mom, my budget had little room for emergencies. My Chevy had broken down and was towed to a garage. My mechanic called me with bad news. "Karen, for about $900 I can put a rebuilt engine in for you."

Numbed by the news, I said, "I'll need time to think."

"Okay. Call me."

"Thank you. I will."

The whole situation was a drain on my finances. If I continued to take a taxi at 5:00 A.M. to work, my monthly transportation bill would be over $200. The problem seemed insurmountable. I prayed, "Lord, I don't have the money for repairs, and I can't afford car payments. You're my only source of help. I relinquish this to You."

After work the next day, my phone rang. It was a friend from church. Jim said, "Karen, I have a car sitting in my garage that I don't use. It's in good mechanical condition. I would like to give it to you."

"Oh Jim, that's an amazing answer to prayer! Thank you." Tears filled my eyes, and my heart beat with excitement.

That evening, Jim delivered my car. He said, "I forgot to tell you that it's a stick shift. Do you know how to drive a stick shift?" "No. But, I'll learn."

After Jim left, I prayed, "Lord, I'm filled with joy. My red Pacer is a gift from you, and red is my favorite color!"

> . . . the Lord will watch over your coming and going both now and forevermore.
>
> —PSALM 121:8

Thought . . . Do your circumstances have you backed into a corner from which there appears to be no escape? Ask the Lord to "part the Red Sea" of your obstacles. You will miraculously walk through on dry land . . . or perhaps drive through in a red Pacer!

Wisdom

The Tapestry of Life

BY GWEN ELLIS

It is the loose ends with which men hang themselves.

—ZELDA FITZGERALD

I walked the halls of Versailles—covered with tapestries. I thought of tapestries as old fabrics with not much color and a lot of confusing images.

I realized I was looking at needlework of women who made beautiful hangings as a record of their lifetimes.

I walked closer for a look at the intricacy of tiny stitches. I realized why we use the term tapestry of life. Life is a tapestry made up of tiny actions, thoughts, words, each contributing to a lifetime.

When we talk about tapestry, we are talking about needlepoint. Needlepoint is worked on canvas, filled with tiny stitches. Canvas provides the sturdy, unchanging background upon which creative design can be worked.

Christ provided the canvas of life. He laid down the background, stability, and rules upon which your Christian walk is built. We are free to make choices in the design of our lives as we continue to grow in Christ. The Master Designer encourages us to be creative.

He wants us to explore possibilities, to live our lives so that they become beautiful tapestries. God has also given us a pattern, rules known as the Word. As we follow these rules, God promises to work in us.

A needlepointer could say, "I'm not going to follow the pattern." Doing so might create a mess that can't be untangled.

God gave us His rules, not because He is mean, but because He knows the consequences that occur in a life without structure. While rules may seem confining, they can bring great peace when followed.

Continue to work out your salvation with fear and trembling, for it is God who works in you to will and to act according to His good purpose.

—PHILIPPIANS 2:12B-13

Thought . . . Do you follow God's rules? Discover them by reading His Word. God's rules are for your benefit and He promises blessings for your obedience.

The Unexpected Channel

BY MARTHA B. YODER

Let God perform His own beautiful music on the strings of your heart.

—RAYMOND P. BRUNK

*A*s I prepared our lunch I pondered, *Will Mark's speech ever be clearly understood? Does his speech therapy do any good? This must be caused by his neurofibromatosis.*

Oh, Lord, I need Your comfort, I cried within. *Send someone to be Your channel of help to me today.*

Suddenly, leaving his contented play with his trucks in the next room, four-year-old Mark came dashing up to me. He grabbed my skirt in eagerness to get my attention.

"Sing, Mama!" he commanded in his garbled speech that only I could decipher.

I was startled!

"Sing, Mama," he repeated earnestly.

"What shall I sing?" I asked in uncertainty at this sudden unusual request.

"Sing *His Name Is Wonderful,*" Mark stated with grearter clarity than I had ever heard from him. I was amazed!

As I sang this familiar song, I suddenly realized that God had used the unexpected channel of Mark's halting speech to bring both him and me the very words that would provide us the comfort we so much needed. How great is our God and how unexpected are His blessings!

"For My thoughts are not your thoughts, neither are your ways My ways," declares the Lord.

—ISAIAH 55:8

Thought . . . Are you alert to life, attentive to surprising ways in which God might be speaking to you? So often after we pray, we don't listen and miss the very answers of God.

Moments Matter

BY RACHEL ST. JOHN-GILBERT

"I come in the little things," saith the Lord.

—EVELYN UNDERHILL

I was quite the fashion plate—an alluring mixture of Early Morning Mommy, with a smidgen of Homespun Housefrau thrown in for good measure. Admittedly, I was a bit self-conscious as I approached the charming and chatty coffee barista, but today it didn't seem to matter—Mommy had some moments to herself!

Beams of sunlight streamed through the high, oak-framed windows of *Prince Books and Coffee Shop.* I listened to the quiet. *I feel so happy right now*, I thought, *so fulfilled, right here in this very moment in time.* A stiff cup of Sumatra, a freshly baked nutmeg muffin, James Taylor softly serenading me through the speakers— I was struck by the thought that these moments felt sacred.

How many moments like these had I missed because I didn't pause to value them? So often I had felt pushed by time. But today, I was basking in the luxury of *unhurried time*—time to enjoy the gift of my senses—the taste of rich coffee, the feel of a warm mug between my hands, the sight of sunlight streaming through antique glass windows—time to check my internal compass and ponder over the direction in which it was pointing.

How often the responsibilities and tasks of everyday life have my compass pointing due east, while my heart cries out, "Go west, young woman!"

This is the day the Lord has made; let us rejoice and be glad in it.

—PSALM 118:24

Thought . . . Are you making the most of each moment God gives you? Mundane routines become sparkling experiences. Chance meetings become divine appointments. As you *live on purpose*, every season becomes sacred with meaning. Make the moments matter!

Flirting with Danger

BY LUCI SWINDOLL

It is God who must guard and rescue. If the Lord does not rescue you from a desperate circumstance, you may be sure He is guarding you instead.

—Dr. George O. Wood

The highlight of any safari is seeing a leopard. Most people never do. Nocturnal, solitary, and enormously independent, the leopard is also secretive and seductive, athletic, intelligent, and breathtakingly beautiful. An incomparable beast!

My friend and I had been on a photographic safari for a week. It had been perfect except for one thing: no leopard.

On the last day, we saw a gorgeous leopard strolling toward us with all the arrogance in the world. He turned and sat upright next to us. He was posing.

His cold, intense, unblinking stare gave us goose bumps as we made eye contact with the beast.

After snapping three rolls of film, we reluctantly drove away. Almost immediately the driver whispered, "Oh, theh is anotheh le-o-pard. You are veddy lucky with this miracle."

As we watched our second one in the same day, I relaxed and felt bold. He was so . . . close. So comfortable in our presence. So . . . charming. I wanted to pet him. I considered him a friend. I knew he was wild, but he seemed tame.

How many times have you been in a similar situation? Something seems so innocent, safe. You don't realize that what feels right has the potential to destroy.

Predators are real. That's not a problem as long as we keep our distance. But when we drop our guard, we are lured, hooked, then devoured. We wonder how something so charming could have been the messenger of death.

God's way of escape for His followers is to keep our eyes on the Lord, to fear and reverence Him.

He will not let you be tempted beyond what you can bear.
—I Corinthians 10:13a

Thought . . . Have you dropped your guard by innocently flirting with temptation? There is nothing innocent about it. Stop! Flee before you are caught in Satan's trap.

Tired of Pretending

BY BETTY J. JOHNSON

My business is not to remake myself, but to make the absolute best of what God made.

—ROBERT BROWNING

After racing through a typical day in this over-committed season—Bible study in the morning, lunch with a friend, errands and writing in the afternoon, choir practice at six—I snuggled into my recliner for a long-awaited quiet time. The phone rang. I answered with a weary hello.

"Hi, Mom! I want to tell you the latest 'Clayton-story,'" my daughter-in-law said, giggling. "What did my charming five-year-old grandson do now?" I asked.

"Since he's fascinated with super-heros, I cut up an old sheet, tied a piece around his shoulders, and sent him out to play. With his "superman cape" trailing behind him, he ran around the yard, totally wrapped up in his world of make-believe. After about thirty minutes, he wandered back into the kitchen—without his costume on. When I asked him where his cape was, he said, 'I took it off. I'm tired of pretending to be somebody I'm not.'"

Later, I began reflecting on Clayton's comment and wondered, *Am I like my grandson? Am I tired from pretending to be superwoman— believing I'm indispensable and indestructible? Is there someone else who wants to lead the Bible study? Which writing deadline does God want me to meet? Have I asked Him?*

I decided to imitate my grandson by quitting to pretend I'm superwoman and just enjoying being a child of God.

If anyone thinks he is something when he is nothing, he deceives himself. Each one should test his own actions. Then he can take pride in himself, without comparing him- self to somebody else . . .

—GALATIANS 6:4

Thought . . . Do you ever wear a "pretense mask". . . pre- tending life is fine when it's not . . . that you can juggle multiple roles when you can't? Take off your mask and discover the *real you*. You will be glad you did. And people will be glad to help you when they know your need.

Trusting the Unseen

BY JUDITH COUCHMAN

Prejudice is the child of ignorance.

—WILLIAM HAZLITT

I recognized the youngster on my porch as a new neighbor.

After eyeing her clashing shorts, shirt, and socks, I wondered what kind of mother would unleash this outfit on an unsuspecting neighborhood. Now the fashion fiasco stood thrusting a note into my hand. It read: *I am your new neighbor downstairs. I have the flu, and my daughter Mallory has only eaten a sandwich. Could you please take her to McDonald's? Thanks. Amanda.*

"Of course," I told Mallory. "Tell your mom it's okay." I thought, *Weird clothes. No food. Sending her daughter out with a stranger. What kind of mother is Amanda?*

Mallory and I drove off together, and the funky outfit faded from my judgmental vision. She filled our conversation with tidbits about her nine-year-old interests. Mallory boggled me with information about weather patterns, the space shuttle, and our local economy.

This kid is really something, I thought. I mentally chided myself for concluding that mismatched clothes meant mixed-up mothering.

Amanda knocked on my door to thank me for helping her daughter.

"My pleasure," I replied. "Mallory's a special little girl."

"I think so," she smiled.

Over the next weeks I observed Amanda as an attentive, creative, loving mother and undeserving of my hasty, critical impressions. I'd mistakenly assessed a few physical qualities instead of acquainting myself with her soul. Without knowing it, Amanda reminded me to delve into the truth about people, rather than what floats on the surface. She reminded me that God asks us to see what resides in the heart.

. . . God does not judge by external appearance . . .

—GALATIANS 2:6

Thought . . . Do you judge parents by their children's actions? Rather than criticize, offer to babysit. You may learn that there is more to the parenting season than meets the eye.

163

Do Not Judge!

BY RUTH E. MCDANIEL

Do not judge, and you will never be mistaken.

—JEAN-JACQUES ROUSSEAU

I watched through the window as my next door neighbor blew leaves off his driveway. Row after row of dead leaves were deliberately blown closer to my house until, finally, they were stacked up high—smack dab against my siding! *What nerve!* I thought, fuming, as my blood pressure rose.

Our neighbors were strangers until 1991 when I became my husband's caregiver. On sunny days, I like to park his wheelchair on the front porch to watch the kids play and the people walk by. It wasn't long before we became acquainted with the bypassers and those who lived around us. We saw the man next door regularly, and (I thought) we had developed a warm friendship. I couldn't believe he would be so inconsiderate.

Suddenly, just as my hostility level was reaching its peak, he began to bag both our leaves and his, then hauled the bags out to the curb for trash pick-up!

What a lesson! I was judging him and finding him guilty, when all along he was performing a service for us. I promptly asked the Lord's forgiveness, grateful that my neighbor would never know how I had jumped to conclusions.

I want to remember this lesson for the rest of my life. So, to make certain I never forget, I memorized Matthew 7:5: "You hypocrite, first take the plank out of your own eye, and then you will see clearly to remove the speck from your brother's eye."

Duly noted!

Do not judge, or you too will be judged.

—MATTHEW 7:1

Thought . . . Have you ever been misjudged? It's a terrible feeling. The next time you are tempted to judge, remember what it feels like. You can never understand someone unless you have walked around in her high heels!

164

The Right Armor

BY SHARON P. MOORE

... whose armor is his honest thought, and simple truth his utmost skill.

—SIR HENRY WOTTON

I have worked as a secretary for many years, but never for anyone as unpredictable as my last boss. His bad moods always took me by surprise and whenever he snapped at me, I was at a loss to know what to say or do. Getting along with others was ingrained in me from childhood, so I found this especially distressing.

When I read a self-help author's opinion that everyone wears different "masks," depending upon with whom they are interacting, I thought that maybe "hiding behind a mask" was the way to work with my boss. I would pretend that everything was fine, even if I were seething inwardly. That same week I read Romans 13:14 (KJV): "But put ye on the Lord Jesus Christ . . ." God's Word went straight to my heart, refuting my worldly wisdom. I began to pray for inner calm and confidence and the right words when the time came. Confrontation was not my forté!

An opportunity came following my yearly employee review. After presenting a favorable evaluation, my boss asked if I had any comments.

"I'm on your side," I calmly stated, "but I don't know what to do when you're 'gruff.'"

He then admitted that he had some "rough edges," but intended no harm. It wasn't exactly an apology, but I believe that we reached an understanding. After that, his bad moods seemed to disappear.

The workplace teaches some hard lessons, but how to "put on Christ," instead of a mask, is one of the sweetest I have ever learned.

Rather, clothe yourselves with the Lord Jesus . . .
—ROMANS 13:14

Thought . . . Do you openly express your feelings in the workplace with both boss and coworkers? If you are having a difficulty with someone, ask the Lord whether to speak in love or to remain silent. There is a place for both options, under God's direction.

Roses or a Right Heart?

BY TWILA PARIS

Man sees your actions, but God your motives.

—THOMAS À. KEMPIS

I learned the lesson of this passage [I Samuel 15:22, below] as a very little girl.

One day when I had been bad, I hit upon a brilliant plan. Little did I know it was the same plan used for thousands of years by children everywhere—including my mother. I rushed out to the garden to pick a bouquet of roses, knowing she would be so overwhelmed with gratitude and delight that she would not be able to find it in her heart to punish me for my crime. With a little luck, she might even be so distracted that she would forget about it altogether.

Of course, you're already way ahead of me, because you tried to do this, too. You know that my mom graciously thanked me for my gift, then sat down and took the time to teach me that obedience was much more important than sacrifice, not only to her, but to God.

We all know that God wants our obedience, not our sacrifices, but sometimes, the Enemy can still tempt us to bribe God with our adult versions of a bouquet from the garden. The next time you offer a sacrifice to the Lord, take a moment to check your heart and make sure it's a sacrifice of love, not a substitute for obedience.

Does the Lord delight in burnt offerings and sacrifices as much as in obeying the voice of the Lord?

—I SAMUEL 15:22

Thought . . . Do you give God the sacrifice of your service, instead of your very self—your devotion and adoration? Obey God by worshiping Him. Then let your *doing* flow from your *being*. He will show you the right thing to do.

Go Back!

BY PAMELA DOWD

The heart is happiest when it beats for others.

—ANONYMOUS

*S*he was an ordinary-looking person, about middle-aged. I glanced at her handmade garage sale sign and kept driving. *Go back*, my internal sensor prompted. Circling the block, I pulled into the parking lot of a building that I didn't recognize.

She wobbled over, profusely thanking me for stopping. Her warm welcome flooded my heart with joy. As I got out of my car, she led me inside. The front room was lined with jumbled piles of "miscellany" and a handful of mentally challenged citizens. They watched as I examined their castaway possessions. I looked through rumpled clothes and dented pots that I didn't need. *What do you want me to do, God?* I breathed.

I made a donation and started to leave. It felt good to offer them money that I, myself, needed, as well. On my way out, the director stopped me and said, "We're having a free car wash out back; pull your car around."

Water sprayed randomly as ten happy adults wrestled buckets, sponges, and soap. It took them thirty minutes, but I had the cleanest van in town. One lady ran into the building and hauled out a bag filled with sweatshirts. Some used them to dry the van, but one puzzled fellow tried his on first. As the torn hose sprayed sprinkles into the sunlight, I smiled. With what a joyful surprise God had blessed me that day!

A happy heart makes the face cheerful . . .

—PROVERBS 15:13

Thought . . . Do you sometimes hesitate in reaching out to those who are different from you? In so doing, you miss experiencing the unique delights with which our creative God bestows all His children.

Good News Bearers

BY PAT DEVINE

Beatitude-people are kingdom-people. They call us forth and urge us on toward that kingdom [to] bless the world.

—MACRINA WIEDERKEHR

On a recent visit to the drugstore for a headache remedy, I found myself facing a friendly cashier who asked, "How are you today?" Not about to give her a report on my medical condition, I smiled rather weakly and said, "Just fine, thanks, and you?" She said, "Just great!" and went on to philosophize: "It's amazing what words can do. There's a man who comes in every day who says, 'I'm tip-top.' Another says, 'Fit as a fiddle; all tuned up.' People with attitudes like that keep me going." I left the store thinking, "It's catching." I felt better even before I had a chance to take a pill.

This reminded me of other people in my life who have offered words that brought life and light to many an otherwise dreary season—the Good News Bearers.

Dick—greets friends with "How are you, you wonderful you!" Suddenly, I feel wonderful.

Ellen—when asked "Who are you?" answers "I'm the King's Kid!" It reminds me that I, too, am a child of God—heir to the Kingdom. I smile and stand a little taller.

Marylou—always answers the phone with "Praise God!" It causes telemarketers to forget their spiel, others to grump, "Just say hello!" But it inspires many to say "Amen!"

Ann—a favorite aunt, always answers my phone calls with "What's on your good mind?"—words that tell me I am special.

No forced or phony compliments meant to flatter—just words of joy from a deep well of God-ness, bubbling up, spilling over and out—blessing everyone in their path. "Beatitude People," Macrina Wiederkehr calls them.

God saw all that He had made, and it was very good.

—GENESIS 1:31A

Thought . . . Are you feeling down and out? It has been said that attitude determines your altitude. Think positive thoughts. Speak encouraging words. And in no time, you'll be flying high and lifting others up with you!

I Want That Refund!

BY KATHY COLLARD MILLER

I have held many things in my hands, and I have lost them all; but whatever I have placed in God's hands, that I still possess.

—MARTIN LUTHER

My husband and I had made a major purchase from a Christian business. Later, they informed us that they couldn't supply the item, and promised a refund. When we didn't receive it after repeated requests, I was furious. I couldn't believe that God would want His money treated this way.

One day as I had my devotions, my thoughts again turned to the situation. I wrote in my journal, "This is a test of whether we are stewards or owners of God's money. Father God, this is not hidden from Your sight and neither are Your eyes closed and uncaring. Thank you that I can surrender this to You."

I decided to find a verse to memorize so that when my anger welled up again, I could meditate on that verse. The Lord whispered in my heart, "Look at Jeremiah 17." At first I resisted because I knew that passage didn't deal with this situation. But when He whispered it again, I turned there. At the top of that page, a verse I'd marked in yellow many years earlier caught my eye. "My eyes are on all their ways; they are not hidden from me, nor is their sin concealed from my eyes (Jeremiah 16:17)."

Those were some of the very words I'd just written in my journal! God was telling me that He truly was aware. In time, we did receive the refund, but God had already done the important part: helping me to release His money.

> No one can serve two masters. Either he will hate the one
> and love the other, or he will be devoted to the one and
> despise the other. You cannot serve both God and Money.
> —MATTHEW 6:24

Thought . . . Do you believe that God owns all your money and possessions? If you hold your assets loosely, you will not lament their loss. You will consider anything you receive as an undeserved blessing in any season.

Being Neighborly

BY SANDI GORDON

After the verb "to love," "to help" is the most beautiful verb in the world.

—BERTHA VON SUTTNER

I often wonder who learns more from whom—children or their parents—for children are superb teachers. One memorable lesson I received from my nine-year-old came during the fall season when I peered out the window and saw my daughter single-handedly raking the neighbor's yard. The middle-aged woman lived alone. Her home sat on a huge corner lot, shaded by gigantic oak and maple trees—definitely one of the toughest leaf-raking yards on the block.

In all honesty, I was not pleased to see Stephanie across the street, clearing away a path in the leaves, while our own lawn remained untouched. I wondered if my daughter expected to be paid for a job for which she had not been hired. Yet, I held my tongue as Stephanie painstakingly worked all day, dragging one rake-load of leaves at a time to the curb. Surprisingly, she stuck with the task until the job was done.

When our neighbor arrived home, she was obviously pleased and offerred to pay Stephanie. Refusing money, Stephanie shuffled home, tucking her rake in our garage. Curious, I asked Stephanie why she had taken on such an overwhelming job. She replied, "I just figured the woman lived all by herself and had no one to help her with all those leaves."

I knew then that my daughter had been paid well, having experienced the blessings of giving. I profited, too, having received a needed refresher course on neighborly love.

. . . Love your neighbor as yourself.

—MATTHEW 22:39

Thought . . . Do you champion the old adage, "Good fences make good neighbors?" Take a Biblical refresher course on neighborly love and *mend* fences, instead. Take your neighbor a "Love Basket" filled with teas, scones, and jams. Enjoy tea and sympathy together.

You Can't Take It with You

BY LYNN D. MORRISSEY

Wherever you find the treasure, you will find the heart.

—RICHARD J. FOSTER

I fumed out of the house spouting angry words at my poor, patient husband. "That's it! I'm not putting up with a used car breaking down one more time! I want a new one!"

Headed for work in my decrepit Mustang, I regretted words I'd vented at Michael, yet felt justified, stubbornly holding my ground. After all, I worked, and deserved decent transportation. We would just have to make the budget stretch somehow. I didn't want a "better" used car. I wanted the best—a *new* one! I refused to be in a position to have to worry incessantly over repairs.

Just then, a large trailer passed me on the highway transporting a colorful array of new cars. They sparkled in the sun like jewels and I coveted them. Literally seconds later, a similar trailer passed, hauling rusted wrecks to the recycler.

In that fleeting moment, God gave me an object lesson in establishing values. Why was I "spinning my wheels" when even the "lilies of the field" didn't spin, labor, or worry? Yet, God provided for them and even for birds of the air. Wouldn't He provide for my needs, too? Why was I fretting over material things that would eventually be destroyed and wouldn't accompany me to Heaven anyway?

That day I prayed that God would change my heart to value things of eternal worth. I still haven't bought a new car and haven't regretted it for a minute!

Do not store up for yourselves treasures on earth, where moth and rust destroy, and where thieves break in and steal.
—MATTHEW 6:19

Thought . . . What do you truly value—God, Himself, or His material blessings? Stop, take a heart-check, and realize that the only blessings you will "take with you," are the spiritual ones.

Lifting the Veil

BY SUE MONK KIDD

I've always regarded nature as the clothing of God.

—ALAN HOVHANESS

On a clear afternoon in February, Ann called me outside from my desk and all my "important" work to "see something."

"See what?" I asked, reluctant to be interrupted.

"Come and I'll show you."

A year or so before I might well have refused such an "unproductive" breather from work, but today I followed her to the backyard where she pointed to a strangely shaped cloud. Her eyes were dancing with discovery. "It's a unicorn!" she announced as if she had sculpted it herself.

I gazed at it, trying to peel the veil away, turning loose the idea that this was simply a shapeless mass of condensed moisture in the sky. And when I did, I saw it perfectly: the four legs, the graceful neck, the head with its long single horn.

"Why, it *is* a unicorn," I cried. Ann and I sat on the cold ground, shivering against each other, and watched him. As the wind blew the clouds along the sky he appeared to be walking on air.

"Did you know that long ago the unicorn used to be a symbol for Christ?" I asked her.

"My teacher read a story about a unicorn who died so all the other animals could live," she said.

We sat and thought of Christ, seeing Him in the shape of a cloud, feeling the beauty of His love. What joy! And certainly far more important work than the papers on my desk.

The heavens declare the glory of God; the skies proclaim the work of his hands.

—PSALM 19:1

Thought . . . Do you see Jesus in magical moments throughout life's seasons? When you are saved, Christ lifts the veil from your eyes (II Corinthians 3:14). Keep your vision unclouded by expecting to see Him in unlikely places.

Marriage

A Season for Everything under Heaven

BY BECKY FREEMAN

More marriages might survive if the partners realized that sometimes the better comes after the worse.

—DOUG LARSON

I sat alone in a hotel garden room, enjoying a French pastry and a cappuccino. Being alone with a pastry and good coffee is about as close to Heaven as this busy wife and mom gets. As I munched and sipped, my Bible fell open onto the table. Sunlight, from the skylight overhead, illuminated a familiar passage from Ecclesiasties beginning, "There is a time . . ."

As I basked in God's presence that lovely, unhurried morning, it dawned on me that if a marriage is to grow strongly and fully—like a bountiful oak tree—it must go through its own times and seasons. For example, there is, in marriage—*A time to weep.* I'm not sure I understood what it meant to be "one" in marriage, until Scott and I wept together in a time of deep sorrow.

A time to laugh. Equally as unifying was the time we got so tickled, that we fell off the bed in a shared fit of laughter.

A time for war. Unfortunately, we've experienced both hot and cold wars in our marriage.

A time for peace. Is there anything like the delicious relief and joy when "all is calm, and all is bright" between a man and wife? A season to savor!

Just as spring follows winter, so often the most enjoyable seasons of marriage follow a time of coldness—for one season does not a marriage make. Even dead-looking plants have a way of blossoming to life again, in time. And so do husbands and wives.

> There is a time for everything, and a season for every activity under heaven.
>
> —ECCLESIASTES 3:1

Thought . . . What season are you experiencing in your marriage? Difficulties will *season* you for endurance as a couple; shared passion and joy are *seasonings* that "spice up" your union. Entrust all seasons to God. Your marriage and times are in His hands.

174

Bad Hair Day

BY DORIS C. CRANDALL

We like someone because. We love someone although.

—HENRI D. MONTHERLANT

"*I* believe my number of bad-hair days could be listed in the *Guiness Book of Records*," I fretted, but my husband made no reply. "It's sticking up in all the wrong places!" Silence.

I decided to go back to the beauty salon and have it cropped. A really short haircut should be easy for me to style. "I'll be back in time for lunch," I called, but I didn't wait for Richard's reply. I knew he'd say, "Not too short."

He had wonderful hair. He could run a comb through it and it would fall into place like the ripple of a wave.

Back home, I slunk past Richard while he watched television. He didn't say a thing. The cropping hadn't worked. Now my hair resembled a kitchen mop on which a puppy had chewed.

"Richard," I said, "I think I'll get a permanent wave. But suppose it turns out frizzy? Then what will I do?"

"Stop worrying," he replied. "Remember one thing—no matter what happens, come on home."

His words lifted my spirits like a visit to *Baskin-Robbins. Come on home.* The words echoed in my mind. *Richard loves me even when I'm unattractive. That's like God's love,* I thought. God loves me all the time and He is always ready to encourage me and welcome me home—even after a bad hair day.

Love is patient, love is kind . . .

—I CORINTHIANS 13:4

Thought . . . Are you measuring your phyiscal attractiveness or others' according to society's "artificial" standards? Remember that God cares about your *heart* and He loves you unconditionally.

Remember When . . .

BY PATTY STUMP

A life worth living is worth recording.

—LYNN D. MORRISSEY

Shortly after we were married, my husband and I began a tradition of ending each day briefly recapping highlights and hurdles. We jotted these items down in a small notebook, categorizing them as either thanksgivings or requests, and then spent a few moments praying about each entry before we headed to bed.

We recently read through some previous entries: . . . Remember when our dryer broke and we couldn't afford to have it repaired? Just days later we found an almost-new washer/dryer set for an incredible price at a yard sale! . . . Remember the Christmas we couldn't afford a tree? You brought home a toy tree in a bucket! Our two-year-old daughter cried at the sight of it. We watched *A Charlie Brown Christmas* and afterwards enjoyed decorating our tree. The next day we received a written invitation to stop by the corner tree lot to pick out any Christmas tree we wanted, a gift from a friend! But by now we had grown so attached to our Charlie Brown tree that we declined their generous offer! . . . Remember when mechanical problems kept our cars in park? . . . Remember when our daughter was ill? . . . Remember when our marriage . . . ? . . . Remember when . . . ?

It has been ten years since we first began ending each day in prayer. These moments together have been a wonderful way for my husband and me to stay in touch. Our prayer journal has become a keepsake reminding us of God's faithfulness in seasons of thanksgiving and need.

> Oh that my words were recorded, that they were written on a scroll, that they were inscribed with an iron tool on lead, or engraved in rock forever!
>
> —JOB 19:23–24

Thought . . . Is life meaningless, joyless, boring? Does God seem absent? Keep a prayer journal and/or joy journal, recording your blessings and God's faithfulness. Your walk with God will become the most fascinating story ever written! Pass it on to the next generation.

Lord, Please Help Me

BY RUTH E. McDANIEL

The strongest principle of growth lies in human choice.

—GEORGE ELIOT

In 1989, my husband was diagnosed with multiple sclerosis, a debilitating disease that attacks the central nervous system. Two years later, I became his only caregiver.

Constant prayer and compassion carried me through the early days, but then the days turned into weeks, the weeks became months, and compassion began to fade. Friends and relatives rarely visited; it was too painful to see his decline. My caregiving role expanded daily with no respite. Soon, my prayers started and ended with, "How long, Lord?"

Then one day when confronted with a particularly unpleasant mess, I rebelled. I had had enough! I fell to my knees and cried, "Lord, please help me! I can't take it anymore!"

Suddenly, a quiet inner voice asked, "Could you do it for Christ? As Jesus bathed His disciples' feet, could you bathe His?" Stunned, I repeated the question to myself. *If Jesus Christ lay on that bed instead of my husband, would I resent caring for Him?* My spirit cried, *No! Of course not!* In that instant, my resentment and rebellion melted away and were replaced by the love of Jesus.

I'm still experiencing a season as a full-time caregiver, and friends and relatives continue to avoid us. But now, whenever a task seems too burdensome, I claim Philippians 4:13: "I can do everything through Him who gives me strength." Then I see Jesus Christ in my husband, and the task becomes my love-offering to God.

If anyone serves, he should do it with the strength God provides, so that in all things God may be praised through Jesus Christ.

—I PETER 4:11B

Thought . . . Have you had enough?—of work?—of ministry?—of difficult people?—of illness? See trials as an opportunity to serve Christ, and He and you can do *together* what you never could have done alone.

You Are Useful

BY LIZ CURTIS HIGGS

The Lord can use any vessel, even if it's cracked, as long as it's clean.

—A.W. TOZER

I was not prepared for *any* good work that day. Bill and I had had an unpleasant exchange in the car on the way to my presentation—one for sisters in Christ! It was rather mean-spirited.

It ended in silence. My six-year-old Lillian asked, "If you knew when you got married that it would be like this, why did you?"

I felt I'd been nailed. "Good question!" was my lippy retort, which I regretted instantly. I took a deep breath, tried not to look at Bill, and said carefully, "Lillian, even though Mama and Daddy disagree, it doesn't mean we don't love each other. We do. Very much."

I thought this answer might serve as an "I'm sorry" to Bill, but it didn't, because there wasn't a repentant syllable in it.

We'd reached the hotel, and I bounded out of the car. I went, leaving him to find a parking space so the poor dear could unload my books. I'm lucky he didn't toss them after me.

As the morning progressed, it was my turn to be introduced. I smiled, I spoke, they laughed, all was well, except for one problem: My vessel was clogged with the dirt of unconfessed sin and I knew it. True, the women seated before me didn't know it, but I knew.

Finally, I told them so they'd know too. Thankfully, they understood. We laughed even more, but this time my own laughter had wings instead of weights. I couldn't wait to see Bill, ask his forgiveness, and clear up things between us.

If a man cleanses himself . . . , he will be an instrument for noble purposes, made holy, useful to the Master and prepared to do any good work.

—II TIMOTHY 2:21

Thought . . . Is unconfessed sin inhibiting your relationship with God and with others? Confess. Ask forgiveness. You will never find freedom until you do.

Talk to Her, Lord

BY GAYLE CLOUD

Husband, your wife needs to hear these same things from
your lips . . .

—ED WHEAT, M.D.

I know for a fact that the Lord has a sense of humor. A few
years back, my husband and I were at odds over a particularly
bothersome decision. His proclivity to avoid conflict was bump-
ing against my tendency to confront issues head-on, and we
were definitely at odds.

One day while he was at work painting a wall, his mind drifted
to the recent frustrating conversation he had had with me. He
was sure that the Lord had shown him a direction for our lives
and he felt that I wouldn't like it. So, he was praying, "Lord,
reveal your will to my wife!" He was surprised by the quick response he felt that he heard: "You tell her, she's your wife."

Meanwhile, the Lord was dealing with me. The Lord had already whispered to me to listen to my husband, but I was feign-
ing deafness. When he came home and broached the sensitive
subject, I was ready to rationalize. And then, he shared God's
instructions. WOW! God did listen to my husband's prayers and,
even more encouraging, my husband listened to God . . . as I
then was able to do! The tension was broken as we both chuck-
led at God's wonderful sense of humor.

> Wives, in the same way be submissive to your husbands so
> that, if any of them do not believe the word, they may be
> won over without words by the behavior of their wives . . .
> —I PETER 3:1

Thought . . . If you and your husband are having difficulty in resolving a problem, pray together for God to
guide your thinking. He will often reveal His solution
by giving you both the same answer.

God's Prerogative

BY JONI EARECKSON TADA

No man can justly censure or condemn another, because indeed no man truly knows another . . . No man can judge another, because no man knows himself.

—THOMAS BROWNE

While my husband and I were eating in a fast-food restaurant, discussing gardening plans for the afternoon, we overheard a couple at a nearby table having a heated argument. "You dumb-bell," the woman hissed, "why don't you ever listen to me?!"

I mentally slammed down the gavel and pronounced the woman guilty. The nerve of her talking like that. However, the sentence we render on others may turn around and condemn us. For example, when Ken and I were gardening in the back yard that afternoon, I found myself getting irritated with his tech-nique of pruning. I started to complain. I hardly uttered a word when God stabbed my memory with the woman in the restau-rant. I felt the gavel come down on me, and it hurt.

We must not judge rashly, assuming the worst in people. We cannot judge unmercifully or with a spirit of revenge. Finally, we must not jump to conclusions and judge the hearts of others, for it is God's prerogative to try the heart.

Yes, we ought to weigh between right and wrong. Yes, we should hold our brother accountable to Scriptural standards. But judging goes far beyond discerning and carries with it an atti-tude of condemnation. Let Jesus be the judge of men's hearts, and instead of rendering a sentence on others, let's pray for them.

If any one of you is without sin, let him be the first to throw a stone at her.

—JOHN 8:7

Thought . . . Have you ever eaten your own words? Humble pie isn't tasty, but it's convincing. The Bible teaches that we reap what we sow. Instead of criticism, sow compassion. You'll receive kindness in return—a sweet-tasting fruit, in any season!

Just Like a Rainbow

BY TERESA ARSENEAU

Standing on what too long we bore with shoulders bent and downcast eyes, we may discern unseen before a path to higher destinies.

—HENRY WADSWORTH LONGFELLOW

*A*s I hacked away at my rose bushes (otherwise called pruning) and yanked up scores of weeds, Terry listened patiently, penitently. He even rolled up his sleeves, dug in, and started helping me.

Once again we were faced with a problem that had plagued our marriage for years. Eventually my anger sizzled out through my work, tears, and words.

I picked up the hose to water what I had transplanted. As I watched, a rainbow appeared in the water's stream and I remembered something I had told my friend's child last summer as she played in my garden. I called Terry over and, after tilting this way and that, he could see the rainbow, too. I shared with him what I had told Mikayla: "God gave the first rainbow to remind us of His promise to never destroy the Earth by flood again, but rainbows also remind me of His other promises to us, as individuals. We can't always see them, but they are always there."

We both reflected on that as we watched the sparkling wonder of God's creation. Somehow God would overcome the hurdle in this season of our marriage, too, just as He had already fulfilled so many other assurances to us over the years.

His promises are gloriously shining in the beauty of His love. And if we look at just the right angle, we will see them. But even when we can't, they are still always there . . . just like a rainbow.

I have set My rainbow in the clouds, and it will be the sign of the covenant between Me and the earth.
—GENESIS 9:13

Thought . . . Are you having difficulty in seeing anything but clouds in this troubled, rainy season? "Tilt" your perspective and look for God's rainbows, instead: His fulfillment of past promises, comfort from His Word, and the love and support of friends.

Let God Be Cupid

BY DORIS SMALLING

Enjoy your own life without comparing it with that of another.

—MARQUIS DE CONDORCET

My two younger sisters laughed happily as they concentrated on a marble game with their boyfriends. *Why can't I be pretty, too? Why can't I have a special boy friend?* I wondered. I felt unattractive.

My sister's reddish-auburn curls bounced like autumn leaves spinning in fall sunshine. My other sister, unbelievably blonde and unaware of her striking beauty, stroked her hair, fashionably styled in a page-boy. Mother tried curling my mousey-brown hair, but I looked as if I'd tangled with a lightning bolt. What I needed, I decided, was a fairy godmother to come quickly and make me tall, slender, and radiantly lovely.

Feeling ashamed that I even harbored such thoughts, I asked God to forgive me. "Lord, I'm sorry. Teach me to be content as I am. Fill my life with service to You. Remove all my self-concern and center my thoughts on You."

The following Saturday I attended our town's annual Fall Festival.

"Are these seats taken?" asked an incredibly handsome, tall, muscular young man, touching the seat beside me.

"No," I answered, turning quickly to watch the rodeo. As we cheered the participants, he asked me questions. We began conversing and felt an immediate affinity for each other. He suggested that I attend other festival events with him. Later, it seemed so right when he asked to visit my family.

My sisters peeked at him after our wedding. "He is so-o-o handsome, sis!" I had needed no fairy godmother to transform me. God, Himself, arranged a fairytale romance. We've been "married happily ever after" for the past forty years. And I agree wholeheartedly with my sisters. My husband is so-o-o handsome!

Love is . . . kind. It does not envy . . .

—I CORINTHIANS 13:4

Thought . . . Do you envy others? Find contentment as you realize just how special and unique you are. You are God's one-of-a-kind woman for all seasons. With you, He threw away the mold!

Storm Warning

BY SHEILA WALSH

He who kicks up a storm should expect rough sailing.

—ANONYMOUS

*B*arry and I lay in bed one night in a hotel watching television. *Drip! drip!* One of us hadn't switched off the bathroom tap.

I determined not to get out of bed. But I felt as if I were being tortured!

"All right!" I cried. "I surrender." I turned off the offending lethal weapon, at which point Barry said, "Thanks! That was bugging me."

Is there anything in the Bible about not smothering your husband with a pillow?

I decided it was time to visit a godly counselor. "Life can be so great, and then I get mad over some stupid little thing," I told him. "I hate who I am in those moments."

"Have you asked God to help?" he asked.

"I don't feel like talking to God when I'm mad."

"That's when you need to," he said.

A few days passed. I decided God must have answered my prayers. Then . . .

"Did you mail that insurance form?" I asked Barry.

"I forgot," he said.

"Why would you forget something as important as that?" I asked, feeling old emotions rising.

"I'm sorry. I just forgot," he said.

I went upstairs to our bedroom.

"Lord, what do I do here?" I cried. "I'm angry. Please help me."

I made a conscious choice to let my anger go. I was filled with joy.

I heard Barry's footsteps. I could honestly say, "It doesn't matter. We can sort this out tomorrow."

I want to be the fragrance of Christ in the midst of the storms of life, not part of the storm.

> . . . a quarrelsome wife is like a constant dripping.
>
> —PROVERBS 19:13

Thought . . . Do you explode at your husband over minor irritations? Release them to God. Praise your husband's good qualities, instead.

Can Chickens Fly?

BY REBECCA BARLOW JORDAN

Hope never spread her golden wings but in unfathomable seas.

—RALPH WALDO EMERSON

My husband, Larry, and I believe that all things, good or bad, will work together for our benefit. But there were times when we questioned that promise.

One night, when we were on a high school date, a speeding pickup truck hit us broadside. The impact crushed the driver's side of the car just behind Larry's door. The couple in the back seat huddled on the opposite side and sustained some deep cuts and bruises. But Larry and I escaped with only a minor cut or two.

The highway patrolman who investigated the accident just shook his head as he looked at the twisted wreckage. "Son, I hope you realize you could have been killed." We didn't forget his words. The car collision that almost had demolished our dreams of sharing life together, instead prompted a new dream.

Through those circumstances, Larry began to sense God calling him to full-time ministry, and this preacher's daughter became a preacher's wife. Twenty years ago I prayed, "Someday, Lord, I want to write a book and work together with my husband in marriage ministry."

The path to fulfilling that dream has taken more than a wing and a prayer and has, at times, been painful. We had to overcome major flaws in our marriage and God had to build courage in my chicken heart. But today we lead marriage enrichment retreats together. Because of God's grace, He allowed me to write not just one book (one with Larry on marriage), but three, including a CBA bestseller—*Courage for the Chicken Hearted*. With God's enabling, chickens can fly—they can even soar!

For nothing is impossible with God.

—LUKE 1:37

Thought . . . Do you have a deep longing, coupled with a deep fear that you are unable to fulfill it? The bigger the dream, the more likely it is from God. He can do impossible things through impossible people!

Forgiving Everything

BY KAREN O'CONNOR

Life lived without forgiveness becomes a prison.

—WILLIAM ARTHUR WARD

The last person I would have expected my lesson in forgiveness to come through was Lynn—the woman my husband left me for.

Rage and resentment were draining life out of everything. I did everything except forgive and let go.

I was drawn to a seminar. The leader asked us to bring to mind one person we needed to forgive. Lynn. I lashed out at God. How can you expect me to forgive her?

I can't. She stole my husband. I didn't deserve what she did.

I wanted to release this woman, but I also wanted to punish her.

I couldn't bear the burden of my hatred any longer. Without warning, an incredible shift occurred. I just—let go. I surrendered—and the Holy Spirit empowered me to do something I had resisted. I released Lynn. I let go—just like that. It was clear that as long as I separate myself from even one person, I separate myself from God. How arrogant!

I wrote to Lynn. I apologized for the hateful thoughts I had harbored.

The phone rang. "Karen?" There was no mistaking her voice. "It's Lynn."

I listened more than I talked—unusual for me. I found myself interested in what she had to say. She told me how sorry she was.

I appreciated her response, but it was suddenly unimportant. I had discovered the assurance that God was with me, encouraging and strengthening me.

No one can take my good away. My life is a gift from God, and every experience, no matter how painful, can draw me closer to Him.

Do not say, "I'll pay you back for this wrong!" Wait for the Lord, and He will deliver you.

—PROVERBS 20:22

Thought . . . Is it impossible for you to forgive? Despite your offense, Jesus forgave you. He asks you to do the same.

Vinegar and Water Don't Mix

BY SUZY RYAN

Faith never shrinks in hot water.

—BARBARA JOHNSON

I nabbed my husband's blue shirt from the dryer and tossed it in my ironing pile. Then I saw it—a large bleach spot! I scrambled to find the permanent blue marker, trying to color the problem away. It only looked worse.

Oh NO! How did this happen? My friend suggested that I put a little vinegar in the rinse cycle to sanitize the dark wash. Now my man is going to hang *me* to drip-dry!

The anxiety in my heart brought back childhood fears of disappointing my mother. She only praised me for *stellar* behavior as I grew up. Unfortunately, this made me endeavor to achieve perfection, which spilled over into my adult life.

When these insecurities surfaced, past experience taught me to pray. "Oh Lord, I know you love me unconditionally, but I get so angry when I botch things. Help me forgive myself!"

God said to my heart, "Suzy, I love you regardless of your blunder. Give me the unrealistic expectations you place on yourself. You only have to please me. You did your best, now let it go!"

My anxiety melted and, thankfully, I realized the humor of adding vinegar to the rinse cycle. It went straight for his "Tommy Hilfiger," leaving the rest of the load untouched. Unbelievable!

Oh by the way, if you see a handsome man with blue ink on his shirt, just tell him you like his outfit. Then smile knowingly and walk away.

My expectation is from You.

—PSALM 62:5

Thought . . . Do you try to please God or "man"? People are a "tough audience" whom you will never please; when you please one person, you disappoint another. But God loves you just as you are and sees you as already perfect in Christ.

Victory

The Prayer of Helplessness

BY CATHERINE MARSHALL

God comes in where my helplessness begins.

—OSWALD CHAMBERS

I believe the cliché, "God helps those who help themselves," is not only misleading but often dead wrong. Spectacular answers to prayers have come when I was so helpless as to be able to do nothing for myself.

The Psalmist says: *When I was hemmed in, Thou hast freed me often.* I have learned to recognize this hemming-in as one of God's loving devices for teaching us that He is gloriously adequate for our problems.

One such experience occurred during the writing of my first book. As the young widow of Peter Marshall, pastor and Chaplain of the United States Senate, I was attempting the audacious project of writing his biography. Midway in the manuscript, I received devastating criticism from one whose judgment I trusted. He told me, "You haven't even begun to get inside the man Peter Marshall." And he was right. The realization of my inadequacy as a writer was not only an intellectual one. It was also emotional; there were plenty of tears. But out of the crisis came a major realization.

In my helplessness, there was no alternative but to put the project into God's hands. I prayed that *A Man Called Peter* be His book, and the results too.

I still regard as incredible the several million copies of *A Man Called Peter* circulating around the world. But that and the successful motion picture were of little importance compared to what I hear of lives changed through this book of men entering the ministry through the inspiration of Peter Marshall's life.

That is why, for Christ's sake, I delight in weakness, in insults, in hardships, in persecutions, in difficulties. For when I am weak, then I am strong.

—II CORINTHIANS 12:10

Thought . . . Are you ready to give up because something is too difficult? Good! When you surrender your helplessness to God, He gives you His strength.

Letting Go

BY JEANIE CONNELL

All change, even the most longed for, has its melancholy. For what we leave behind is a part of ourselves.

—ANONYMOUS

*R*eceiving professional counseling had been part of my life for a ten-year season. As I began to heal from childhood trauma, I realized that I had become addicted to therapy. I did not think that I could live without relationships with my psychiatrist and therapist.

One day in church, I heard my pastor talk about fasting. Later I read the story of Noah's ark. It seemed that God was speaking to me, as the story described a forty-day waiting period. The waters receded and the ark rested on top of a mountain. No one did anything!

The voice that I had come to recognize in my thoughts as the Lord's, directed me: "Jeanie, I want you to fast from therapy for the next forty days . . . no visits, no calls, no correspondence." Those days became precious as I sensed God's presence with me.

On day forty, I received prayer in a little chapel with seven people. My life has never been the same. I saw the power of prayer accomplish more healing in two hours than I had seen during ten years! Truly, I was resting on the mountain top!

At the close of the prayer time I was asked if I wanted a hug from Jesus. I eagerly answered, "Yes!" With no human being touching me, I saw and felt myself embraced by my Savior.

Whoever loses his life for My sake will find it.

—MATTHEW 10:39B

Thought . . . Do you need help sorting through emotional confusion? First seek the Wonderful Counselor and then, if God so directs, seek a Christian counselor. God's words in the Bible are also your "counselors" (Psalm 119:24).

Sounds of Silence

BY KATHY TROCCOLI

I like the silent church before the service begins better than any preaching.

—RALPH WALDO EMERSON

I experienced great anxiety over career decisions I had to make. I wanted to follow my heart, but I wanted it to be God's heart. I decided to take time to fast and pray.

I've lived on Long Island most of my life. I love having access to New York City about sixty miles away, and I love the ocean, trees, and seasons. I reserved a hotel room for a couple of days in Montauk Point.

It was October, and I knew hardly a soul would be there during the fall season. It would be quiet, which would make it easier for me to focus on hearing God. I loaded a bag with my Bible, books, legal pads, pens, and cassettes. It was God and I . . . I was on a mission. I had prayed He would truly meet me.

Halfway through my trip, over the music blaring in my tape deck, God spoke to my spirit. "Shut the music off. I want you to sing to Me. Please sing to Me." My hand reached for the power button and I drove in silence. I wept at the Lord's gesture, at His beckoning for me to worship Him. My voice filled the car.

I sang and sang. I cried. He was preparing me for my time with Him. He was filling me with peace and the certainty of His presence. The following three days were sweet and serene. I wrote and read and prayed. I received answers to my prayers, gained wisdom, and grew closer to Him.

As the deer pants for streams of water, so my soul pants for you, O God.

—PSALM 42:1

Thought . . . What is the best antidote to worry? Worship! Get alone with God and pause in His presence— praising and praying. Anxiety will be replaced by adoration, pressure by peace.

A Winner for all Time

BY MARJORIE LEE CHANDLER

Love: in tennis, nothing; in life, everything.

—FRANK TYGER

I opened my last birthday gift, a long cylindrical package, and looked at it with puzzlement. "Just some tennis balls for our next game—whenever," my husband explained. Wistfully, we both wished we were on the court instead of facing my recuperation from major surgery. Those tennis balls became our symbol of hope for the future.

Slowly my physical strength returned and with each surge of vigor, I whispered, "Thank you, God." In my weakness, He gave me His strong gifts of love and gratitude. New Year's Day, I walked onto the court clutching the vacuum-packed can of tennis balls. Mechanically popping it open, I stared at the three balls in my hand, wondering if I could possibly race from one side of the court to the other, hitting these little fuzzy spheres. I had to try! I returned a few slow balls, but missed the rest. "40—Love," declared my partner. My racket dipped as I nipped his last serve. "That's game!" shouted my husband, the victor.

My score was "love"—meaning zero. But love, a spiritual fruit, never totals "no score." I had learned that gratitude and triumph filled my heart. I knew this never-failing power would help me handle the hard serves of daily life. Sometime I might win a tennis match again, but right now I was a winner for all time! I was filled with the One Who *is* love.

> . . . let us love one another, for love comes from God. Everyone who loves has been born of God and knows God.
> —I JOHN 4:7

Thought . . . Is love the motivation behind your actions and accomplishments in this season of life? No one is poor or unsuccessful who is rich in love.

Working for Jesus

BY JILL BRISCOE

Patience is a bitter plant but it bears sweet fruit.

—GERMAN PROVERB

I remember being a student teacher with a slave driver supervisor! She worked me harder than I had ever worked and got rid of her dirty work by dumping it on me. She was unfair, demanding things I found impossible to give. She reminded me of Egyptian slave masters who demanded the Israelites make bricks without straw.

If I had not just been converted to Christ, I would not have put up with this treatment. Now I had no option; God had led me to choose teaching as a profession and what I did was all part of God's will involving my training. Preparation of character included my attitude toward this lady, who was my "master."

Seeing I was now the slave of Christ, I tried to look at each task as if Christ had asked her to ask me to do it. If she demanded the impossible—asked me to make bricks without straw—I would try, for I was the Lord's freedwoman!

The difference was incredible! I cleaned out the hamster and mice cages singing, "All things bright and beautiful, all creatures great and small," focusing on the mice, not the muck! I began to pray fervently that my taskmaster would become a slave of Jesus like I. I tried to treat each day as a challenge instead of a chain. It worked! I am always amazed how this mind-set—what I am doing for others I am doing for Him—transforms the actual task and lightens the load.

> Moreover, I have heard the groaning of the Israelites, whom the Egyptians are enslaving, and I have remembered My covenant.
>
> —EXODUS 6:5

Thought . . . Are you the Lord's freedwoman? Ironically, the only way to become one is to be His slave, obeying Him in all things in all seasons, no matter how difficult it may be.

Victory via Interruption

BY ELAINE CUNNINGHAM

God develops spiritual power in our lives through pressure of hard places.

—ANONYMOUS

My husband, Cloyce, and I were traveling from Indiana to Puerto Rico with a group from our church. Our plan was to help our missionaries in San Juan conduct a two-week Vacation Bible School.

Over Miami, Cloyce began having severe pain. When the plane landed for refueling, I called a taxi and took my husband to the hospital. The rest of our group, along with our luggage, continued on to Puerto Rico.

While doctors examined Cloyce in the emergency room, I looked for a telephone to call the airlines and find out what to do about our luggage. Stranded in a strange city with not even a toothbrush and very little cash in my purse, I felt frustrated, lonely, and frightened.

I located the phone booth. Inside, I noticed a Gospel tract someone had left on the shelf. *Others May, You Cannot* was the title. I picked it up and read these unforgettable words, "When you are content with any food, any climate, any society, any solitude, any interruption by the will of God—THAT IS VICTORY."

Tears washed my face as I realized that God had not forgotten us. The next day, with my husband safely situated in the hospital, I flew to San Juan to retrieve our luggage. I returned the following day and took Cloyce to Indiana where he had successful surgery.

Even though our trip was interrupted, God taught me a valuable lesson. He can give victory over any circumstances.

That is why, for Christ's sake, I delight in weaknesses, in insults, in hardships, in persecutions, in difficulties. For when I am weak, then I am strong.

—II CORINTHIANS 12:10

Thought . . . Are you content in this season of life? Contentment lies in obeying the Lord of your circumstances and remembering that it is He Who has ultimately orchestrated them for your good, to make you strong in Him.

You Are a New Creation

BY LIZ CURTIS HIGGS

Preaching the Word of God is as great as hearing it.

—JOHN WYCLIFFE

When I received Christ, you can imagine what my coworkers thought! They watched me like a hawk. A curious cohort asked, "Liz, what does it mean to be a Christian?"

Glancing at a ceramic pumpkin perched on her desk, I said, "Oh, it's just like being a pumpkin!"

"What do you mean?"

I gulped, having no idea what I meant.

I was determined to move forward with the Lord's leading, never imagining the fruit this answer would produce.

"Well, pumpkins have the same options people do. They can wither on the vine, bake in an oven, or be turned into something new. Which one would you choose?"

"Oh, to be made into something new," she responded.

I plunged on. "Just like a farmer who brings a pumpkin from the field, God cleans us up inside and out, gives us a happy new face, fills us with light, and puts us in a dark world to shine for Him."

"That is so simple. It sounds like God does all the work."

"Exactly," I assured, my heart pounding wildly. Within days, my friend received Christ as her Savior and was baptized. Although many influences were involved, I do thank the Lord for that pumpkin.

A published version came rolling off the press—*The Pumpkin Patch Parable*—a "how to be made into a new creation" book for kids. Since the Lord created pumpkins, it made sense to redeem this symbol of the harvest season for His good purpose.

Therefore, if anyone is in Christ, he is a new creation; the old has gone, the new has come!

—II CORINTHIANS 5:17

Thought . . . Are you a new creation in Christ? When you receive Jesus Christ as your Savior, not only do you receive a new lease on life, but you, yourself, become new. Jesus has forgiven every single sin forever.

It's the Red Stuff!

BY MARILYN J. HATHAWAY

Who sins and mends commends himself to God.

—CERVANTES

The raspberry had been dropped during breakfast, but it was late afternoon before I spotted the blob of scarlet mush on the carpet. Even as I grabbed the industrial strength cleaner, I knew that the spot was there forever. This was the indestructible red stuff—permanent, period!

The largest red stain, now hidden beneath a throw rug, was my grandson's spilled juice. The rambling trail on the dining room carpet, Christmas punch. The ring by the window was a long-since melted Valentine candy. As I silently berated the "berry dropper," a chorus burst upon my mind: "Sin had left a crimson stain; He washed it white as snow."

Had sin actually left its mark on my flesh, I fear I would be one "red hot mama!" All effort to scrub away my stains, even using my strongest industrial cleaner, would be in vain. The red stuff cannot be washed away—it's indelible.

Since our sins don't actually show, we can often hide them from the world, but not from God. He sees beneath every fleshly throw rug. The entire human race glows crimson in His eyes. Yet Jesus' purifying robe of righteousness not only covers our sins, but removes them from God's sight forever.

As I made a mental note to buy another kitchen throw rug, I said a prayer of thanksgiving that I didn't have to *wear* one! I can live with the red stuff on the carpet but, thankfully, I do not have to live with sin! Jesus has permanently cleansed that.

. . . Though your sins are like scarlet, they shall be as white as snow; though they are red as crimson, they shall be like wool.

—ISAIAH 1:18

Thought . . . How do you cover your sin? Ignore it? Excuse it? Deny it? Blame it on others? Wallow in guilt? None of the above will remove it. Only Jesus can. Confess your sin and receive His complete forgiveness and freedom.

Christmas in Our Hearts

BY DONNA GOODRICH

When the woes of life o'ertake me, hopes deceive, and fears annoy, never shall the Cross forsake me: Lo! it glows with peace and joy.

—JOHN BOWRING

*H*ow could I celebrate Christmas? I didn't have much good news to share in our annual letter; it had been a year of sickness and tragedies.

I had lost several dear friends—some old, some young—and others were undergoing treatment for serious illnesses. Our own family had also struggled with physical problems, and we were all left in a state of shock when my twenty-year-old nephew committed suicide, leaving a six-month-old son.

Lord, I thought, as Christmas drew nearer, *this is supposed to be a season of rejoicing.* I prayed for strength to get through each day.

Then one afternoon I came across a cantata written by my nephew entitled *From the Manger to the Cross.* It begins with Mary agonizing over how to tell Joseph that she was with child. She did not celebrate when she first heard the news from the angel. And, I questioned, would she have celebrated during those nine months if she had known this new Life would end thirty-three years later on a cross?

Then it hit me! *Because* of that cross, we *can* celebrate Christmas, regardless of what we have experienced during the year. We can walk with Mary to the tomb, we can see the stone rolled away, and we can hear the angel proclaim, "He is not here! He is risen!"

And I realized anew that *because* He lives, no matter what happened to us yesterday, we *can* face tomorrow. Through His resurrection, we *can* celebrate Christmas this year in our hearts and in our homes.

Let us fix our eyes on Jesus, the author and perfecter of our faith, Who for the joy set before Him endured the cross . . .
—HEBREWS 12:2

Thought . . . When you face agonizing pain and loss, where do you run? Go to the foot of the Cross. Jesus understands your pain. Go to the empty tomb. Jesus gives you eternal hope.

Adjusting Your Focus

BY ELIZABETH GEORGE

Many a questioning, many a fear, many a doubt, hath its quieting here. Moment by moment, let down from Heaven, time, opportunity, guidance, are given. Fear not tomorrows, Child of the King, trust them with Jesus, DO THE NEXT THING.

—ANONYMOUS

As I've worked on focusing on today and looking to God for strength and guidance, I've realized that my approach to life is much like my approach to running. I plan and prepare. Once I have on the right clothes and shoes, it's time to run. I run to the first corner and then to the next. But as the run gets longer and I get tired, I run not to the next corner but to the trash can I see, to a certain curb, to the next driveway, to the stoplight. As I get closer to home, I concentrate on even smaller measurements and make my goal that streetlight or those trees. I don't look up the huge hill to the stoplight. That goal is too large and unreachable—but I can take one more step. I also don't look all the way home. The distance seems too far to go—but I can run to the next flower. So step by step, I complete my run. I reach my goal. With God to guide and empower, I make it through my day.

Focusing on today helps us live each day to the fullest, and that focus begins with preparation, planning, and prayer. Having done these things, we then proceed—one step at a time, one task at a time—focusing energy on each task as it comes throughout the day. This focus on today helps us competently scale the mountain of today as we refuse to think about the mountain range of tomorrows.

Then he prayed, "O Lord, God of my master Abraham, give me success today."

—GENESIS 24:12

Thought . . . Are you overwhelmed by the big picture? Tackle each project, with God's help, step by step, and before you realize it, the job will be done.

Cinema Life

BY ELLIE KAY

In Adam's fall, we sinned all.

—THE NEW ENGLAND PRIMER

In my home state, our favorite dessert has two syllables. It's called *pi-e*. Apple pi-e is a staple in our neighborhood.

When I was a young bride, my husband, Bob, and I moved to California. He removed me not only from two-syllabled apple pi-e, but from "normal-speaking" folks, as well. In the Golden State, grocery cashiers spoke a foreign language that I didn't understand. They used words like *tubular*, *awesome*, and *totally*.

In our new church, the ladies would listen as I expounded on Biblical theology during our weekly study. They were mesmerized not by my knowledge, but by my Texas accent. Once, I was talking about receiving God's grace for my transgressions. Sharing my own vulnerabilities seemed to greatly impact our group. It felt good to stir up truth in others; at least that's what I thought I was doing.

During one of these discussions, our associate pastor had the look on his face of a man seeking greater understanding. Finally, he could contain his question no longer. "Ellie, in our discussion about transgressions, you talked about Cinema Life. Is that a magazine about the movies? And how does it cause you grief?"

I was confused. "What do you mean Cinema Life?" I queried. Then, suddenly, it dawned on me, "Oh, I see! We have a language barrier. I'll spell it for you. I was talking about s-i-n i-n m-y life."

No matter what language you speak, I believe that self-evaluation is still important. In every season, I ask God to reveal unconfessed sin in my life, so that I can enjoy the just desserts of rightly relating to Him. Now that that's settled, would someone please pass that apple pi-e?

. . . Blessed is he whose transgressions are forgiven, whose sins are covered.

—PSALM 32:1

Thought . . . No matter what you call it, sin is sin. Call it like it is, as God sees it. Then you can confess it and receive His complete pardon.

The Most Important Goal

BY GRACE WITWER HOUSHOLDER

The triumphant Christian does not fight for victory; he celebrates a victory already won. The victorious life is Christ's business, not yours.

—REGINALD WALLIS

The rain was coming down in sheets, and my husband and I could barely see the soccer action from the protection of our car.

After about ten minutes we moved the car to a better position. The windshield wipers and the fog and the rain made everything hazy. But I could tell that the ten-year-olds were giving it all they had.

It appeared it was going to be a 0-0 tie. I felt sorry for our boys. They were attempting many shots, but the other team's skillful play made it seem as if making a goal would be impossible.

All of a sudden, the players were running off the field. My son came to the car and said that the game was over because lightning had been seen.

"We won!" he added.

"You did?" I said in amazement. "I thought it was 0–0."

"We got two goals at the beginning. Didn't you see them?"

At the beginning of the game our car had been too far away for us to see anything.

That evening I realized the soccer goal I didn't see illustrated the sermon we had heard that morning in church.

Day by day, often in dismal situations, we and others struggle to "win" the game of life. We are often tired and discouraged.

We fail to remember that Christ's victory on the Cross—His winning goal for all mankind—has already made us victors. We receive new strength when we realize that the battle is already won.

The thief comes only to steal and kill and destroy; I have come that they may have life, and have it to the full.

—JOHN 10:10

Thought . . . Are you letting Satan's defeats get you down? Though he may win a few battles, Christ has already won the war! Get up, stand firm, and claim Christ's victory.

Overcoming the Power of the Past

BY LESLIE WILLIAMS

If thou hast a fearful thought, share it not with a weakling, whisper it to thy saddle-bow, and ride forth singing.

—ALFRED THE GREAT

*W*hen our son Jase was two, his aunt and uncle took him to see the traveling Dinosaur Dinamation display at the museum, a room filled with towering replicas of ancient reptiles, moving and growling in life-like imitation. That night, Jase lay in his crib, alone, talking to himself. "They aren't real. They can't hurt you," he repeated over and over. I tiptoed in and bent over his crib. "Are you all right, honey?" I asked. "Oh, yes. They won't hurt you," he replied, hugging his raggedy bear and sucking his thumb.

Jase had learned a valuable technique for dispelling the power of frightening memories. The dinosaurs, a recent memory, scared him, so he extracted a more distant memory of a time his father or I had calmed him down on another occasion—and employed the same method to calm himself. His self-talk reduced his fear and put him to sleep. That night, Jase incorporated two memories—the now-unfrightening memory of the dinosaurs and the memory of being calmed. He became a stronger, more resilient little human being for it. We can learn much from Jase about the power and positive use of self-talk and memories.

The crucial question becomes how to access and use our memory in order to become the people God would have us to be. As adults, we cannot go back and change things. The choice is whether we sort and examine our past, gleaning health and meaning from the events, or whether we allow the past to rob us of the pleasures of the present.

Forget the former things; do not dwell on the past.
—ISAIAH 43:18

Thought . . . Do you lament your past? Learn valuable lessons, and then move on, determined not to repeat mistakes. Do your best now and think positively. Then when your present becomes your past, you will never regret it.

Strong and Courageous

BY KAY ARTHUR

You can measure a man by the opposition it takes to discourage him.

—ROBERT C. SAVAGE

Slides were part of my childhood—trips to the parks with playgrounds for picnics. We'd feast on mother's wonderful fried chicken.

It was fun to race up the slide and throw up your hands and careen down. What was more fun was to get wax paper that Mom had wrapped food in, slip it under our bottoms and really take off. The higher the slide and the waxier the paper, the wilder the ride!

Mom shouted for us to be careful. Children had been hurt on slides—bones broken, bottoms bruised.

As I think about what happens when we don't pay attention to what our Heavenly Father says about dealing with disappointments, it reminds me of what happens when you put wax paper on an already slippery slide. You go down—quickly!

When you don't handle disappointment with meekness, you'll find yourself sliding right into discouragement.

Disappointments are fires governed by our Refiner for the purpose of conforming us into the image of His Son. While it isn't wrong to be disappointed, we must be careful not to let disappointment bring us into discouragement.

What hope is there for us if we've plunged from disappointment to discouragement? Can we still reverse the slide?

Yes, even though a battle has been lost the war can still be won. It is *not* God's plan for you to be discouraged.

God's way out of discouragement is to simply *follow* Him.

God's path of escape is to determine—in dependence upon Him and His promises—to *be strong and courageous.*

Have I not commanded you? Be strong and courageous. Do not be terrified; do not be discouraged.

—JOSHUA 1:9

Thought . . . How do you handle a season of disappointment? If you see disappointment as *His* appointment, you will accept it as God's will and allow Him to work through the situation to teach you important lessons for your good.

Bigger Every Day

BY JANE FOARD THOMPSON

One's attitude toward a handicap determines its impact on his life.

—JAMES C. DOBSON

Tracey was born with webbed toes, one toe enlarged beyond the big toe. As she grew, that toe grew faster than the others.

When Tracey was four, a new family moved in next store. We baked fresh bread and took them a loaf to welcome them. The girls watched each other as the mother and I chatted.

"Why don't you take Tracey out to your trampoline, Sarah?" She opened the screen door for the girls. We watched through the kitchen window as they climbed up and began jumping.

Suddenly, Tracey stopped and stared at Sarah's left arm, which ended at the elbow.

"What happened to your arm?" she asked.

I felt Sarah's mother stiffen next to me. She reached for the door knob.

"I was born that way. It's a birth defect," Sarah explained, continuing to jump.

"Oh, good!" Tracey exclaimed. She bounced to the mat and pulled off her left shoe and sock, proudly displaying her protruding middle toe. "I've got one, too!"

Sarah grinned and hugged Tracey. Relieved, her Mom sighed, tears brimming in her eyes.

Later, Tracey chatted in the bathtub. "Mommy, now I know why God gave me this foot." She poked her webbed, ever-growing toes through the bubbles. "I have this so I can understand people who have worser problems."

I didn't even know that she was asking the question, yet already Tracey understood better than I that God always has a plan, and His plan is good.

. . . Who gave man his mouth? Who makes him deaf or mute? Who gives him sight or makes him blind? Is it not I, the Lord?

—EXODUS 4:11

Thought . . . Are you embarrassed by your body? You were created *by* God for *His* glory (Isaiah 43:7). Your body is *His* temple. Celebrate yourself in Christ!

The Sacrament of Surrender

BY CLAIRE CLONINGER

If the basis of peace is God, the secret of peace is trust.

—JOHN BENJAMIN FIGGIS

*W*hen I married, I had a notion life would be idyllic. That notion short-lived, we have faced many surprises and challenges.

One was to discover that my two sons were not robots I could raise by remote control. Each was equipped with God-given free will to make choices—even destructive ones.

When Andy was in high school, his free will to choose led him into what became a serious alcohol and drug problem.

During those heartbreaking years, I moved from the kind of prayer that was really nagging God to prayer that admitted my powerlessness and put Andy into God's hands.

It was a surrender I had to make again and again. Even after God had worked miracles in Andy's life, I would find myself trying to be in control. That was when I discovered a tool I called my "God Box."

My God Box is a shoebox with a slit. I would write Andy's name and the situation I was fretting about on a slip of paper. I would commit it to God by slipping it into the God Box. It was a visible "sacrament" of surrender, putting it into God's hands.

Though I am much improved in my need to control, I have not outgrown my need for the "God Box." When I feel strangled by that old urge to butt in, I know where to go. At the top of my closet, it waits. A shoebox full of folded slips of compulsiveness, each reading, "Your will, not mine."

And the peace of God, which transcends all understanding, will guard your hearts and your minds in Christ Jesus.
—PHILIPPIANS 4:7

Thought . . . Have you surrendered your troubles to God, only to "take them back" again? Tangible gestures reinforce your commitment to let go: use a "God Box"; write problems on pieces of paper, tearing or burning them up as you give them to God; write a prayer of surrender.

The Privilege of Sacrifice

BY JENNIFER KENNEDY DEAN

Prayer is the expression of our dependence upon God, our whole-souled reliance upon His power to sustain us, His mercy to forgive us, His bounty to supply us, and His glory to overwhelm us as we reflect on who He is.

—C. SAMUEL STORMS

The pursuit of any goal requires a narrowed focus. Choosing to live a praying life—a life through which the power of God is free to flow—involves sacrifice. In this, it is no different from any other rock-solid commitment. Whatever you choose to pursue will mean that you sacrifice something else. The key is this: if the goal is sufficiently attractive, the sacrifice required will be irrelevant. In fact, the more focused on your goal you are, the less you will perceive the requirements as "sacrifices."

When my son Stinson was a toddler, I picked him up from a birthday party he had attended. He came out proudly clutching a red helium-filled balloon. "Stinson, what a wonderful balloon!" I said. "Don't let go of it or it will go way up in the sky and we won't be able to get it back."

I turned around for a moment, and when I turned back, there was Stinson, watching his wonderful red helium-filled balloon float higher and higher. "Oh, I'm sorry you lost your balloon, Stinson," I said.

"I didn't lose it, Mommy!" was Stinson's reply. "I gave it to Jesus!"

The person who is living a praying life learns that nothing you give to Jesus is lost. Giving the thing you love best to the One you love most is what brings exuberant joy, the hallmark of the praying life.

Therefore, I urge you, brothers, in view of God's mercy, to offer your bodies as living sacrifices, holy and pleasing to God—this is your spiritual act of worship.

—ROMANS 12:1

Thought . . . To what have you been stubbornly clinging which Jesus requests? Joyfully give it to Him. He will give you Himself! There is no comparison.

Friendship

Oxygen for My Soul

BY FRAN CAFFEY SANDIN

Science cannot restore the joy of life and help us laugh again. Joy and laughter are the products of faith. Men can laugh only when they believe.

—GERALD KENNEDY

*W*hen I met Elizabeth Garland, an ugly clear plastic tube in her nose delivered supplemental oxygen from a tank on rollers that she dragged everywhere she went. But she did not let that interfere with her enthusiasm for life. She and I attended *Bible Study Fellowship* classes together and, subsequently, became prayer-partners and close friends.

One day while sipping coffee and chatting with Liz at her home, I asked, "Liz, how did you adjust to using supplemental oxygen?"

"At first, I was so discouraged, I didn't even want to go to church," she confessed. "I was embarrassed about my contraption and feared that no one would even talk with me."

She explained, "I finally went and sat on the back row. Just as we were leaving, Kris gave me a warm smile and a hug. Because she focused upon my personality and not upon my disability, I gained enough courage to return."

Liz smiled as she recalled her first trip to the grocery store. "I felt so awkward as I drove. Then when I arrived, I jumped out of the car and slammed the door on my tubing! First, I looked around to see if anyone were watching. Then I began laughing at myself."

As I recall our conversations through the years and our prayer times together, they are like oxygen for my soul. In 1990, Liz began breathing on her own and moved to her Heavenly home. Her cheerful countenance, contagious laugh, and sparkling blue eyes are among my fondest memories. As my friend, she left a legacy of joy and the luster of a holy life.

Do not grieve, for the joy of the Lord is your strength.
—NEHEMIAH 8:10B

Thought . . . Are you making lemonade out of your lemons and turning your scars into stars? All this is possible, and more, when the Lord is your strength!

Lover of Hospitality

BY FLORENCE LITTAUER

Strangers are friends that you have yet to meet.

—ROBERTA LIEBERMAN

I have always been a "lover of hospitality." I've had parties for any possible reason known to man.

After our family dedicated their lives to the Lord, He moved us from our social position in Connecticut, to "Bungalow One" in California. When we had been asked to go on staff with *Campus Crusade for Christ* I pictured Fred and me on a spiritual cloud floating through life while a choir sang majestically. How quickly I fell off the cloud when I was to live in "Bungalow One." There wasn't even a kitchen so I had to cook on a hot plate. How could anyone be a lover of hospitality in such a setting?

What a lesson the Lord had for me! He had to teach me that it wasn't surroundings but the spirit that made genuine hospitality.

With eight around a crowded table every night, could we add even one more? Psalm 101:6 says, "I will make the godly of the land my heroes and invite them to my home (TLB)." The godly of the land passed through and I found what they wanted most was a friendly, home-cooked meal. Since I spend much time traveling and eating by myself, I can understand how they enjoyed our home. I see why the spirit of togetherness was more important than the space.

I became "Martha of the Hill," cooking and serving the godly of the Lord. Could I entertain in "Bungalow One"? Oh, yes. I could and did. Hospitality doesn't depend on size, but on spirit.

> Then the Word of the Lord came to him: "Go at once to Zarephath of Sidon and stay there. I have commanded a widow in that place to supply you with food."
>
> —I KINGS 17:8–9

Thought . . . Do you dread having company? Consider the condition of your heart, not your house. When you share Christ's love, warmth, and compassion with your guests, and receive theirs in return, you will soon forget the last time you dusted.

There Goes the Neighbor "Hood"!

BY BONNIE COMPTON HANSON

It is never too late to give up our prejudices.

—HENRY DAVID THOREAU

Plucking off some dead leaves, I stood back to admire my roses. Those flourishing bushes along my picket fence were my pride and joy.

"Excuse me!"

Startled, I looked up. Towering over the fence right in front of me stood a young man. His jeans and tee-shirt were ragged, his hair long, lank, and tangled. Tattoos covered his arms. His ears were circled with rings—and so was his nose.

In sudden panic, I looked around for another neighbor. Was he just looking for a handout? Or was his intent assault and robbery? Or worse?

I jumped back from the fence. "Yes?" He smiled shyly. "Sorry. I just wanted to tell you how much I love your roses. I live up the street with a bunch of guys. None of us has a green thumb."

Suddenly, under all that counter-culture garb I saw a homesick college kid. I smiled back (in relief!), then cut him off a rose to take with him.

"Wow, thanks!" he cried, accepting it as gratefully as if it had been made of diamonds.

As he hurried away, I was filled with shame. How quick I was to judge him by his outward appearance, seeing a "not-one-of-us" danger instead of a lonely young man for whom Christ had died.

If only I had not been so fast to criticize, and so slow to love! "If you give me another chance, God," I prayed, "next time I'll tell him of Jesus—our wonderful Rose of Sharon!"

> . . . Always be prepared to give an answer to everyone who asks you to give the reason for the hope that you have . . .
> —I PETER 3:15

Thought . . . Are first appearances important to you? Try not to form an opinion based on how someone *looks*. See each individual as Christ does—as someone He loves and for whom He died!

Love Your Enemies

BY LORI WALL

God always ignores the present perfection for the ultimate perfection. He is not concerned about making you blessed and happy just now; He is working out His ultimate perfection all the time—"That they may be one even as We are."

—OSWALD CHAMBERS

"If they transfer anyone, I hope it's you," a coworker said to me one day while I helped out in her office.

This was the greatest compliment I could ever receive from her. Years before, when we worked together in the same office, we had had a personal misunderstanding. It created tension so great that I looked for another position within the company.

My faith became the subject of conversation and joking among non-believing coworkers. While devoted friends prayed regarding the situation, I prayed simply, "Lord, get me out of here!"

The Lord provided my "way of escape" by sending me to another office for nine months. After He put me through a healing process where I learned to deal with people more effectively, He sent me back. During the time that I was away, I came to realize that God is the One Who validates me and not other people.

Slowly my relationship with the woman began to mend to the point where we were able to speak with one another again. But when I was moved to the desk directly across from her, I didn't know what to expect. I wondered what the Lord was doing.

Amazingly, the woman and I became friends. When she was transferred to a different office, I could genuinely say that I would miss her! Now I realize that God was teaching me to love her all along.

In return for my friendship they accuse me, but I am a [woman] of prayer.

—PSALM 109:4

Thought . . . Are you enduring a tense season of insults or avoidance by a coworker? These tactics might be her camouflage for pain or self-hatred. Realizing this, it will be easier for you to reach out in love.

The Faithfulness of God

BY CYNTHIA HEALD

Alone, and without other help, God is the foundation and completion of my safety.

—CHARLES SPURGEON

*J*ack and I were attending a banquet when a young man recognized Jack and came to sit down next to him. Two other couples who knew each other, but not us, joined our table. The seating left an empty chair next to me.

Everyone at our table began conversing—except me. I began to feel isolated and alone. I even felt as if people at nearby tables must be whispering about how sad it was that Cynthia was such a pitiful case that no one wanted to talk to her!

As I was feeling sorry for myself, the Lord's gentle voice spoke to my heart: *Cynthia, is it true no one is noticing you?*

I replied, *Oh, Lord, I know You love me and are with me now, but look at these people—they're having a good time and I'm by myself!*

Then came the question, *Cynthia, isn't My love enough?*

Yes, Lord, I answered, *Your love is enough. You only are my salvation, my stronghold, the rock of my strength, my refuge. In You, I am complete and lack for nothing. You are always enough.*

Seating arrangements at a dinner table may seem like a minor episode. Yet the clutch of insecurity I felt was very real. It was the fear of abandonment. My experience at that banquet became a precious reminder to me of how God is faithful to abide with us in every moment of our lives—from the "little" events to the big ones.

And surely I am with you always, to the very end of the age.

—MATTHEW 28:20B

Thought . . . Do you ever feel alone—even in a crowd? Don't find your security in others' company or opinion of you. Let your security be in Christ, Who promises to be your friend (John 15:14) and to stay with you in all seasons.

Cultivating Contentment

BY PATTY STUMP

Whatever God has given you to do, enjoy it! It's His provision for you. It is not in doing what you like, but in liking what you do that is the secret of "happiness."

—JAMES BARRIE

*G*od created me to live in the country, or so I thought. With this in mind, our move from the Carolina countryside to the asphalt of Arizona wasn't my idea of living! Crowds, concrete, and community life seemed foreign. I felt cloistered by walls that characterized our new neighborhood. Surely there had to be a way to make the adjustment more bearable for me and to get to know some of our neighbors in the process.

Determined to make this new venture a positive experience, I typed a handful of informal invitations, placed our two small children in a wagon and, along with my husband, went door-to-door inviting neighbors to a holiday open house at our home. I wasn't sure that anyone would come, but felt I had nothing to lose.

On the day of the event, over fifty neighbors stopped by and enjoyed a simple snack of cookies and cider. Much to my surprise, many had lived on our street for ten years and had never met one another!

Our Christmas drop-in has become an annual event and our tiny yard seems to grow larger the more it's used for "pee wee" baseball games, pool parties in our inflatable pool, and lawn games. I've grown accustomed to community living. While there are still times when I miss the Carolina countryside, investing myself into life where God has placed me has allowed me to feel increasingly content in this season.

. . . I have learned to be content whatever the circumstances.

—PHILIPPIANS 4:11

Thought . . . Are you blooming where you are planted? Life is not a dress rehearsal. See every day as a gift, especially those that provide an opportunity in which to grow.

"Gentle Me," Lord

BY JILL BRISCOE

To live in prayer together is to walk in love together.

—MARGARET MOORE JACOBS

I remember bossing around someone who had been put on a work team with me. I was conscious of a cool response from this friend; she muttered, "I like to be asked, Jill, not told!" I was taken aback and ignored her rejoinder, but when I was alone, I thought about her words. "I am such a controller, Lord," I confessed. "Gentle me with the Spirit's sweet grace. Help me to be a servant and not 'lord it over others—as the Gentiles do.' Make me sensitive. Help me listen to myself talking and giving orders. Temper my strong personality with the Spirit's gentleness."

Then I went to find my friend and offered an apology, which she accepted lovingly, and we prayed about it.

That prayer together, of course, is an essential ingredient if we are to see our relationships mended. Somehow you can't harbor resentment when you're on your knees together at the foot of the cross—it just doesn't work!

Be kind and compassionate to one another, forgiving each other, just as in Christ God forgave you.

—EPHESIANS 4:32

Thought . . . Do you tell people to do things, or *ask* them, adding the word "please"? Before beginning to work, why not ask, "May we please pray together?" Any differences will disappear!

A Garden of Friendship

BY PAQUITA RAWLEIGH

All the best of me belongs to her—there is not a talent or an aspiration or a joy in me that has not been awakened by her loving touch.

—HELEN KELLER (ABOUT HER TEACHER, ANNE SULLIVAN)

*W*hen I was growing up in Spain, my mother kept the most beautiful garden that I have ever seen. She had a colorful corner of roses, carnations, lilies, and geraniums. The smell of those flowers transported me to the exotic places of my dreams.

As a little girl, in the spring of life, I used to sit among that rainbow of colors. Inhaling the sweet fragrance, I'd let my dreams run wild. During one of these escapes, my mother sat beside me and, stroking my hair, said, "The friends we encounter during our lifetime will be very much like this garden." She explained that a variety of people and cultures would intertwine their lives with mine.

During the last forty years in America, I have learned the lesson of my mother's patch of flowers—friends *are* the garden in life. If we gently tend buds of friendship, the beauty of their blossoms will greatly enrich our lives. Like an exquisite flower, our friends' faith must be cultivated as we water it with nurturing kindness. As we allow them to grow on their own, we give our friends room to spread their roots.

I have seen some friends transplanted by God into His Heavenly Glory Garden. Their eternal blossoms show me that the "garden principle" applies to our faith as well as to our friendships. Wisely tending our relationship with Christ, we will walk with Him through the beauty of His earthly creation, growing in His love. Then, one day, we will fully blossom, becoming a sweet-smelling aroma in that glorious garden, joining the colors of friends who await us.

But thanks be to God, Who always leads us in triumphal procession in Christ and through us spreads everywhere the fragrance of the knowledge of Him.

—II CORINTHIANS 2:14

Thought . . . Do you show appreciation for friends, with qualities as colorful as roses? Tend to them while you can, before the rose fades and is transplanted into Heaven.

Just Like Friends

BY RITA J. MAGGART

My mother is a poem I'll never be able to write, though everything I write is a poem to my mother.

—SHARON DOUBIAGO

Long interested in the art of floral design, when I heard that a well-known British flower arranger named Sheila Macqueen would offer classes in Bath, England, I knew that this was a "must" for my continuing education.

Somehow I convinced my mother that this would be a wonderful adventure for both of us. We set out for England in February, which is typically cold, damp, and gray—not the environment one envisions for bonding with one's mother and sampling colorful flowers! But the weather did not dampen our spirits or dim our fellowship. Nor did it obscure the charm of stone buildings, the beauty of rolling countryside.

From beginning to end, we were immersed in "the English way with flowers" as we savored the company of "flower friends," dined on delicious cuisine, and slept under crisp linens.

One memory stands out from the rest. Someone asked me, in that oh-so-British manner, "How is it that you and your mother get on so well?" The answer came to me in an instant: "My mother makes me believe that anything is possible, and she is encouraging with her words and nonjudgmental in her criticism—just like friends."

When people see my mother and me together, they usually comment about our striking resemblance. Because we are alike in ways that run deeper than physical appearance, I respond with these words: "We have met in the middle." Then Mother and I smile knowingly at one another as we think to ourselves, "Just like friends!"

Your mother was like a vine in your vineyard planted by the water; it was fruitful and full of branches because of abundant water.

—EZEKIEL 19:10

Thought . . . Do you have a good friendship with your mother? . . . with your daughter? Center your relationship in Christ and become *sisters* . . . eternally!

214

You Don't Have to Understand

BY MARJORIE K. EVANS

God the Holy Spirit, mould me to Thy will. Use me in the service of my glorious King.

—E. MARGARET CLARKSON

Mrs. Wetzel. Mrs. Wetzel. The name kept coming to my mind.

The Lord had been impressing on me the need to be sensitive and obedient to the Holy Spirit's leading. So each month I asked Him to guide me to the friend He wanted me to invite to our Christian women's luncheon. This month I kept thinking of Mrs. Wetzel.

"But Lord," I protested, "she is just an acquaintance, not a friend." But the feeling that I should ask her to accompany me persisted until I finally called her. She quickly replied, "Yes, I'll be delighted to go with you."

It was pleasant to get acquainted as we drove to the luncheon. The speaker gave an excellent message. She told of the peace that could be ours as we gave up our "rights"—anger, pride, envy, bitterness, resentment, unforgiveness, and jealousy—to God. Several times Mrs. Wetzel secretly wiped away tears.

On the way home she said, "You told me that you didn't understand why you felt led to invite me to the luncheon. But God used the speaker to minister to me in an area of my life where I really need help. Thank you for asking me."

Since that day my prayer has been, "Lord, show me the friend, acquaintance, or stranger whom You want me to invite to our luncheon." Learning to obey the Holy Spirit's leading in all situations and seasons, even when I don't understand why, is exciting. As a result, several of the new friends I have made have accepted Jesus as their Savior!

> . . . those who live in accordance with the Spirit have their minds set on what the Spirit desires.
>
> —ROMANS 8:5

Thought . . . Do you always obey God, even when it doesn't make sense? Follow His lead every time. It will surprise you to know whom you will reach for eternity.

Playing Favorites

BY JONI EARECKSON TADA

Don't judge a book by its cover.

—ANONYMOUS

The other day as I drove into a restaurant parking lot, I was cut off by two beach boys on a brand new motorcycle. They whooped it up as they parked their bike, shaking the sand from their dirty sweatpants and sleeveless tee-shirts. They plopped on the curb to lace up their oversized tennis shoes and rummaged through their fanny packs for cigarettes. I noticed that one boy wore two earrings . . . in both ears. I also noticed they parked on the white line of my handicap parking space.

Strutting into the restaurant, they proceeded to act tough while standing in line. I wheeled up behind them, deliberating whether or not I should say something. I was just ready to open my mouth when the kid with earrings turned, looked at me, and asked in a small voice, "Ma'am, excuse me, is your name Joanie?"

Bother! This snotty kid was about to be nice to me and I suddenly felt like Jonah, who got irritated because those rotten Ninevites started to turn soft. The boy continued, "I saw your movie when I was little and I used to go to Calvary Church up the road."

I sat there convicted as we talked about his wayward faith. I need to remember that the people God places in my path are usually those with whom He wants me to share His love—even lost and lonely beach boys in California.

> Don't show favoritism. Suppose a man comes into your meeting wearing a gold ring and fine clothes, and a poor man in shabby clothes also comes in. If you show special attention to the man wearing fine clothes and say, "Here's a good seat for you," but say to the poor man, "You stand there" or "Sit on the floor by my feet," have you not discriminated among yourselves and become judges with evil thoughts?
>
> —JAMES 2:1B-4

Thought . . . Do you judge people before you even know them? When you remember to see them through Jesus' eyes, you will feel deep compassion and be able to act accordingly.

He Supplies Our Needs

BY ELAINE CUNNINGHAM

Faith that is sure of God is the only faith there is.

—OSWALD CHAMBERS

One Friday when our two children were toddlers, we discovered that our milk was gone and we had no money to buy more. Our home mission salary never seemed to stretch far enough. We knew that our babies needed milk, so we got on our knees and asked God to supply our need.

In our desperation, we claimed the promises of God. "You said in Your Word, Lord, that we would lack no good thing." We prayed, making our request known to Him.

We were still kneeling when the doorbell rang. Our next door neighbor stood there holding two gallon jugs of milk. "I feel foolish asking," she said, "but could you possibly use some extra milk? Our milkman left this, and we're going away for the weekend."

"You're the quickest answer to prayer I've ever seen!" I exclaimed.

Some might say it was coincidence. Never! I believe it was a loving Father's direct answer to a plea from two of His children. God is near us when we pray. We will probably never know the many times that God has intervened on our behalf. I have learned to trust Him daily. Those who seek the Lord lack no good thing in any season!

The lions may grow weak and hungry, but those who seek the Lord lack no good thing.

—PSALM 34:10

Thought . . . Are you lacking some good and necessary thing? Have you asked God to provide it? Amazingly, sometimes we actually forget to ask. Asking, seeking, and knocking release His power to answer.

Values

BY JEAN FLEMING

People are more important than things.

—ANONYMOUS

My husband's Aunt Barbara lives in a home for mentally retarded women. We planned a trip to familiarize ourselves with the home. We were totally unprepared for what we found.

In a large white house, twenty-two women live with A. W. and Bertha Gaskins, a middle-aged Christian couple. We hoped to find a clean home run by caring people. What we found far exceeded our expectations. Mr. and Mrs. Gaskins, who had prayed for five years to operate a home for women from mental institutions, now give these women a level of loving care that few parents provide for their own children.

After breakfast on Sunday mornings the women line up eagerly outside the dining room. Bertha fixes each woman's hair and applies powder and lipstick. This is no assembly-line operation. Each woman receives Bertha's full attention. The shade of lipstick chosen flatters each woman's complexion and outfit. Bertha talks kindly and upliftingly to each one: "Darling, you look beautiful. Mama loves you. Run upstairs and get the necklace Mama bought for you. Your dress needs something at the neck." Each woman leaves for church looking attractive and feeling loved.

A.W. and Bertha Gaskins believe these women are important and maintain a loving relationship with each of them. Their lives demonstrate that they believe people are important.

> Look at the birds of the air; they do not sow or reap or store away in barns, and yet your heavenly Father feeds them. Are you not much more valuable than they?
> —MATTHEW 6:26

Thought . . . Do you value people more than possessions? Sunday is a great day to spend time with family and friends whom you love, or to visit the "unloved" elderly in a nursing home. In no time, you'll be surprised at how easy it is to love them, too.

Love and Loyalty

BY SHIRLEY A. REYNOLDS

There is no better exercise for strengthening the heart than reaching down and lifting people up!

—ANONYMOUS

Elderly. Disheveled. Jagged-lined face. These were all descriptions of Roy. With hands extended, and shaking voice he cried, "I want my dog back from Florida!" A tear fell down his cheek.

"Went to see my son. Sold everything. Truck broke. We were stranded. My son . . . no help. Called a preacher who took Shadow. Said he'd send him back so I rode the Greyhound. They said, 'Sorry, can't take your dog on the bus!' He's my life . . . all I have!"

We collected money to bring Shadow home. After a six and a half hour plane flight, Shadow arrived at the center.

News cameras greeted Roy. He was their human interest story. But Roy wanted only one thing . . . SHADOW!

Emerging out of the crate was a small, hairless head, shaved because of the Florida heat. Knowing his master's voice, just like a puppy, Shadow jumped into Roy's arms repeatedly licking his face.

Camera crews asked, "Tell us Roy . . . why ask for help with a dog, when you need a home?"

"Shadow is my life, my child. He comes first!"

As I looked at Roy, he leaned over and hugged me. "Thank you from the bottom of my heart."

You know what, Roy, thank YOU from the bottom of my heart! I thought, as he had demonstrated to me the true meaning of love and loyalty.

A man of many companions may come to ruin, but there is a friend who sticks closer than a brother.

—PROVERBS 18:24

Thought . . . Do you go out of your way to help the homeless, the outcast? One of the best ways that you can share Christ's love is to *demonstrate* it and not just talk about it.

Hymns from Childhood

BY MARIE ASNER

When music fails to agree to the ear, to sooth the ear and the heart and the senses, then it has missed its point.

—MARIA CALLAS

I planned a trip through Europe after finishing a music degree. I received a phone call from the mother of a former classmate who had dropped out of high school and joined the military. "Can you write to him while you are there, or phone, or visit? I know he's homesick, but he hasn't answered my letters in months."

He was not someone to whom I wanted to speak, but I took his address. Eventually I found myself within a day's ride of his camp. I wrote, giving him the phone number of my hotel. At least I could tell his mother I had tried. To my surprise, he telephoned and asked me to visit him at the town near his camp. My hotel owner knew the minister there and said she could arrange lodging at the church.

Arriving at the church early, I climbed to the loft, inspected the organ, and began to play hymns from childhood. Suddenly, I heard sobbing. I turned around to find my classmate sitting in the sanctuary. He said it had been a long time since he had heard that music and asked if I would play it again. I played for an hour and he never stopped crying.

Later, my friend went to the chaplain on base, then wrote to his mother. He has remained a church member ever since.

It took a trip to Europe and the courage to reach out, but faith was renewed that day. My vacation had been a springboard for a season of hope.

But while he was still a long way off, his father saw him and was filled with compassion for him; he ran to his son, threw his arms around him and kissed him.

—LUKE 15:20

Thought . . . Do you think that because of your past—or even your present—you can never return to God? It is never too late. Run to Him and confess. His arms remain open to lovingly receive you.

Missing Melody

BY DEBRA WEST SMITH

And the song, from beginning to end, I found in the heart of a friend.

—HENRY WADSWORTH LONGFELLOW

Playing handbells is a humbling, but enjoyable experience, thanks to the wonderful ladies composing our church's handbell choir. At Christmas we often play at elementary schools.

If they lack facilities, we play outdoors. One such occasion taught me a lesson in interdependence.

The morning sun blinded us and wind whipped through the courtyard as the children were seated. Our concert began with *We Three Kings*, in which plunking bells suggested camels plodding across the desert. Then the *camels* ran into a storm!

Suddenly, the wind blew our music, shuffling the pages. Only a few notes were heard as we frantically scrambled to straighten the sheets. We don't memorize music, because it's tricky enough playing several bells with two hands and half a brain. However, we do learn to listen to each other. More than listen—we *depend* on one another.

And that's what saved us. If one person continued, the rest could catch up. One player carried the melody, then another, and another. Our "three kings" may have sounded frazzled and the "camels" lame, but we finished that concert together, despite the wind.

It reminded me that our life's song was never meant to be performed as a solo, but as part of a choir. Though sometimes we falter or may be the only one carrying the tune, if we rely on each other, we'll make beautiful harmony together.

For none of us lives to himself alone and none of us dies to himself alone.

—ROMANS 14:7

Thought . . . In this season, are you trying to carry your burden alone, living independently of others? Reach out and ask for help, and when you do, you'll bless others as well.

This Can Only Be a "God-Thing"!

BY LEA C. TARTANIAN

How calmly may we commit ourselves to the hands of Him Who bears up the world.

—JEAN PAUL RICHTER

I went to bed feeling disappointed with a couple of people who are dear to me. Although sleep came immediately, I awoke in the middle of the night. I grew sadder by the minute, dwelling on how they had hurt me. I prayed to God to restore my faith in humanity. I told Him that I could not stand friends being so disappointing. Pleading, I whispered, "God if you want to use me for Your purpose, please remove my despair. Snap me out of this!"

I turned on the tiny light by the bed and began to read a Christian magazine I had received in the mail that week. Opening to the "letters from readers," I noticed that someone had written, stating that he loved the publication so much that he had sent a gift subscription to a "soulmate." I thought, *What a wonderful thing for a person to say about a friend!* I was stunned to discover that the writer was my penpal from Tennessee. I knew that I was the "soulmate" because he had just given me a gift subscription to the magazine.

I burst into tears. God had shown me that letter at the exact moment I needed His encouragement. My faith in people was immediately restored and my faith in the Lord, strengthened.

> . . . my mouth will praise You. On my bed I remember You;
> I think of You through the watches of the night.
> —PSALM 63:5-6

Thought . . . Do people disappoint you? They are bound to sometimes because they are imperfect. Anchor your hope in our perfect Lord, knowing that when people fail you, He never will!

Nurture

A Time for Awakening

BY EMILIE BARNES

God Almighty first planted a garden; and indeed, it is the purest of human pleasures.

—FRANCIS BACON

Wake up and smell the roses!

"Wake up!" the garden calls to me.

Standing in my garden, breathing in deep and sweet, I realize how often I seem to be holding my breath. So much of our urban air is noxious. What a relief to find a place where taking a deep breath feels safe and pleasurable.

But this is not just a matter of breathing cleaner air. It's about finding a place where it's safe to feel. So much about modern living assaults our senses. We're buffeted by bad news, hurry, anxiety, until we unconsciously pull down our awareness levels like blinds on a too-bright window. No wonder we forget to breathe deeply. No wonder we become half-blind, hard-of-hearing.

No wonder our spirits get hardened to the point that we can discern only the harshest realities.

The garden is a safe place to reverse that hardening process, to become conversant with realities that are softer and more beautiful. A garden is place of tenderness, freshness, joy and delight. The triumphs and sorrows here are on the scale of centuries, grounded in eternal rhythms of the earth.

Here I find myself slowly unfolding, my numbed senses coming alive again. Here it is more than safe. It is wonderful.

My garden is a place that nurtures quiet in the midst of noise and makes it safe to listen to bird song and bee buzz and the trickle of water. People who come here exclaim, "We can't believe we're still in the city."

Now the Lord God planted a garden in the east, in Eden; and there He put the man He had formed.

—GENESIS 2:8

Thought . . . How does your garden grow? If your thumb isn't green, enjoy someone else's garden, instead. Saunter through a park or botanical garden. Spend time relaxing outdoors. *You* will be the one to grow . . . closer to God.

Rest for the Weary Student

BY KELLY KING

Thou hast made us for Thyself, and the heart of man is restless until it finds its rest in Thee.

—SAINT AUGUSTINE

My parents had planned a fall getaway to the mountains of New Mexico during my junior year in college. Driving from the university, the trip did not seem important. My thoughts centered on a test that I had nearly failed, a looming yearbook deadline, and a required science course that was beyond my average "B" student mentality. This was not a vacation, just a long road trip with textbooks in tow.

My parents were ready to leave when I arrived home. They could see from the expression on my face that the last few weeks had taken their toll. Sleepless nights of studying, combined with a hectic schedule of activities had left me with swollen eyes and a weary body. My mother was keenly aware of the situation. As I got in the back seat, I lugged along my heavy backpack. Without warning, mom reached back and took the books. "I think you need a break. Let's put these in the trunk for now."

In that small gesture, my mother became a catalyst of nurture for me. During the next four days I did not focus on what seemed to be the most important thing in my life. Instead, I was able to focus on the beauty of the changing seasons and experience a glimpse of wonder with the first autumn snowfall. I experienced God's presence when I experienced the glory of His creation. I was reminded of His intimate love and that His thoughts towards me are endless and precious.

Come to Me, all you who are weary and burdened, and I will give you rest.

—MATTHEW 11:28

Thought . . . Are you physically exhausted? . . . weary of soul? Simply stop . . . whatever you are doing. Take a nap. Take a bath. Take a walk. But most of all, take time to go to Jesus and rest in Him.

But, Lord, I Don't Want to Be a Secretary!

By Lenae Bulthuis

Every man's work is a portrait of himself.

—Arthur Brisbane

After a season of seven years as a high school secretary, I felt like part of the office furniture. Students graduated and embraced freedom, while I was chained to the school system.

It's not that I didn't like my work. I did. The challenging projects, fun coworkers, and interesting students kept each day fresh. Even so, I struggled to *take my job and love it.*

My dissatisfaction peaked during the graduation preparations. As I listened to the senior class make plans to change the world, I questioned God's plan for me.

My job wasn't changing lives. I wasn't curing diseases, inspiring people into the ministry, or saving famine-stricken countries. I whined in my prayers, "But, Lord, I don't want to be a secretary!" I begged Him to guide me into a soul-changing career.

His answer came through my youngest sister, Shari. On the last day of her senior year, she bounced into my office and said, "Thought you would like to read my final English paper."

The paper focused on the most influential person in her life. To my surprise, it was I! It ended, "I know Lenae will leave her mark at least one place on this earth. It is in my heart."

To Shari this was just a year-end assignment. To me, it was an answer to prayer. "Lord, I never would have received this honor if I weren't the school secretary," I prayed.

God filled me with His peace and the realization that *even secretaries* can leave eternal marks on souls.

"For I know the plans I have for you," declares the Lord, "plans to prosper you and not to harm you, plans to give you hope and a future."

—Jeremiah 29:11

Thought . . . Have you found fulfillment in your career? Ask the Lord to confirm that you are doing His assignment by showing you the effect that you are having on others. We often find satisfaction through service.

Her Sleep Shall Be Sweet

BY BECKY FREEMAN

Nature had not intended man to work from eight in the morning until midnight without the refreshment of blessed oblivion, which, even if it lasts only twenty minutes, is sufficient to renew all vital forces.

—WINSTON CHURCHILL

What is it we women want the most in life?

I think I have the answer. We want a nap, a simple guilt-free nap.

It was an afternoon typical of so many others—loaded with writing deadlines and housework and phone calls and a dozen family obligations. Like a movie producer who yells, "Cut!" I walked away from the middle of the action and went outside to my porch swing where I read and prayed and wrote for awhile, until I realized what I really needed was a nap.

The kids were at school, the day was gorgeous, and I craved the warmth of sunshine on my skin. So I laid out a quilt on the deck, curled up and fell into a deep, peaceful sleep. An hour later I awoke refreshed, without a trace of guilt, ready to tackle the dishes and deadlines again.

The busier I get in this season of mothering and working at home, the more I realize that often the most efficient—and spiritual—thing I can do for my heart, soul, mind, and family, is to pause and observe a mini-Sabbath: in the form of one quiet, uninterrupted nap.

He makes me lie down in green pastures . . . He restores my soul.

—PSALM 23:2A, 3A

Thought . . . Are you being pulled in a million different directions? Don't proceed or prioritize. Simply pause and say, "Time out!" After literally resting, you will emerge refreshed with the needed energy to evaluate and complete your tasks.

Beautify a Space

BY SANDRA PALMER CARR

There should be a practical result of the realization that we have been created in the image of the Creator of beauty.

—EDITH SCHAEFFER

*E*ach evening I make a list of the next day's activities. Even routine tasks such as "shower," "make bed," etc., are included and lined through upon their completion.

Though I have found this a satisfying way to keep track of basic household duties, I decided to liven up my list with an appealing description for projects that I don't do as often as I would like.

Somewhere on the list I write: "Beautify a space." Then I pick one anywhere in the house. My rule is not to choose it when composing the list. I want to be surprised by God's glory.

Perhaps a shelf gets cleaned and polished, a drawer sorted, pictures rearranged, or a dull table brightened with flowers. One by one, lackluster places become beautified spaces—shining with the glory of God. Instead of feeling rushed and overwhelmed, I am at peace.

Since I have begun beautifying my home, I have thought about how the Lord desires to beautify me, the temple of His Holy Spirit. He continually cleanses me with the blood of Jesus and I grow daily in His Word and grace. His lovingkindness is the source of His beauty being expressed through me.

So while I beautify a space in my home, I can trust the Lord to do the same in my heart. I wonder what's on His list today!

He has made everything beautiful in its time.

—ECCLESIASTES 3:11A

Thought . . . What is the condition of your home? . . . of your heart? While you "de-junk" your house, rid your heart of debris such as jealousy, anger, and discontent. Let God make a clean sweep of any sin which disqualifies your heart as being "His beautified space."

With God in the Dark

BY JANE PARRISH

A simple rule, to be followed whether one is in the light or not, gives backbone to one's spiritual life, as nothing else can.

—EVELYN UNDERHILL

*I*t had happened again. The lights went out as I knew they would. *Why did these storms come when my husband, Larry, was out of town? Why did things seem worse at night—especially when I was alone?* I wondered

In the dark, I inched my way toward the kitchen to get matches to light a small kerosene lamp. At least I could dispel the darkness around me. Light from the flames danced on the wall. I sat and stared, thinking about Chris, my son, and questioning again and again where I had failed. He should have been home hours ago.

Outside the wind hurled rain against the windows, picturing the turmoil of my mind. Sirens pierced the night, and I was tempted to think that Chris had been in an accident. We were so estranged these days, and I longed for a close relationship with him again. He had left for the evening, not on the best of terms with me, and once again I was slipping into a "worse-case scenario."

As I sat there God whispered, "Larry may not be home and Chris hasn't returned, but I am here; you are not alone." I opened my Bible and bowed my head, finding comfort as I rehearsed God's faithfulness to me. "Thank you, Father," I prayed. "You are the Lord of tumultuous seasons—both storms of the weather and of the heart. You are here, You understand, and You care. I will trust You, once again, with Chris and with our relationship."

Who among you fears the Lord and obeys the word of His servant? Let him who walks in the dark, who has no light, trust in the name of the Lord and rely on His God.

—ISAIAH 50:10

Thought . . . When you are in the dark, how do you find the way? God's Word lights your path (Psalm 119:105), providing the answer for every single problem of life. Read it daily and discover God's light, truth, and peace.

An Inward Singing

BY KAREN BURTON MAINS

Taking joy in living is a woman's best cosmetic.

—ROSALIND RUSSELL

An earnest teenager, I learned what joy is not.

Someone had impressed me by the fact that one quality of the Christian life is joyfulness, so each day I put on a determined mask of radiance. I practiced in my mirror a spiritual smile, and manufactured a perky greeting for friends.

With forced effort, I was exhausted by midday!

Negative lessons are often ones we long remember. I learned as a teenager that joy cannot be manufactured. Happiness is a quality we control. We can create happy moments; it is beyond our ability to invent joyful ones.

But joy is an inward singing which cannot be silenced by outward negative circumstances—not by boredom, pain, disappointment or distress.

Joy cannot be summoned. It is something we receive rather than something we do. The source of joy is God.

We cannot command, "Be joyful!" Joy is the by-product of a growing relationship between us and God. We must increase our worship of the Father, identify the presence of Christ in our everyday living, and become increasingly obedient to the Holy Spirit: "The fruit of the Spirit is . . . joy (Galatians 5:22, RSV)."

Today, when joy is missing, I don't practice my spiritual smile in the mirror. I don't dazzle the grocery clerk with a dose of megawatt brightness. Instead, I pray, read Scripture, meditate—pushing roots of my fruit-bearing self deeper into spiritual soil.

Then suddenly, while doing dishes, or working against deadlines, joy inhabits me, singing its own child-tune, kicking its glad heels against my heart. Unexpected, unbidden—but a welcome gift—joy is there!

> Sing for joy to God our strength; shout aloud to the God of Jacob!
>
> —PSALM 81:1

Thought . . . Are you joyful? Remove joy-killing weeds, like complaining, worry, or fear, and give joy a chance to flourish in season.

Hungry No More

BY KRISTEN INGRAM

I am a part of all that I have met.

—JOHN MILTON

$\mathcal{B}$ill comes to our church almost every Sunday, carrying a worn Bible whose red-edged pages are falling out. He wears clothes that are ragged and soiled from living under bridges and sleeping on benches. He stuffs all his extra garments into the front of his black plaid shirt; his profile is ludicrous. He is crumpled and stooped and resembles the garbage bag he carries, full of his belongings—whatever "treasures" he has collected from our gutters and dumpsters.

On his worst days he apparently hears voices, muttering to someone the rest of us cannot see. He is foul-smelling, and most of our parishioners shrink away or even demand that he be ejected. These folks complain that at the coffee hour, he pokes twenty cookies into his pockets and stirs numerous spoonsful of sugar into his coffee. At potluck dinners, he relentlessly gorges himself.

When the congregation first issued an invitation to the city's homeless to attend our church, they expected doe-eyed, docile children and clean, struggling adults who were humble and grateful. They certainly hadn't imagined worshiping with an ugly, stinking old man.

One day Bill was beside me in church at Communion. He leaned forward to hear the words, "This is My body," and "This is My blood." As he lifted the Bread to his mouth, I heard him sigh like a weary wind, and tears slid down his cheeks as he ate.

Maybe for once, he was filled.

> Then Jesus declared, "I am the bread of life. He who comes to Me will never go hungry, and he who believes in Me will never be thirsty."
>
> —JOHN 6:35

$\mathcal{T}hought$ . . . How are you reaching out to the poor and homeless? Don't preach. Show Christ's love by meeting their genuine physical needs. Then you will be in a position to share the Gospel.

Sing Your Lungs Out, You're Family

BY SHEILA WALSH

A child in the cradle, if you watch it at leisure, has the infinite in its eyes.

—VINCENT VAN GOGH

I love that my baby boy has no sense of what's appropriate on the noise-making front.

On the first Sunday we took him to church, we opted to sit in the back row, knowing that at the first squawk we could be up and out fast. He slept through the time of worship. We thought we were home free.

Then came the sermon.

Suddenly, Christian burst into a baby version of "Moon River" at a decibel level that could have burst a dog's eardrums. I jumped up so quickly I nearly dropped him. I hurried out whispering, "Shh!" That only seemed to encourage him, and he moved into verse two, grinning.

I was laughing so hard I could barely breathe. There is something so charming about that kind of innocence. When he is happy, we know it, and when he's not, we know that, too. It would never cross his mind to be anything but authentic.

When children are secure, they feel free to be who they really are. That's how you and I can live, too. God is the only One Who knows everything about us. He knows our good thoughts and the thoughts that we struggle to admit. Nothing would dampen God's heart toward you. He knows it all, and He loves you. Surely, this kind of security should set us free to be who we really are.

What a gift in a world where there is so much uncertainty! Why, it's enough to bring on a chorus of "Moon River."

O Lord, you have searched me and you know me . . . you are familiar with all my ways.

—PSALM 139:1, 3B

Thought . . . Do you have the freedom to be yourself before others? Knowing God made you this way for a purpose, you can rejoice in fulfilling it!

A Little Brighter Day

BY MARY BETH NELSON

Fragrance always clings to the hand that gives you roses.

—CHINESE PROVERB

My husband and I enjoy fresh flowers on the breakfast or lunch table. Severe heat experienced in our Texas Panhandle last summer frequently deprived us of this special treat.

Because my yard plants were rather sparse, I actually became excited at the appearance of a lonely rose exhibiting itself on the Talisman bush one morning. Its slightly brown edges did not discourage my taking it to the breakfast table. A few hours later, I noticed a sudden fragrance which only a rose can emit. Who would have thought that that "droughty" little flower could produce an aroma so delectable and potent that it would permeate the entire room? I smiled in unexpected delight.

To me, the rose symbolized one of those tiny blessings that often remains unnoticed. Each time I passed the table, the rose teased me with its fragrance.

I became convinced that if God could provide me with such pleasure through such an incidental gesture, that surely in some way, I could supply some measure of comfort to others.

I remembered a statement by George MacDonald: "If I can put one touch of rosy sunset into the life of any man or woman, I shall feel that I have worked with God." I resolved right then to include his suggestion in my daily life. My encouraging words, understanding heart, or kind deeds might help to provide that rosy sunset and make someone's day a little brighter.

> For we are to God the aroma of Christ among those who are being saved and those who are perishing.
> —II CORINTHIANS 2:15

Thought . . . Do you take time to "smell the roses"? Although this statement has become overused, its value is inestimable. When we take time for beauty, we take time for God. And when you share beauty with a friend, you are doubly blessed.

The Flame of Joy

BY SUE MONK KIDD

Children are not things to be molded, but are people to be unfolded.

—JESS LAIR

*A*fter reflecting one morning on John 15:11 where Jesus speaks about His joy being in us with fullness, I was reminded of what had happened when I picked up Ann at school one day. I saw a little fellow of six or seven walking across the school lawn toward his mother's car. About halfway there he stopped and began to toss his book satchel high in the air, trying to catch it. The joy in this free, childlike act was evident on his face. "Look!" he kept shouting to his mother, who sat impatiently in the car. After ten or so of his tosses, she got out and dragged him into the car, reprimanding him for keeping her waiting. His face fell. She had extinguished something important in him—some important flame of joy.

It made me think of the times I'd done the same sort of thing to my own children, to Sandy, even to myself—puncturing the joy of others with my impatience or thoughtlessness. Jesus Christ desires my joy. He wants our joy to be full. I needed to change my attitude, to make a tangible response to these words.

That afternoon when Bob yanked off his shoes and waded gleefully through a mud puddle he'd created with the garden hose, I had to bite the insides of my cheeks, but I didn't say a discouraging or angry word. Instead, I peeled off my shoes and squished around in the mud with him. We laughed till the puddle dried. Our joy was full.

I have told you this so that My joy may be in you and that your joy may be complete.

—JOHN 15:11

Thought . . . Are you a killjoy? Often we unintentionally snuff out children's joy simply because we're in a season of pressure. Slow sown and "take joy" with them; don't take it from them.

Freedom from Want

BY VEDA BOYD JONES

Solvency is entirely a matter of temperament and not of income.

—LOGAN PEARSALL SMITH

*A*unt Punch was a singular person. Widowed at a young age, she never remarried, but managed her farm with the help of a teenaged son. She was a woman of the land. She took strength from God's outdoors. Most of the time she milked cows, but when her son married and moved to his own home, she turned to raising chickens in one of those long, low chicken houses.

Her home was a run-down old place, heated with a wood-burning stove. A round kitchen table was the center of her home, where she nurtured guests with the best hamburgers in the world and lively discussions. She always spoke her mind, but lent a sympathetic ear to those with troubles. With the first lull in conversation, she would pull out her guitar and in a clear voice sing hymns and country songs.

She had no debts, owned little, and gave freely. She was the first to lend a tool to a neighbor or take food to a family after a death. She once said to me, "I have everything I need and most of what I want."

She was a God-fearing woman who was content with her life and with what God had given her. She taught me that money isn't the way to true riches; fewness of wants makes us wealthy in any season.

Keep your lives free from the love of money and be content with what you have . . .

—HEBREWS 13:5

Thought . . . Is discontent your constant companion? Remember that if you have God, you have everything!

True Love Never Leaves

BY CINDI McMENAMIN

. . . nothing can wedge in between the love of God and the saint.

—OSWALD CHAMBERS

I grew up believing that people who loved me would leave. My mother often left my home after an argument with my father. Sometimes she would come back after a few hours. Sometimes it would be a few days. She explained that people need time away from one another to be able to love and appreciate them more.

During my college years, my boyfriend felt the same way. He believed that absence makes the heart grow fonder, so he would strategically arrange for time away from me. Naturally, I thought separation was a sign of true love.

When I met the man whom I would eventually marry, he told me one evening that he would never ask for time away from me. "Why?" I asked, thinking maybe he didn't love me.

"God never wants time away from you, Cindi," Hugh replied. "So neither will I."

When Hugh spoke those words, my eyes were opened to the amazing love that my Heavenly Father has for me. He never wants a separation from my presence. He loves me so passionately that He never wants to be apart from me. His Word says that there is no place that I can go where He will not follow—nothing I can do that will cause Him to leave.

That is security. It is that for which I have searched all my life. And today, through the wise words of my husband and the promises of God's Word, I am convinced that True Love never leaves—in any season.

. . . Never will I leave you; never will I forsake you.

—HEBREWS 13:5

Thought . . . Do you fear abandonment from God because someone left you in the past? Do not compare God with people. God loves you permanently and will stay with you now and through eternity.

Season of Renewal

BY LYNN KUNTZ

The year's at the spring and day's at the morn; Morning's at seven; the hillside's dew-pearled; the lark's on the wing; the snail's on the thorn: God's in His heaven—all's right with the world.

—ROBERT BROWNING

Up, up, still further up we drive. The trail narrows and tilts, with a bright profusion of wildflowers sprinkling its banks. Approaching our small cabin, dwarfed by towering Douglas firs, the children practically erupt from the car, whooping and hollering. I grab Darryl's hand. Journey's end: we're back!

I look beneath the front porch. The central foundation cement pier, embedded with the long-outgrown handprints of our children, supports much more than four log walls and a roof. It is an integral part of our family's foundation, a reminder of God's goodness in bringing us back, again and again, for a season of beauty and peace and renewal.

Each summer, we retreat to this uncluttered, soul-nourishing world. We rise with the sun, warmed awake by its rays, and energized by the clean mountain air. We gather fresh raspberries, hand-feed trusting chipmunks, and mix nectar for hummingbirds. We watch a shy, tawny doe at the salt lick, a hawk soar from his cliff-top nest.

Days pass quickly, a series of small adventures and quiet miracles. Everywhere we look, we see God's handiwork.

Prayers and dinner are shared around a campfire. Our youngest falls asleep in his father's lap, barbecue sauce and a smile on his face. Stars shine like glitter scattered across black velvet.

Surely, along with the Heavens, we declare God's glory in any season.

How many are your works, O Lord! In wisdom You made them all; the earth is full of your creatures.

—PSALM 104:24

Thought . . . How much time do you spend in God's "great outdoors"? Enjoying God's creation is good for our health, refreshment, and sense of wonder. Nature draws us closer to our Creator.

The Archer

BY SHARON P. MOORE

Thought takes man out of servitude, into freedom.

—HENRY WADSWORTH LONGFELLOW

*R*eturning to my office job after a heavenly retreat in the country, I wallowed in a miserable Monday morning mood, wishing I didn't have to work. I was slogging through paperwork, feeling sorry for myself, when a retired advisory board member stopped by.

Dick stands tall despite his eighty years and three recent back surgeries. He laughs at old age and stays busy.

His response to my "How are you?" was enthusiastic.

"You know I volunteer at the physical therapy center," he began. "I'm working with Dave, a man paralyzed from the waist down after a car accident. He used to be so weak that he couldn't lift his arms. I'm teaching him how to shoot a bow and arrow! He's good enough now that he wants to go hunting with me."

"That's terrific!" I exclaimed. (I was laughing to myself at the picture of an eighty-year-old man smeared with camouflage, pushing a wheelchair, 'stalking' through the woods!)

"Some people in therapy aren't as bad off as Dave," Dick continued. "But so many have given up.

"It's what you do with your *mind* . . . " he emphasized. "You can't let it pull you down."

Zing! Like an arrow, Dick's message hit its mark.

My black mood lifted even before he had finished speaking, and I silently thanked God for His patience. Through Dick, He had reminded me, "Look at all you have!" The greatest blessing is Himself, a loving Heavenly Father Who knows me and tells me what I need to hear in every season.

. . . we take captive every thought to make it obedient to Christ.

—II CORINTHIANS 10:5

Thought . . . How is your thought-life? Do what author Kay Arthur advises and "Philippians Four-Eight"any thought that knocks on your mind's door. "Frisk it" and if it isn't noble, right, pure, lovely, etc., then send it packing!

Monday Musings

BY LUCI SWINDOLL

Attitudes are capable of making the same experience either pleasant or painful.

—JOHN POWELL

Mondays . . . too many chores. Since I travel most weekends, Monday is the day I unpack. That's always a mess, with stuff strewn everywhere and suitcases lying about. Being a neat-nick, I hate that.

On Monday I must make stops at the grocery store, the post office, the service station, . . . Deliver me! Mondays annoy me.

But . . . not completely. In another way, I love Mondays. I love unloading all my stuff out of the suitcase and organizing it back where it belongs. That satisfies me.

I love grocery shopping. I love anticipating the preparation of wonderful meals. Every now and then, I add a jar of pickles, can of hairspray, or package of liverwurst to another shopper's unattended cart, just to entertain myself and give that person whiplash at the checkout counter.

Even the post office can be rewarding. Last week, I bought ten stamps and gave two each to the five people behind me. I was giving them a little present. My own little random act of kindness.

On Monday nights, I feel genuine joy, a sense of accomplishment. Plus, I've had a few good laughs, enjoyed a meaningful chat or two, and expressed love in a tangible way to total strangers.

So what's the difference? Why do I sometimes get bogged down hating the day? . . . at other times, loving the day? Perspective! Perspective is everything. Paul encourages us to do whatever we do with all our hearts. When you do, you can do anything. The busiest days can become our most joyful.

> Whatever you do, work at it with all your heart, as working for the Lord, not for men.
>
> —COLOSSIANS 3:23

Thought . . . What is your perspective on chores? Change your "troublesome tasks" to "joy jobs." Once completed, they will bring a season of order and pleasure to life.

Healed for His Service

BY ROSALIE J.G. MILLS

Every miracle in the Old and New Testaments began with a problem. If you have a problem, you are a candidate for a miracle.

—JOHN MAXWELL

"We trust you with this minister's license." My pastor's words spoken just a few short months ago penetrated my heart to its core, humbling me before a gracious God. I hadn't realized until then how deeply distrusted I had felt for so many years.

More than thirty years before, I had heard God's voice for the first time and it changed my life's direction. Over two ensuing decades, I sang, taught, served on various boards, and eventually was ordained into the ministry. Still, I felt there was something else for which He was uniquely preparing me. What I hadn't realized was the hard road I would need to travel as He perfected traits in me that were interfering with His call.

Eight years after being ordained, I resigned from the ministry, disillusioned, ashamed, and broken. I thought that the season of immorality in which I had engaged had ruined any hopes of serving Him again. Yet, I had not counted on His matchless love, grace, and ability to transform my life.

Healing came over the next six years in my new church as I experienced Christ's love firsthand through women friends' loving accountability, support, and encouragement to try my wings again. And when I did, it was with a deeper sense of understanding for other broken women without hope.

Through it all, He has given me my life's work and message: If God can transform my life, there is hope for you, too.

> And the God of all grace, Who called you to His eternal glory in Christ, after you have suffered a little while, will Himself restore you and make you strong, firm and steadfast.
>
> —I PETER 5:10

Thought . . . Do you, having experienced immorality as a Christian, think that God will never forgive nor use you in service again? Jesus forgives *every* sin from which you repent. But He also tells you to "go now and leave your life of sin (John 8:3)."

Parenting

Priorities

BY BECKY FREEMAN

Dishes and dusting can wait 'till tomorrow, for children grow up we've learned to our sorrow. So quiet down cobwebs and dust go to sleep, I'm rocking my baby—and babies don't keep.

—NURSERY RHYME

$\mathcal{I}$'d delayed as long as I could. It was time to stop by the school library to complete records for my three school-aged children.

Why the procrastination?

Take four children, numerous shots per child, and an absent-minded mother who had no idea where she'd filed "children's immunizations." Fortunately, I looked under "T" for "Traumatic Experiences." Locating birth certificates was equally challenging.

I asked the school secretary if I could just show her my stretch marks as proof of my children's birth. By the time I had finished filling out forms, I was so tired, I put "undecided" in the blank next to "name," and "not applicable" in the blank beside "sex."

My pre-schooler, Gabe, who'd come along on this errand, was remarkably quiet. When I looked up I saw the reason: he'd been happily licking and sticking postage stamps to the library shelves.

A half hour later, shelves de-stamped, I scooped Gabe into my arms and dashed for the car muttering, "Gabe, Momma's got to stop by the store and clean the house and . . ." Lowering him into the car seat, I felt his arms tighten around my shoulders and his warm breath on my neck. "And love on me," he whispered. I felt as if I'd been running at top speed and had hit a wire stretched across the road. Looking into Gabriel's upturned face, I brushed his soft, dark hair from his forehead, grateful for a three-year-old with clear-cut priorities.

"Yes," I answered as I hugged him closely, "and most importantly, love on you."

> . . . whatever other commandement[s] there may be, are summed up in this . . . : "Love your neighbor . . ."
> —ROMANS 13:9

$\mathcal{T}hought$ . . . Do *your* priorities match God's? Do what *He* considers important and you will have done what really counts!

Sibling Rivalry

By Fran Caffey Sandin

What generates so much conflict between brothers and sisters? With rare exception, it is not the result of poor parenting. Much of it is an expression of basic human nature.

—James C. Dobson

*O*ne day, while working in the kitchen, I heard my children yelling at each other. In the midst of a big fuss between my eight-year-old son and six-year-old daughter, I tiptoed to the cassette recorder, inserted a blank tape, and captured the commotion on audio. They didn't notice what I had done.

After a few minutes, I called for a truce. "Okay. Stop fighting now. I want you to hear yourselves."

The children's eyes widened as I played back the tape. Their "mad voices" sounded so hilarious, that they laughed uncontrollably while listening to the tape over and over again. They even dropped to their knees and, while holding their sides, rolled around on the kitchen floor.

When they finally regained composure, I seized the opportunity to teach a short lesson, "Be ye kind to one another, tenderhearted, forgiving each other . . . (Ephesians. 4:32 NASB)."

That verse did not become a magic wand to wipe out the last argument. But after numerous reminders of its message through the years and by God's grace, they survived. Now, as young adults, Steve and Angie are best friends. Their loyalty has extended to consultations on every topic from how to dress for a certain occasion to how to make the best impression on a date. As a mom, I am glad that the hair-raising season of sibling rivalry has passed. But, most of all, I am happy that they have each chosen kindness as a way of life.

Train a child in the way he should go, and when he is old he will not turn from it.

—Proverbs 22:6

Thought . . . Do your children exhibit kindness towards each other? The best way to encourage that trait, is for you to be kind to them.

God's Training Manual

BY LAURA SABIN RILEY

You did not lose your identity when the laundry room replaced the boardroom as your center of operations. Your true identity is in Christ.

—DONNA OTTO

*W*hen I first made the transition from corporate executive to full-time mom, I felt a little like an oak tree losing its colorful autumn leaves. This new season of life left me feeling bleak and unproductive.

Those early days of staying home with my son were very difficult for me. I lacked the affirmation and on-the-job training that I had enjoyed in the corporate world. And I missed the support. *Where's the training manual for motherhood?* I often wondered.

I was confident in *why* God had called me to stay home and care for our family, but what I was missing was the *how*. I was an expert sales coordinator, not a home-management expert. The colossal demands of such a tiny person exhausted me and left me feeling inadequate.

One day, as I was feeling particularly overwhelmed by my new responsibilities as a mother, I was sitting in my favorite chair telling God all about it. Suddenly, I had the urge to open my Bible. I read aloud, "All Scripture is God-breathed and is useful for teaching, rebuking, correcting and training in righteousness."

Relieved, I lifted my eyes to the ceiling. "I get it God," I exclaimed. "This is my training manual!"

My search for guidance in the area of parenting is an ongoing process, one that has led me time and time again to God's Word. There, in the training manual written by the greatest Father of all time, I have always found the answers I need to best equip me as a mother.

> All Scripture is God-breathed and is useful for teaching, rebuking, correcting and training in righteousness, so that the man of God may be thoroughly equipped for every good work.
>
> —II TIMOTHY 3:16-17

Thought . . . To what expert do you refer when seeking parenting tips? The Bible has every answer for life and godliness.

Sharing a Mother's Heart

BY ROSALIE J.G. MILLS

Mom, you and I are going to be much better friends after I leave home.

—JASON MILLS

He looked so scared and vulnerable, my six-foot-tall *child*, huddled in the back seat of the Navy recruiter's car. Jason didn't like to get up early, but when he questioned the 3:30 A.M. pickup time, the answer was short and to the point: "Get used to it." Now the time was here, and the car was pulling out of the driveway.

I only made it halfway up the stairs to the apartment before I began sobbing.

It felt as if someone had torn out my heart. I knew that there was one person in this world who would understand my pain and be able to comfort me. As I dialed my mother's phone number, I realized that the job of mothering never ends.

When Momma answered and heard my anguished sobs, she, who had experienced the same tearing of her heart when I had left for college, now patiently listened to the one who had so glibly said good-bye that day so long ago.

I am so thankful to God for the healing closeness Momma and I have gained as she has empathized with my struggles of parenting a teenager, and as I have been able to understand and forgive her parenting mistakes.

My son and I have developed similar closeness, as I compassionately related to his struggles in each season along life's journey, and as he forgives my parenting mistakes.

A mother's work is truly never done.

Do to others as you would have them do to you.
—LUKE 6:31

Thought . . . Now that you are an adult, can you understand why your parents made certain decisions? This wiser perspective can also help you better trust your Heavenly Father and to realize that, as your parent, He makes decisions about you that are for your good.

The Winning Team

BY SUZY RYAN

This is going to hurt me a lot more than it will hurt you.

—EVERY MOTHER'S WORDS AT SOME POINT IN THE PARENTING PROCESS

I crave for my children to experience the childhood that I always wanted. Since my parents divorced when I was young, I desired to provide a stable environment, full of joy and fun. With this idyllic home-life, I knew that my offspring would never require much discipline. Right?

Wrong! Last week my seven-year-old son made the only two goals on his soccer team. He rode high while he led his team to victory. Yet his victory was short-lived when, the next day, he resisted his time-out for "sassing." He defiantly threw items out of his room and refused to remain in his mother-imposed solitary confinement.

I made it clear that if he did not cease this conduct, he would not play in the weekend's soccer match. Sadly, he sealed his "benched fate" when he hurled another item out into the hallway.

By Friday, his stellar performance all week tempted me to rethink the consequences I had established for his earlier behavior. I flipped through my calendar and saw a Bible verse about discipline, reinforcing my earlier decision.

"Oh Lord, give me the strength to hold him accountable for his poor behavior. I *just* don't want him to feel badly," I prayed.

"Suzy," God said to my heart, "You must make him stay home. That doesn't mean you don't hurt with him, but that you love him enough to hold him accountable for his actions."

With new understanding, I decided that we would stay home. Amazingly, it poured that September San Diego Saturday. I'm sure glad I'm on God's team; He always wins the game!

Endure hardship as discipline; God is treating you as sons. For what son is not disciplined by his father?

—HEBREWS 12:7

Thought . . . Do you cringe at the notion of disciplining your children? It does hurt you *now*, yet, it will hurt your children far more in the long run if you neglect that responsibility; God will give you both grace to endure it.

How Does Your Garden Grow?

BY GRACE WITWER HOUSHOLDER

Mary, Mary, quite contrary, how does your garden grow?

—NURSERY RHYME

When I was in fourth grade a boy with a buzz-cut loved to tease me by calling, "Hey, Grease—I mean Grace!" I disliked the way my name could so easily be reduced to a slimy substance. But that intentional word mix-up and a story about my cousin, Lisa, help illustrate God's love.

When Lisa was four, she lived near a gentleman who spent many hours keeping his lawn and garden beautifully manicured. His grass resembled a velvet carpet. His flowers were huge. One day Lisa came home and announced, "Do you know why Mr. Lee's yard is so nice? He puts elbow grease on it!"

I have never been one to keep an exceptional yard or garden. When I planted carrots, they grew short and round like radishes. When I grew radishes, they burned our mouths like hot peppers. Those were my "successes." Most of the time nothing came up.

But there are many different kinds of gardens. We don't all have "green thumbs" in the traditional sense of the word.

One of my "gardens" is my four children. The soil is the nurturing from me and my husband; the rain is baptism; and the sunshine is God's love.

Tending my children takes commitment, time, sacrifice and strength. It requires lots of "elbow grease." But more important than elbow grease is a generous dose of grace!

God's grace and my elbow grease will make my garden grow!

Let your conversation be always full of grace, seasoned with salt, so that you may know how to answer everyone.

—COLOSSIANS 4:6

Thought . . . How do your "gardens" grow? Whether tending your gardens of family, ministry, or career, do you start by weeding, feeding, and watering them? And don't forget to ask God to send His "Sonshine," seasoning them with grace.

Parenting in the Spirit

BY KAREN O'CONNOR

I have many times been driven to my knees by the overwhelming conviction that I had no where else to go.

—ABRAHAM LINCOLN

*T*he year my son turned twenty I was frantically worried about his life, his choices, his behavior. His father and I had recently divorced and he was upset, feeling displaced, and terribly hurt.

Jim smoked pot, lived out of his car for a time, hung out with irresponsible young people, and sank deeper into his pain. To top it off, he and his dad were not getting along.

One morning at a women's prayer group I couldn't contain my fears any longer. I broke down in front of the group, sobbing with frustration, anger, guilt, remorse. I wanted to help my hurting son, but didn't know what to do. Within seconds of my speaking, an older woman approached me, putting her arm around me. "Hush," she said sweetly, stroking my hair as she would a child's. "Your parenting in the flesh is over. This is between your son and his father. Stand back. Let them work it out. Your parenting must now be in the spirit."

"Pray," she said, "like you've never prayed before. Leave the results to the Lord."

An unexpected peace came over me in that moment. I knew she was right. I knew what to do and I began doing it—daily. My life turned around that day, and in the years since, so has my son's. He is no longer the victim of his circumstances or his parents' choices. The Lord listened and answered my prayers—and it all started with one woman's willingness to speak the truth at a time when I most needed it.

Then you will call upon me and come and pray to me, and I will listen to you.

—JEREMIAH 29:12

Thought . . . Is your child too old to discipline? Don't despair. You possess one of the most powerful spiritual resources available—prayer! Use it every time you have the chance and watch God work.

Praise the Lord! Please!

BY GLENDA PALMER

God always answers us in the deeps, never in the shallows of our soul.

—AMY CARMICHAEL

He's acting like such a brat, I thought as the praise-singing concluded and my twelve-year-old son, Scott, plopped down in the pew beside me. He hadn't sung a single note. He fumed because we had made him sit with his family in church. Every time I tried to talk to Scott about the Lord, he gave me "that" look from behind his long bangs.

I believed that Scott was a Christian, but he certainly showed no joy in the Lord. Mine was fading fast!

On the verge of tears, I remembered when Scott was six and had walked boldly to the front of the church to accept Jesus. He was so excited to get baptized. How he had changed!

Scott probably didn't hear the sermon that day, but I did. It was centered on the verse, "He who has begun a good work in you will complete it." Our responsibility was to train this child and Jesus' responsibility was to complete the work that He had begun in him. In my silent prayer, I gave Scott back to God.

Over the years, we went through other trying seasons with Scott, but I knew that God was working. When someone gave Scott an old guitar, it became the "instrument of change." A year later, he led singing in his high school church group. After graduating from college, he married and now works with junior high kids in a growing church. I continue to watch with amazement as God completes the work that He began in Scott.

> . . . He Who began a good work in you will carry it on to completion until the day of Christ Jesus.
>
> —PHILIPPIANS 1:6

Thought . . . Can you entrust your rebellious child to Jesus? Your job is to train him; Jesus' job is to *change* him.

What Would Jesus Do?

BY NANCY L. BORJA

Yes, our children need intentional lessons in life—but sometimes the unexpected moment hands us the greatest opportunity of all.

—DEAN AND GRACE MERRILL

"Mommy, why can't someone else do your job and you stay home and take care of me?" My youngest daughter clung to me as I tucked her into bed. Her words ripped through my heart. I felt guilty. She must have sensed my dilemma.

For quite some time I realized that I neglected my children by not being available for them when their needs arose. My career in the corporate business world advanced, but my family suffered. We thought because we were financially able to give them whatever they wished, we were successful parents.

One day my older daughter unwittingly gave me a look at myself. She said she didn't like the way I dressed for work because it made me look mean and cold. Was that the way my children perceived me? Why didn't I understand that while I may be succeeding in my career, I was distancing myself from my family? The children were wiser than I. I sensed a decision in the making.

In asking myself, "What would Jesus want me to do?" I found my answer. Jesus was available to me day or night—anytime. He put nothing ahead of me, His child. He even gave His life for me.

I found the answer to my decision in Him. The least I could do for my children was to be an all-the-time mom during their childhood season. I know that God enjoys being a full-time Father. And now I enjoy being a mother at home full-time.

And she who remains at home will divide the spoil!
—PSALM 68:12 (NASB)

Thought . . . If you are a mother of young children, do you struggle to know whether or not you need to stay home full-time with them? Relay your struggle to God. Follow whatever direction He gives you.

Show Them Respect

BY KATHY COLLARD MILLER

We need to be careful that we in no way make light of our children's problems. When they are facing difficulties, we have a unique opportunity to influence them.

—JOSH MCDOWELL

*W*hen Darcy was in elementary school, I walked by her room and heard her crying. "Oh, no," I moaned. "Something's wrong."

I opened her door and peeked in. She was sitting on her bed, tears spilling down her cheeks. "What happened?" I asked, imagining some horrible thing. She looked up at me with a quivering lip and cried out, "I don't have anyone to play with."

Anyone to play with? That's what this is all about? I realized. A laugh of relief, then disbelief began rising within me. *How ridiculous*, I thought. But then I caught myself.

I had begun understanding that Darcy's temperament is the "Expressive." Expressives love people and prefer to be having fun with other people constantly. Having the opposite temperament as the "Analytical," I prefer being solitary and would rather make life perfect than have fun.

In that moment, I reminded myself that Darcy's expressiveness made her miserable without anyone with whom to play. That's okay. Although I didn't feel the same way, I could respect it. With that reminder, I was able to sympathize with her and understand the reason for her tears.

For we do not have a high priest Who is unable to sympathize with our weaknesses, but we have One Who has been tempted in every way, just as we are—yet was without sin.
—HEBREWS 4:15

Thought . . . Do you treat your children with respect, recognizing them as unique individuals designed by God? Showing respect involves understanding their feelings, not criticizing them.

Footprints

BY LAURA SABIN RILEY

Lives of great men all remind us we can make our lives sublime. And, departing, leave behind us footprints on the sands of time.

—HENRY WADSWORTH LONGFELLOW

*A*s Seth and I trudged through the mountain forest, he noticed the deep tracks his boots left on the path. "Look Mom," he pointed, "there's my footprint! It means I've been there, huh?" I smiled, musing over Seth's words.

I had been discouraged, wondering if I were leaving proof I'd "been there" on his heart. Developing Seth's godly character was my priority, but as he grew it became more difficult . Since he had started kindergarten, our old "couch-potato-sit-and-talk" method of instruction didn't seem to work; other influences vied for his attention. *What does he need?* I wondered. *How can I impress God's commands on his heart?*

Seth's rapid-fire questions broke my reverie: "Hey, mom did you know that when you sin, you have to kill an animal? . . . that no one knows where the Garden of Eden is today? . . . that Satan is a fallen angel?" Without taking a breath or missing a beat, he smiled triumphantly, then stomped forward.

Seth's interest in spiritual matters stunned me. Delighted, I realized that God had answered my questions. Seth is entering a season where "walk-and-talk" instruction is replacing the "sit-and-talk" kind. He's a growing boy *on the move*, with much to discover.

I'm growing, too; motherhood is stretching me. And if I'm going to show that I've "been there," I'd better keep up!

I quickened my pace to catch up with my son, now leaping from boulder to boulder. There is more than one way for a mother to leave a set of footprints; sometimes I walk, and sometimes I run!

These commandments that I give you today are to be upon your hearts. Impress them on your children. Talk about them when you sit at home and when you walk along the road, when you lie down and when you get up.

—DEUTERONOMY 6:6-7

Thought . . . Are your child-training methods for one season outdated in another? God never changes. He is always there to give just the counsel you require.

Be Still and Know

BY SUE MONK KIDD

God is a tranquil being and abides in a tranquil eternity. So must your spirit become a tranquil and clear pool wherein the serene light of God can be mirrored.

—GERHARD TERSTEEGEN

In the texture of an ordinary day, we can learn to meditate. Almost anything can become a prompter to point us to God, if we pause and let it draw our minds to Him.

I remember a "be still and know" moment that popped out of the unexpected blue. There is not a time at my house full of more fuss than the children's bath time. They have always hated baths and I have done ridiculous things to persuade them into the tub, including letting them bathe with goggles, snorkels and inner tubes! So it wasn't entirely strange that I bribed Ann into the tub one evening by suggesting a bubble bath and candles. When the tub was snowy with bubbles, I lit candles around the bathroom and cut off the light.

Instantly Ann and I fell absolutely silent. The light was pink and golden and enchanted like a spell of magic from a fairy tale. I sat down and watched her move in the little bubbles of light. As I began to be still and focus on one round bubble dancing around her head, spinning and shimmering in the candlelight, I was drawn to God . . . the God of little girls and bubbles and light reflecting around and through us. Sitting there in the bathroom I was surrounded by His love.

A raindrop winding across a window or a tear winding down a face can take on a holiness if we use them to focus our attention and interface our moment with God's.

No eye has seen, no ear has heard, no mind has conceived what God has prepared for those who love Him.

—I CORINTHIANS 2:9

Thought . . . How can you know that God is God? Scripture explains, by being still (Psalm 46:10). When you enjoy a season of quiet, you allow God to reveal Himself in all His fulness.

An Angel in Our Anguish

BY VIRGINIA M. BATY

The angels are the dispensers and administrators of the divine
beneficence toward us; they regard our safety, undertake our
defense, direct our ways, and exercise a constant solicitude that
no evil befall us.

—JOHN CALVIN

Breakfast was over and my husband and I were discussing
final plans for our vacation. The last chore to be finished was
the lawn-mowing and two of our boys were doing that. Everything seemed just perfect.

Then, we heard a blood-curdling scream. Our daughter, Opal,
had been watching her brothers cut the grass. When they were
finished, they decided to pour gas on a match book, light it, and
see what happened. Opal was standing near the gas can when it
ignited. Flames followed the fumes around her right leg and her
dress caught on fire. Having had scouting experience, the boys
knew that to quench the fire, they must roll her in the dirt.

We rushed Opal to the hospital. She had suffered second and
third-degree burns and was hospitalized for eleven days. The
next day, we noticed that although her hair and eyebrows had
been singed, there were no burns on her face! It was then that
we understood the Scripture—that God commands His angels
to guard us. We knew that an angel had been guarding Opal.

Although her recovery was lengthy, and we were not able to
take that vacation, she did walk again and live a normal life. We
have often thought about the "angel" who guarded *our* little angel, Opal, that day—and we will always be deeply grateful to
God for initiating His command.

For He will command His angels concerning you to guard
you in all your ways.

—PSALM 91:11

Thought . . . Have you ever just barely escaped some life-
threatening accident? It could well be possible that God
sent an angel to protect you. Thank Him now for His
special care.

From Briefcase to Baby

BY CINDI MCMENAMIN

There is no nobler career than that of motherhood at its best.

—ANONYMOUS

I never wanted to be a mother. It's not that I didn't like children. I just always wanted to do something different with my life.

As an editor in a bustling newsroom, I was happy to be married and childless. I was accomplishing my goals in life, being productive, making a difference. Motherhood, however, would involve change and sacrifice—two things of which I wasn't very fond.

But God had other plans. He wanted me to be productive in another way. Two months after a big promotion at work, I got the news: I was pregnant.

I cringed at the thought of exchanging my suits for sweats and dollars for diapers. But nine months later, the inevitable happened. After a tumultuous labor and an emergency C-section, I was handed a bald, wet, wrinkled creature, screaming at the top of her lungs. I immediately fell in love with Baby Dana!

It didn't take long for life to change—incredibly. But as I began carrying a baby instead of a briefcase, God changed me and the ideas that I once held about motherhood. What once seemed so productive about a career, in retrospect, seemed like a season of barrenness. And today, when I look into the big brown eyes of my daughter, and realize that God has given me the privilege of shaping her life, it is hard to imagine why I never wanted to be a mother!

But women will be saved through childbearing—if they continue in faith, love and holiness with propriety.

—I TIMOTHY 2:15

Thought . . . Do you fear or resent becoming a mother? No child is an *accident*, but a precious gift *planned* by God (Psalm 127 and 139). Motherhood is a high, yet difficult calling. If God chooses you, consider it a great privilege for which He will thoroughly equip and reward you.

Earthly Homes and Heavenly Mansions

BY LENAE BULTHUIS

The great use of life is to spend it for something that outlasts it.

—WILLIAM JAMES

"*W*here are your church shoes?" I shouted at my daughter. "If you would put them where they belong, we wouldn't always be searching for them!"

My nerves were raw. As my husband helped me get our three young daughters ready to leave for the funeral home, my patience wore thin. Sorrow over Grandma's death, combined with a stress-filled day, were more than I could handle.

After the family's service, we joined my grandmother's children, grandchildren, and great-grandchildren in reminiscing about her life. Again and again, the conversation turned back to thankfulness—thankfulness for Grandma's faith—thankfulness that her faith was being passed on from season to season—generation to generation.

Although I was grateful, too, I questioned whether or not my children and future grandchildren would say the same thing about me. Would my daughters remember my love for Christ or my impatience over lost shoes?

I watched them stand by their great grandmother's casket. Deep in thought, Stephanie, my eight-year-old, stood there the longest.

When I tucked her into bed that night, she said, "Do you know what I was thinking, Mom? Someday that's going to be me in that box. Whenever my mansion is finished, Jesus will take me to heaven, too."

Tears flowed freely as I hugged my daughter and thanked my Lord. Only God could have used even my imperfect efforts to begin leading another generation to His perfect, heavenly mansion.

> He . . . established the law in Israel, which He commanded our forefathers to teach their children, so the next generation would know them, . . . and they in turn would tell their children.
>
> —PSALM 78:5-6

Thought . . . What will your children inherit from you? Leave the legacy of your faith. It will last for all eternity.

Children Are Priority

BY JEAN FLEMING

Children are not a short-term loan, they are a long-term investment!
—ANONYMOUS

I began waking at 3:30, unable to sleep, my mind whirling with coming events and deadlines. Sometimes I lay in bed praying, committing these details to God. Other times I got up, made lists, and did a few things before returning to bed. While the children were at school, I zipped around trying to keep ahead of the accumulating work.

I became painfully aware of the harsh tone of my voice in my dealings with the children. I felt anguish each time I answered sharply.

I talked about this with a friend. "Wouldn't it be ironic," she said, "to write a book about mothering while being cross with your kids?" Her pithy reply served as a pointed reminder again and again.

Writing was only part of the pressure I felt, but it was part. I decided to put it aside until other pressures subsided.

My friend's comment has core truth applicable to many situations. For example, have you ever been trying to get the house pulled together because company was coming—and the children seemed bent on nullifying your efforts? I think you know what I mean. You've just mopped the floor and someone tracks through leaving grass clippings and leaves everywhere.

How easy to allow the pressure of company to determine my values. My guests will only be here for a few hours, but I will live with my children many years. I've decided not to let what company thinks of my housekeeping to become more important than "walking blamelessly in my own household."

Commit to the Lord whatever you do, and your plans will succeed.
—PROVERBS 16:3

Thought . . . Does your parenting style revolve around impressing others? Determine, instead, to please God by the way in which you treat your children. Your children will rise up and call you blessed.

The Original Starship Trooper

BY SUZY RYAN

Though times may change, the Lord is constant.

—CHARLES R. SWINDOLL

"There is no one to drive the Starship Trooper ship," my four-year-old son, Trent, protested after his sister, Lauren, skipped off to kindergarten.

After he ripped up the paper kite she had made at school, I knew I had to dig for the cause of his defiant behavior. That is when he lamented over the fact that there was no longer a pilot. The poor rascal was lonely because he had lost his playmate.

I thought Trent would relish "alone time" home with mom since he is only a year younger than Lauren. After all, he had shared "mommy" from his birth. However, just the opposite occurred; his anger blasted darts of fire every day when we picked up Lauren from school.

Many days I feel like Trent, anxiously navigating my way through this season of motherhood. Alone. How much discipline is appropriate? What are too many extracurricular activities? How will I help develop discerning children while shielding them from the evil world?

Then God reminds me that He, Who began the work in my children and me, will finish it (Philippians 1:6). He is steadily steering the plane of parenthood, His hands maneuvering the control panel of childhood.

Indeed, it is time Trent and I learn that we have the original Starship Trooper waiting to guide our earthly adventures. As His co-pilots, we have two permanent seats with our names on them. With this security, how can we go wrong?

. . . for the sake of Your name lead and guide me.

—PSALM 31:3

Thought . . . Do you feel out of control? Ask God to maneuver the "control panel" of your life, steering you on course. Steady He goes! (And, therefore, steadily you will go, too!)

Baby Demands

BY KATHY COLLARD MILLER

Making the decision to have a child—it's momentous. It is to decide forever to have your heart go walking around outside your body.

—ELIZABETH STONE

When my daughter, Darcy, was a few months old, she demanded constant attention. Discouraged, I looked at my messy house and had visions of this little dictator controlling my life forever.

I felt hopeless. She's always going to demand my attention! Lord, why did I want to be a mother?

A friend suggested I wake up planning to hold Darcy all day. If she didn't need me, I should regard it as a bonus.

The next day I decided to hold Darcy and read a book to pass time. Darcy took a long nap! I was disappointed. I didn't have an excuse to read.

Children sense when we are anxious to be free of their demands. If we meet their needs, they sense security, which makes them less demanding.

On the other hand, children shouldn't rule our lives. There needs to be balance. There will be times baby must wait. It is up to us to make wise choices.

I found a baby carrier helpful. Darcy felt close to me and received security she needed.

Little by little, I used the baby carrier less. Darcy stopped needing me constantly. She could crawl and explore. Eventually she walked and played with friends.

Now Darcy is thirteen and I have more freedom. She is independent. When I think of those times when she demanded so much, I remember a time of closeness. With the perspective of time, what seemed like a dismally long season was actually quite short. The attention I grudgingly gave now becomes love I'm glad I shared.

He settles the . . . woman in her home as a happy mother of children.

—PSALM 113:9

Thought . . . Do motherhood demands overwhelm you? This season, too, shall pass. Childhood is fleeting. Enjoy every moment while it lasts. You won't regret it.

A Hand in the Dark

BY LINDA CARLBLOM

How often we look upon God as our last and feeblest resource. We go to Him because we have nowhere else to go. And then we learn that the storms of life have driven us, not upon the rocks, but into the desired haven.

—GEORGE MACDONALD

My toddler daughter lay beside me, her fierce independence keeping her from snuggling in as I wished. I let her sleep with me, hoping to provide her security in this unsettling season during her father's and my divorce.

I, too, needed the comfort of a hand to hold, no matter how small it was. I reached over and took hold of Jessica's hand. She jerked it away. Reluctantly, I pulled my hand back.

Immediately, as if in a silent cry, Jessica's hand darted upward into the night, fingers spread wide, as though she were desperately reaching for the things she had so recently lost. She seemed to cry, "Don't leave me! Even when I push you away, I still need you."

I quickly took her hand in mine. I slept that night holding my little girl, whose need finally outweighed her independence and pride.

There in the dark, I realized that I am often like Jessica, so in need of my Heavenly Father's hand, yet so independent that I am sure I can make it on my own. Thankfully, in those moments, fear propels me to reach out to God. He continues to lift me up as long as I keep extending my hand toward Him.

> Humble yourselves, therefore, under God's mighty hand, that He may lift you up in due time. Cast all your anxiety on Him because He cares for you.
>
> —I PETER 5:6-7

Thought . . . Is the enemy, fear, immobilizing you? Think of it as a friend who leads you to God. Run to Him. He is waiting to comfort you.

A Tribute to Papa

BY MARTHA B. YODER

A holy life is the best theology.

—RAYMOND P. BRUNK

*A*nticipating his upcoming marriage, our youngest son had just finished packing to leave the nest for a distant state. In the kitchen I was preparing his favorite meal one more time. "Papa, come here," he said, calling his father to the living room.

Why was he calling him? I wondered, as I grabbed my pen and pad. *What parting words would he share with his father?* I had sensed intensity in his voice.

"Papa, I want to tell you something very important. We know most people perceive what God is like by what they see in their fathers. You, Papa, are always showing me what God truly must be like.

"Although your speech is garbled, you are always kind, always helpful, always gentle. And yet you are firm, you are just, and you expect obedience. Few of my friends have fathers like you. Oh Papa, thank you so much for being so faithful—for showing me God!"

A warm embrace sealed this loving tribute, a healing balm for Melvin who had endured others' misunderstanding for years. Because of his unclear speech, many thought him retarded.

On that memorable day, it was clear that my son had understood Melvin's words—God's words—to him. And, more important than words, my son was changed by his father's godly example.

I understood in that moment that God truly preserves the simple who love Him because He hears their heart and their voices, although their words may be distorted to man.

> . . . so that you, your children and their children after them may fear the Lord your God as long as you live by keeping all His decrees and commands that I give you, and so that you may enjoy long life.
>
> —DEUTERONOMY 6:2

Thought . . . Have you ever misunderstood or avoided someone because he is physically *different* from you? Each person is God's unique gift to the world. Forget the wrapper, and be amazed at the soul within.

Thanksgiving

BY MARITA LITTAUER

Children have more need of models than of critics.

—FRENCH PROVERB

My husband, Chuck, and I spent Thanksgiving week at the home of some friends. Chuck spent his time working on motorcycles with John. I worked in the house with Christie. She and I decorated and cooked. Chuck showed John how to repair and restore his motorcycles.

On Thanksgiving morning, after several days of working with Christie sponge-painting and hanging pictures, I demonstrated how to make pie crust. Incredulously, Christie asked, "How do you know how to do all this?"

That evening, Chuck and I shared our daily "choleric projects." I asked him, "How do you know how to do all this?" Chuck said, "My dad taught me how to use all those tools."

For me, my dad taught me lots about cooking and my mom gave me an interest in decorating. Together, my parents raised me to believe that I could do anything I wanted to do. Although it wasn't preached, it was a subtle, perhaps unspoken, message.

Thanksgiving is a great time to review our lives, making special note of the things for which we are thankful, of the special blessings we have received. I am thankful for the wonderful foundation my parents gave me. I have many skills and abilities which I can attribute directly to the training and modeling I received as a child.

While all parents make mistakes, mine included, there are many things they did for which I can be grateful. In what ways can you be thankful for the foundation that your parents gave you?

Honor your father and your mother.

—EXODUS 20:12A

Thought . . . How can you show gratitude to your parents? Spend time with them, offer verbal and written thanks and, most importantly, follow their good example.

Solitude

Unity

BY ANNE MORROW LINDBERGH

Whatever task God is calling us to, if it is yours it is mine, and if it is mine it is yours. We must do it together—or be cast aside together.

—HOWARD HEWLETT CLARK

For a full day and two nights I have been alone. I made my breakfast alone. Alone I watched the gulls at the end of the pier, dip and wheel and dive for the scraps I threw them. A morning's work at my desk, and then, a late picnic lunch alone on the beach. And it seemed to me, separated from my own species, that I was nearer to others: the shy willet, nesting in the ragged tide-wash behind me; the sandpiper, running in little unfrightened steps down the shining beach rim ahead of me; slowly flapping pelicans over my head, coasting down wind; the old gull hunched up, grouchy, surveying the horizon. I felt a kind of impersonal kinship with them and a joy in that kinship. Beauty of earth and sea and air meant more to me. I was in harmony with it, melted into the universe, lost in it as one is lost in a canticle of praise, swelling from an unknown crowd in a cathedral. "Praise ye the Lord, all ye fishes of the sea—all ye birds of the air—all ye children of men—Praise ye the Lord!"

Yes, I felt closer to my fellow men, too, even in my solitude. For it is not physical solitude that actually separates one from other men, not physical isolation, but spiritual isolation.

How good and pleasant it is when brothers live together in unity!

—PSALM 133:1

Thought . . . Are you alone, alienated from other women? Frantic schedules and frequent moves can isolate us from one another. Reach out to women on "spiritual ground," joining Bible studies and prayer groups to build a firm foundation for friendship.

Hidden Promises

BY BETTY J. JOHNSON

O Lord, Thou knowest how busy I must be this day. If I forget Thee, do not forget me.

—SIR JACOB ASTLEY

It's five o'clock in the morning and I can't sleep. "Okay, Lord, I'll spend some quiet time with you," I murmur as I crawl out of bed, tiptoe down the hall, and nestle into my rocker.

Raising the blind, I watch pink and silver clouds slide across the horizon. They create a shadow of light, a reflection of the sun I can't see, but know is there.

Opening my Bible, I begin reading. My mind wanders, trailing back to the harsh words I spoke to my husband last night, then zooms ahead to the scheduled speech for the young mom's meeting later this day. My stomach churns as my least favorite companions, fear and anxiety, join me during this early morning reverie.

"Lord, help me concentrate," I pray. "I need your presence so I will speak loving words to my family and words of encouragement to young mothers."

My eyes focus on Hebrews 13:5, "Never will I leave you; never will I forsake you."

"Slide away, clouds of fear," I whisper. "Make way for two welcome companions—courage and strength." Like the unseen sun promises light and warmth, God reassured me that even though I can't see Him, He promises to be with me during this entire new day.

I sought the Lord, and He answered me; He delivered me from all my fears.

—PSALM 34:4

Thought . . . Do you take advantage of the fact that God is always available, ready to reassure you of His love? Call on Him in prayer and He will answer with His presence and help.

Slow Me Down, Lord

BY SUSAN TITUS OSBORN

The universe is full of magical things patiently waiting for our wits to grow sharper.

—EDEN PHILLIPS

I watched the waves roll into shore, breaking a few feet from my sand chair. At last, I had captured some time for myself! I dug my toes into the warm sand and breathed the cool ocean air.

I thought of how I had almost canceled this day at the beach. Working part-time, volunteering for church activities, and being a full-time wife and mother left me frazzled. I rushed from one activity to another, never feeling a sense of accomplishment. Was I always too busy *doing* to take time to enjoy God's gifts to me?

Perhaps I crammed too much into my schedule. How could I know God's will for my life when I wasn't taking time to be in touch with my own feelings? I bowed my head and said a silent prayer, asking God to slow me down.

Raising my eyes to the horizon, I watched another wave surge into shore. A sense of God's peace rolled in with it and enveloped me. The tension in my neck and back muscles vanished. For the first time in months, I stopped worrying about all the undone chores at home. I concentrated on the present moment. I experienced the mystery and wonder of God's creation, the ocean.

God's voice is often a whisper. We must slow down and be silent to hear Him speak to us. Only then can He show us His will for each moment of our lives.

Be still and know that I am God.

—PSALM 46:10

Thought . . . Are you so busy performing that you haven't slowed down to enjoy the music? Often the most climactic moments in the score are in the rests. Are you observing the rests? When you do, you will have energy to finish the song and life's music will sound far sweeter.

# Locked Out

BY VICKIE PHELPS

Prayer is the link that connects us with God.

—A.B. SIMPSON

Click. The door closed behind me. *I'm locked out*, I realized in dismay. I turned the knob, but it wouldn't budge. In my hurry, I had left my keys inside. It would be hours before my husband came home from work. Frustration set in as I contemplated the long stretch of time ahead of me.

In addition to my frustration, it was a sweltering summer afternoon—much too hot to move around. I found a shady place to sit and settled down for the duration. I began observing the beauty of the landscape around me. I had much for which to be thankful—a beautiful home in the country, a wonderful husband, a fine church, and good friends.

This morning, in a rush to get to church to help with a children's project, I had neglected to pray and have my usual devotions. Could getting locked out of the house be God's way of getting my attention? He had it now, regardless. As my thoughts began focusing on Him, the fact that I couldn't do any of the things I had thought so important gradually drifted into the background.

I'd been taking God for granted, accepting His blessings without showing my appreciation. I had locked Him out of my day, just as I had locked myself out of my house. Now everything on my schedule had come to a halt, except communing with God. I looked at my watch. Over an hour had passed. All frustration had melted and I felt at peace with the Lord and myself.

Here I am! I stand at the door and knock. If anyone hears my voice and opens the door, I will come in . . .

—REVELATION 3:20

Thought . . . How do you lock God out of your life? Two keys to "letting Him back in" are Bible study and prayer. Set aside time everyday to focus on God. He will never lock *you* out!

A Space for Worship

BY CLAIRE CLONINGER

When someone says, "Oh, I can worship God anywhere," the answer is, "Do you?"

—JAMES A. PIKE

The more I learn about worship, the more I realize that whatever is on the "to do" agenda will flow more smoothly when my day is first grounded in praise. The more I have to face, the more I need it.

When I was under pressure of a writing deadline, my friend Pam told me, "Claire, invest your prime time before the Lord, and He'll get you through the rest. Pray for two hours. Write for one. That's a good ratio."

Pam's praise prescription seemed idealistic to me, but I have found that the closer I come to following it, the better my work goes. Work flows from praise. Doing flows from being.

Oswald Chambers said that the lasting value of what we do for God "is measured by the depth of the intimacy of our private times of fellowship and oneness with Him."

You are probably thinking that Oswald may have had plenty of time to worship God, but you don't. In the busyness of daily life, there is not plenty of time for anything, much less sitting alone focusing on God's goodness while the dirty dishes, dirty clothes, and dirty children seem to multiply around you.

But I truly believe that if you ask God to make a space for worship in your day, He will answer that prayer. I believe that because I know it is His will that you worship Him, and He will move heaven and earth to bring about His will when we desire it.

Come, let us bow down in worship, let us kneel before the Lord our Maker.

—PSALM 95:6

Thought . . . How do you worship God? Choose a solitary place, a specific time, and a special plan—such as Bible-reading, prayer-journaling, and hymn-singing. Praise God for Who He is and for what He has done for you.

Desired Sacrifice

BY EVA MARIE EVERSON

Take time to be holy, speak often with God; find rest in Him always, and feed on His Word.

—WILLIAM LONGSTAFF

Have you ever opened your mouth and spoken words you wished you could immediately retract? Have you ever done so to God?

I was serving my second year as a choreographer and dancer for *Son City Players*, a mime-drama troupe in Albany, Georgia. During those two years, the thirty-five-member group had steadily toured the Southeast and had just returned from a tour of the Bahamas. In addition to my duties with *SCP*, I was a full-time wife, mother, and nurse. My life was so packed with responsibilities that I barely had time to think. Sleep was a foreign word. My prayer life was a joke. If not for the prayers before and after practice, I would have had virtually no prayer life at all.

One evening, after throwing something on the table and calling it dinner, I jumped into my car and headed toward rehearsal. Thoughts of dance steps and timing jumbled in my brain when the sweet voice of my Father whispered in my ear, "You never talk to Me anymore."

I slammed my hands against the steering wheel and exclaimed, "Talk *to* You?! I'm doing all this work *for* You!"

I threw my hands over my mouth, jerked the car over to the shoulder of the road and cried, "Forgive me! Forgive me, Lord!"

I resigned from my position that night. For a season of a couple years, God lovingly disciplined and discipled me. It was not an easy experience. In fact, at times, it stung. But God taught me that my time is more precious to Him than my talent.

The sacrifices of God are a broken spirit; a broken and contrite heart, O God, You will not despise.

—PSALM 51:17

Thought . . . Has your time spent *for* God replaced your time spent *with* Him? He longs for intimacy with you. Your service will be a natural outflow of the inflow of His presence.

Managing the Unmanageable

BY KATHY PEEL

Organizing is what you do before you do something, so that when you do it, it's not all mixed up.

—A.A. MILNE

*S*ending your first-born to kindergarten is a big deal. Not so much for the child but for the parents. John's kindergarten year was a major turning point in my life.

I hurried to the kitchen, dumped Cheerios in a bowl, and reached into the refrigerator for milk. Convincingly I said "John, I have a fun idea! Let's pretend our space ship crashed and we only have dried food."

"Mom, are you out of milk again?"

Watching him eat each bite of dry cereal, I grew uptight. "Hurry up, Honey, you don't have all day! Your car pool will be here." I pulled him out the front door, and shoved him into my friend's car. "Don't worry, Kathy. The kids will be on time. I'll use my radar detector."

It didn't take me long to figure out our schedule had to change.

Every morning I wanted my family to experience a peaceful environment that prepared them to take on the pressures of the world.

It didn't happen overnight. I began by praying myself out of bed.

It was a cooperative project between God and me.

In the years since I prayed that, we've come a long way. Mornings are my favorite time now. I get up at 5:45, pour a cup of coffee, and enjoy unhurried time with God. I read a chapter from the Bible and a devotional book, and write in my prayer journal. I write down my daily "to do's." I've found that a list of everything I want to accomplish each day helps me stay focused.

Teach us to number our days aright, that we may gain a heart of wisdom.

—PSALM 90:12

Thought . . . Mary, Mary quite contrary, how do your mornings go? A little Bible study, prioritizing, and prayer will make mornings, afternoons, and evenings flow better. (Don't forget your coffee!)

The Womb of God

BY PAT DEVINE

Let us hope that after we reach fifty, demands have lessened and we can slow down and let our souls catch up with our bodies.

—SUE PATTON THEOELE

*L*ong ago I read the words of Psalm 46—"Be still and know that I am God." As a young wife, daughter, sister, and mother of six, I longed to be able to do just that. Time alone is precious to a woman besieged by so many demands on her time and energy.

That longing for a season of solitude, silence, and solace has now come to fruition. Each week I travel just a few miles to a little Adoration Chapel. I arrive early each Saturday to experience the joy and serenity of spending an hour with my God—alone. Yet now that I have the time and the solitude, I find that I am not alone. I am surrounded by all the prayer and praise, the despair and joy that have been offered from the secret places of many hearts. Here, silence enfolds the bended knees and folded hands—blessing—anointing—inspiring—forgiving.

And I bring with me those who cannot or will not come. I carry them in my heart—the sad, the lonely, the hungry and thirsty, my children and grandchildren, friends and foes.

Outside are sounds of scurrying traffic, people rushing to jobs and shopping; the whistle of trains carrying freight and passengers bound for faraway places; sirens wailing the sad fate of fires and tragedy.

Yet in that little room, all is muted to my ears. I am like a baby resting in her mother's womb, waiting to be born again—because nothing is impossible with God.

"How can a man be born when he is old?" Nicodemus asked. "Surely he cannot enter a second time into his mother's womb to be born!"

—JOHN 3:4

Thought . . . Is finding an entire season of solitude impossible? Try, instead, cutting snippets of solitude from life's fabric—conversing with God in solitary moments—on a walk, in the car, in the shower, the minute you wake, and just before you drift off to sleep.

Faith's Influence

BY BECKY TIRABASSI

Faith is a strong power, mastering any difficulty in the strength of the Lord Who made heaven and earth.

—CORRIE TEN BOOM

I was living with a man I thought I would eventually marry.

The moment I asked God to come *into* my life, I felt I should move *out* of the house we were sharing. My decision took my boyfriend off guard. He voiced a strong opinion that God might be a crutch only weak people needed.

I painfully chose to let go of my boyfriend.

I moved back to Ohio to pursue a path of following God. My boyfriend remained in California.

[Twenty years later . . .]

While in California, in 1995, I attended a lecture series by Dr. Earl Palmer.

Dr. Palmer gave us a golden nugget about faith. He said, "Over time, the gospel, which is the good news that Jesus loves us and died for us, will vindicate itself."

This caused me to reflect upon my life during the past twenty years! Once I had lived as a completely addicted, emotionally wounded, self-destructive young woman.

Had the gospel, over time, been vindicated in and through me? Yes, beyond my wildest expectations.

At forty, I was healthier and more fit than I had been at sixteen *or* twenty-one!! I had been sober for eighteen years.

I hadn't turned into a freak or failure. Faith had completed me, bestowing purpose and meaning into my life. I had become a successful author of ten books, owned my own company, had been faithfully married to one man for eighteen years, and was the mother of one great son. Yes, faith's influence *had a wonderful effect on my life over time!*

. . . but the righteous will live by his faith.

—HABAKKUK 2:4B

Thought . . . Do you question faith's influence in your life? Rather than focusing on your failures, focus on God and see how much He has caused you to grow.

Alone, Women Worship

BY ANNETTE SMITH

It is by these holy mysteries that I live, that I am sustained.

—MADELEINE L'ENGLE

I can see her alone in a tiny upper room. Mary surveys her surroundings, stands at the open window, and prays. Her voice is a whisper, silvery and soft. Slowly, she raises her bowed head and sunlight bathes her face. Her knees are tremulous and her breath quick. Mary leans out the window and stretches her hands upward as if to grasp a portion of God's own breath. Her body swirls in a dance of unspeakable joy.

On Sundays in households all over the world, from Arizona to Zimbabwe, my sisters and I prepare ourselves for worship. Usually we are inspired, uplifted, and refreshed by the services we attend. But sometimes worship is a struggle. During various seasons of my life, I have been distracted by squirmy toddlers on my knees, note-passing teenagers, cranky sound systems, and an impatient bladder. And yes, admittedly, my worship has been challenged by off-key choir members and irrelevant prayers.

But because I am an imperfect woman struggling to know a perfect God, I keep trying.

Like Mary, I am drawn to God in worship. His indescribable love and mystery knock me to my knees before Him. God is my oasis, my refuge, my quiet place.

We sisters come together on Sundays, but for me—for all of us—Sunday is only a part of our worship lives. Because when Sunday becomes Monday and the earthly calls louder than the heavenly, we still worship. In the most unlikely places, in the most trying of circumstances, we find a holy place.

Alone, we worship.

. . . My soul glorifies the Lord and my spirit rejoices in God my Savior.

—LUKE 1:46–47

Thought . . . How do you worship God if you are not in church? Make your life, itself, a prayer, a holy offering. Lift up your heart in praise. Love God with all heart, mind, and soul. Then, alone, you worship.

The Grace of Patience

BY CYNTHIA HEALD

. . . [The] grace of patience—which is either the meek endurance of ill because it is of God, or the calm waiting for promised good till His time to dispense it comes—[is] the full persuasion that such trials are divinely appointed, are the needed discipline of God's children, are but for a definite period, and are not sent without abundant promises of "songs in the night."

—ROBERT JAMIESON

When our children were small, we memorized Galatians 5:22–23, which describes the fruit of the Spirit. To make it fun, we numbered each fruit in order: "love" was one . . . "patience" was four . . . and so forth.

We found ourselves calling numbers to each other. As I was driving in a hurry, my children would say, "Mom—number four!" This was the number we announced most. For many, patience is one of the more difficult fruits to bear!

My idea of developing patience is to spend time with the Lord . . . then rise up and just be patient! I forget that as I abide in the Vine, the Vinedresser *prunes* my branch to bear more fruit. Pruning means to reduce by eliminating superfluous matter; to cut back for fruitful growth. Pruning produces patience.

Having three children in three years was a great pruning experience. I had to learn patience in a practical way. Having eventually a fourth child was a major way of teaching me to concentrate on what was most important. As I look back now I can hear Him saying to me, "Cynthia, that was for number four!"

God wants to cut back nonessentials so we will draw our life from one source—the Vine. This can be painful, but it is always for our good. As we yield to God's loving desire to sever extraneous branches in our lives, we learn endurance. This develops within us a patient spirit—evidence of His fruit in our lives.

But the fruit of the Spirit is love, joy, peace, patience, kindness, goodness, faithfulness, gentleness and self-control.

—GALATIONS 5:22

Thought . . . Are you a patient person? Determine to endure His pruning season. Besides patience, you will receive an abundant harvest of other fruits, as well.

Confessions of a Hurrier

BY JEANNE ZORNES

Though I am always in haste, I am never in a hurry.

—JOHN WESLEY

It was a typical "errands day"—a dozen places to go in two hours. I checked off the items listed in my planner. *Don't turn red*, I warned traffic signals. *Checkout lines had better be short*, I insisted, storming into stores.

I was so focused on getting things done that I forgot to smile at people. I didn't thank God for a gorgeous sky, a car that ran, and money to spend.

Finally at noon, my stomach rumbling like an impending storm, I decided to grab a fast-food lunch. After all, well-prepared, I had a coupon in my planner. I sneaked in the back way to our local row of fast-food places. Pulling up to a monitor, I lowered the window and said coolly and quickly, "One roast beef on a 99-cent coupon, please."

A long silence ensued, then the voice from inside said, "Ma'am, do you know where you are?"

"Yes," I replied, a bit huffy. "I'm in my car ordering a roast beef on a 99-cent coupon, *please*."

"Ma'am," replied the kindly voice, "this is *Kentucky Fried Chicken*. We don't do roast beef."

I looked up and realized that my intended drive-through was two businesses away.

Oh, the red-faced ways God uses to get our attention when we pack our schedules too tightly!

That day He reminded me how, even when I am in the midst of hectic seasons, that I need to slow down and smell the roses—or at least the fried chicken!

> It is not good to have zeal without knowledge, nor to be hasty and miss the way.
>
> —PROVERBS 19:2

Thought . . . Have you ever made a fool of yourself because, in your hurry, you overlooked an obvious detail? God is a God of order and calm. You can receive His calm through prayer. And if you don't have time to pray, then you are too busy.

O Come, Let Us Adore Him

BY ROSILAND RINKER

Every act of worship is its own justification. It is rendering to God that of which He is worthy.

—ERIC L. MASCALL

It took a negative form of worship to open my eyes to the meaning of true worship. I was visiting my first Chinese temple. Inside, it was dark and shadowy and lined with dusty idols on pedestals. A giant gilded idol was set among heavy draperies that covered all but its feet. A Chinese women came in to worship. She burned incense, waved it before the dumb idol, prostrated her little self before the huge fifty-foot god and waited for an answer. Was there any? There was none.

So that was "worshiping idols." Suddenly I knew that the God I worshiped was alive, that He was a person Who responded to me and to Whom I could respond.

Suddenly I wanted to get out of that temple and go home. I wanted to go into my own room and close the door. I wanted to get on my knees with my face to the floor, like that little Chinese woman. But unlike her, I wanted to worship the living God Who created and sustains life, who has revealed Himself in the Person of Jesus Christ. I wanted to be quiet and let all the love and adoration and worship of my heart go out to Him in a way that I had never done before.

I have learned that it is in holy silence, that my heart pours out its best love and worship to God. Worship is that honor, respect and adoration a small earthling like I can feel and give to the Almighty Creator.

But the Lord is the true God; He is the living God, the eternal King.

—JEREMIAH 10:10

Thought . . . Whom do you worship? There is one true God, Whom we may only worship by first receiving Jesus Christ, His Son, as our Savior. Worshiping any other religion, cult, or god is false and will cause us eternal separation from God.

276

Tune Out or Miss the Real Program

BY ANN M. VELIA

We tend to speak of image emulation as applicable only to children, as though at some fixed age one ceases to learn in this way. This is absurd.

—JERRY MANDER

*W*hen I was in college, my anthropology professor described the Nacirema tribe, which built shrines of chrome, ceramic, lights, and mirrors.

My bathroom, however, bears less resemblance to a shrine than does my television set, stationed prominently in our living room with all the furniture grouped to face it.

At a community Bible study recently, our leader posed these offhand questions before we opened our lessons:

"Do you feel refreshed after you have spent time watching TV? Do you look to television for the rest that Jesus wants to provide?"

His challenge nagged at me over the next few days. To my dismay, I realized that I did expect TV to reward me for the attention I gave it. I held the world's belief that "vegging out" equates with rest and recreation.

I still watch television in moderation as a source of concise daily news or a breaking story, for weather reports, and, occasionally, for excellent drama and entertainment.

But I am careful not to sacrifice time I owe to other responsibilities and to human relationships in order to worship the interminable tube. I punch the "off button" when a show introduces material that cheapens values and character.

I remember God's purpose for me: not to "vege out," but to bear fruit. That requires setting my gaze on the Lord Jesus Christ and finding my rest through learning of Him.

> I will set before my eyes no vile thing. The deeds of faithless men I hate; they will not cling to me.
>
> —PSALM 101:3

Thought . . . Which television programs would you invite Jesus to watch with you? Should you be watching them? Has TV become an idol that replaces your time with God? Turn it off.

I Remember It Well

BY LUCI SWINDOLL

God's ability to remember or not remember is a part of the divine mind or knowledge which filled the Biblical writers with awe.

—DAVID A. SEAMANDS

I've snapped pictures of whales, foreign cities, autumn leaves, parties, weddings, children playing, snowfalls, family, friends, strangers. I hardly go to the corner without my camera. Wherever I go, I'm in search of a memory.

I've journaled for many years because I want to remember meaningful times and people dear to me. I treasure these volumes more and more, and count on them to reveal everything as it actually happened. They are a concise chronicle of my life.

And guest books? I have the writings of my mom and dad (now with the Lord), accounts of parties and holidays, and thank-you notes from countless friends. Each page is a wonderful memory captured on paper.

Remembering is important to God. In Joshua 3–4, we read the account of the Israelites moving the ark of covenant across the Jordan River. After the water parted to allow the ark and Israelites to cross, God commanded the leaders of the twelve tribes to take one stone each from the river and to place it where the priests had stood with the ark when they arrived safely on the other shore. "These stones are to be a memorial to the people of Israel forever (Joshua 4:7)."

Scripture is replete with verses on remembering. We're encouraged to remember days of old, the wonders of God, the Sabbath, God's deeds and our struggles, our Creator, our youth, and that life is short.

God is faithful. Don't ever forget that.

He has caused His wonders to be remembered; the Lord is gracious and compassionate.

—PSALM 111:4

Thought . . . What seasons of remembrance can you establish as a memorial to God's faithfulness? Observe Holy days like Christmas with family devotions, write a prayer journal, letters, or poetry to preserve your memories for generations to come.

Season of Sacredness

BY BRENDA WAGGONER

We wake, if ever we wake at all, to mystery.

—ANNIE DILLARD

It was Passover week. In a moment of serendipity, I asked my husband to join me for a private Easter Eve celebration of holy communion in our own living room. With a bit of reluctance, he accepted. After finishing dinner, I put on some appropriate background music—a Celtic lament—and dimmed the lights. "Lord Jesus, we welcome You to a celebration in your honor," Frank prayed.

After handing him a cracker and cup of juice, I set my own cup on the cushioned footstool, and—oops! The grape juice spilled. As it literally leapt into the air, waves of purple crested into rivulets, then transformed into another shape. As if in slow motion, the drops of liquid began hitting the carpet. The next instant, a mass of purple liquid, brought down by gravity, lay in a glimmering pool at our feet.

Splattered purple grape juice. Spilled blood of our Savior. Life-giving sacrifice for the gravity of our sin. Red. Shimmering. Liquid. I could almost hear the cry of Jesus, "My God, My God, Why have You forsaken Me?"

Somehow, the sacredness of that moment mysteriously overtook the urgency of clean-up. We merely offered our presence to Jesus in a moment of serendipity, and He came to us in a surprising way—a mysterious way of His choosing. I wouldn't have missed it for all the spotless carpets in the world.

. . . And I never realized that grape juice could spill so beautifully.

In the same way, after the supper He took the cup, saying, "This cup is the new covenant in My blood, which is poured out for you."

—LUKE 22:20

Thought . . . Do you *routinely* take the Lord's Supper, with no thought to its meaning? Scripture teaches us to examine ourselves. Come with a grateful, repentant heart. Jesus spilled His blood for you!

Contributors

Many gifted women contributed their stories to *Seasons of a Woman's Heart*. Below is some information about each contributor, and the pages on which their stories can be found are listed in brackets at the end of each entry.

Patricia A. J. Allen is a grandmother who graduates from college May, 1999. She believes we are never too old to dream, believe, and begin. Contact: 1848 East NC 10, Newton, NC 28658. [37]

Beverly J. Anderson is a freelance writer active in her church and community, author of numerous articles and stories for adults and children. Contact: P.O. Box 6291, Auburn, CA 95604. (530) 389-2416. bja@foothill.net. [36]

Ruthie Arnold is a freelance writer and mother of three. She has published numerous magazine articles, newspaper supplements, and Sunday school materials. With her daughter, Becky Freeman, she has co-authored the bestseller *Worms In My Tea* and *Adult Children of Fairly Functional Parents*. [102]

Teresa Arseneau is a wife, mother, and author of short stories and radio dramas. She is currently nearing completion of her first novel and in the planning stages of her second. Contact: 486 Wellington St., Sarnia, ON N7T 1H9. tnt@rcv.org. [8, 76, 181]

Marie A. Asner is a church musician, poet, workshop clinician, entertainment reviewer, and author of five poetry collections. Contact: P.O. Box 4343, Overland Park, KS 66204-0343. FAX (913) 385-5369. [34, 101, 220]

Eunice Ann Badgley is the mother of three grown children, and grandmother of two. Her published writing centers on family experiences and inspiration. She enjoys the country, reading, and making crafts. Contact: 1322 Stonecrest, Kearney, MO 64060. [121]

Marlene Bagnull is a wife, mother of three adult children, and author of five books. She directs the *Greater Philadelphia* and *Colorado Christian Writers' Conferences*, teaches writing seminars around the nation, and ministers to caregivers of aging parents. Contact: mbagnull@aol.com. [39, 53]

Vickey Banks is a wife, mother, inspirational *CLASSpeaker*, and the author of the upcoming book, *Love Letters to My Baby*. Contact: 6400 Sudbury Drive, Oklahoma City, OK 73162. (405) 728-2305. Vbinokc@aol.com. [33]

Kacy Barnett-Gramckow also uses the pen name Elizabeth Larson. Some of her writings have appeared in *A Moment A Day*, and *The Women's Devotional Bible*. She and her husband, Jerry, have two sons. Contact: grrjk@pacifier.com. [110]

Virginia M. Baty is assistant editor for the *Nazarene World Mission Society*, Kansas City, MO. She has written personal interest stories, devotions, and poems for publication since 1983. Contact: 412 Meadowbrook Lane, Olathe, KS 66062. (913) 782-4097. vmbwrites@juno.com. [254]

Janet Chester Bly has authored and co-authored over 20 books, including *The Heart of a Runaway, Awakening Your Sense of Wonder,* and *God Is Good, All The Time.* She also speaks at writers' conferences and women's retreats. [42]

Nancy Borja is a wife and mother of three children. Nancy enjoys gardening, cooking, writing, and spending time with her family. Contact: 8618 SE Evergreen Hwy., Vancouver, WA 98664. Momnanc@aol.com. [250]

Delores Elaine Buis has sold over 1900 articles and stories in 27 years of writing. She is a widow and speaks at writers' conferences and women's meetings. Contact: 6400 S. Narrangansett Ave., Chicago, IL 60638. (773) 586-4384. [100]

Lenae Bulthuis, writer and speaker, specializes in prayer, personalities, and women's topics. She is writing a prayer/devotional book for girls. The tentative release date is January 2001. Contact: 8400 210th Ave. SW, Renville, MN 56284. (320) 978-6906. [32, 226, 256]

Dianne E. Butts, a freelance writer, lives with her husband, Hal, and their German shepherd/husky mix, Profile, in southeastern Colorado. When she's not writing, Dianne enjoys Bible studies, photography, and motorcycling with the *Christian Motorcyclists' Association.* Contact: (719) 336-4403. Dbwrites@juno.com. [31, 75]

Linda Carlblom is a freelance writer, wife, and mother of three and is active in her church's women's and children's ministries. Her book of children's messages will be released December 1999. Contact: 1403 E. Westchester Dr., Tempe, AZ 85283. lcarlblom@yahoo.com. [260]

Irene Carloni writes newsletters, devotionals, poems, lyrics, and leads a Bible study. Irene enjoys photography, crafts, and writing. The Carlonis have three children. Contact: 6 Cambridge, Manhattan Beach, CA 90266. Aicarloni@earthlink.net. [30]

Sandra Palmer Carr is a wife, mother, and grandmother, and a member of the *Christian Writers' Fellowship of Orange County.* She brings the hope of Jesus through poetry, stories, drama, and devotionals. Contact: 9421 Hyannis Port Drive, Huntington Beach, CA 92646-3515. (714) 962-0906. [38, 228]

Marjorie Lee "ML" Chandler: ML and her husband Russell Chandler parent a blended family of six adult children. ML is author of *After Your Child Divorces* (Zondervan, 1997) and writes the on-line column "Family Matters" for HarperCollins. Contact: ChandlerML@aol.com. [191]

Cathy Clark, together with her husband, Duane Clark, ministers in music around the world. She is a freelance writer, songwriter, and homeschool teacher to her two children. Contact: PO Box 461, Lancaster, CA 93584. duaneclark@qnet.com. [98]

Joan Clayton is the author of five books and over 350 published articles. She and her husband Emmitt reside in Portales, New Mexico. "Emmitt is God's gift to me," she says. "I am so blessed!" [4, 120]

Gayle Cloud is a credentialed teacher and mother of six children. She writes about education and family issues. Her varied interests include quilting, gardening, reading, speaking . . . and, occasionally solitude! Contact: 4237 Second Street, Riverside, CA 92501. cloud9@pe.net. [81, 179]

Jeanie M. Connell, Worship leader, author (*I Can Grow Up*, and *I Wasn't Sexually Abused, So Why Am I Hurting?*), and songwriter (professional tapes: *All I Have to Share* and *Roots*).Contact: 104 Onondaga Ave., Warren, PA 16365. (814) 726-7459. [189]

Doris C. Crandall, an inspirational writer, lives in Amarillo, Texas. Co-founder of the *Amarillo Chapter of Inspirational Writers Alive!*, a group dedicated to Christian writing, Doris devotes much of her time to helping beginning writers hone their skills. [73, 175]

Elaine Cunningham is a wife, mother of two adult children, author of seven books and over 100 articles in 26 publications. Contact:1008 Wedgewood Ave., Wenatchee, WA 98801. (509) 662-5621. elainecunn@aol.com. [118, 193, 217]

Barbara Curtis, mother of 11, is also a prolific writer. In addition to her books *Small Beginnings* and *Ready, Set, Read!*, she has also published 300 magazine articles. She speaks before a wide range of audiences, including *MOPS* groups. [72, 117]

Evelyn W. Davison, Host of *Love Talks* radio and TV programs, publisher of *Good News Journal*, is an author and speaker on the personality of Jesus and offers help for becoming His love image on parade. Contact: 9701 Copper Creek, Austin, TX 78729. goodnews98@aol.com. [115]

Jennifer Kennedy Dean is the author of several books, including *Heart's Cry: Principles of Prayer* and *He Restores My Soul: A Forty Day Journey Toward Personal Renewal*. She leads in-depth conferences on prayer and the inner life. Contact: jkdean@prayinglife.org. *God Is Always Ready* and *The Privilege of Sacrifice* from *Live a Praying Life*. [96, 204]

Pat Devine, author, poet, memoirist. She delights in husband, home, travel, grandchildren, and leading workshops to encourage others to explore their faith history and prayer journey through journal writing. Contact: 419 Argent Ave., Ferguson, MO 63135-2205. (314) 521-0419. [3, 168, 271]

Pamela F. Dowd is a wife, mother of three teenaged daughters, a freelance writer of articles, devotionals, and greeting cards and the author of five books yet to be published! Contact: 1016 Shadowood Dr., Marshall, TX 75672. (903) 935-0439. dowpub@juno.com. [167]

Sylvia Duncan is a storyteller, published essayist, poet, and curriculum writer. She teaches four-part journaling. She reviews books for the *St. Louis Post-Dispatch*. Contact: 6216 Potomac Ave., St. Louis, MO 63139. (314) 353-5815. [29, 91, 129]

Karen Dye is a wife and mother who also owns and manages a restaurant with her husband in Lone Pine, California. She leads worship at church and teaches a women's bible study. Contact: P.O. Box M, Lone Pine, CA 93545. [112]

Pamela Enderby has five children. Her writing credits include devotionals in *Why Fret That God Stuff?*, short stories, and articles. She is a Bible study teacher, and speaks at women's meetings on prayer, evangelism, and time management. Contact: 8209 Haskins, Lenexa, KS 66215. (913) 492-5935. enderbyhome@compuserve.com. [2, 82]

Marjorie K. Evans is a former school teacher and a freelance writer of many published articles. She enjoys grandparenting, reading, church work, her Welsh corgi, and orchids. She and Edgar have two grown sons and five grandchildren. Contact: 4162 Fireside Circle, Irvine, CA 92604-2216. (949) 551-5296. [215]

Eva Marie Everson is a wife and mother, writer, teacher and speaker, publishes a daily Internet devotional, is currently collaborating with Carmen Leal on a book, *Pinches of Salt, Prisms of Light*, and is writing her second novel. Contact:(407) 695-9366. PenNhnd@aol.com. [269]

Becky Freeman is author of seven books including *Worms in My Tea*, *Marriage 9-1-1*, *Still Lickin' the Spoon*, *Courage for the Chicken Hearted*, *A View from the Porch Swing*, and *Real Magnolias*. For booking information, contact: beckyworms@compuserve.com. [174, 227, 242]

Cheri Fuller is an inspirational speaker and the author of over 20 books, including *When Mothers Pray* and *When Children Pray*. She is a contributing editor for *Today's Christian Woman* and other publications. Contact: cheri@cander.net. Web site: www.cander.net/~cheri. [109]

Vernette Fulop is a retired nurse, mother of three adult children, a mission speaker, and writer of inspirational articles and cameos. She has traveled in 21 foreign countries and advises foreign students. Contact: 17601 West 70th Street, Shawnee, KS 66217. [71]

Linda J. Gilden, wife and mother of three, is managing editor of *The Encourager* and contributing editor to two magazines. She is the author of numerous articles and a special consultant for children's ministry with the *South Carolina Baptist Convention*. [112]

Verda Glick, missionary in El Salvador, praises God for protection during war, kidnaping, and armed robberies. Her book, *Deliver the Ransom Alone*, tells how her son met with the kidnappers and pleaded for his father's release. Contact: brenald@vianet.com.sv. [10]

Donna Clark Goodrich, professional writer, teaches at Christian writers' seminars across the U.S. She also types, proofreads, and edits manuscripts for writers and publishers. Contact: 648 S. Pima, Mesa, AZ 85210. (602) 962-6694. DGood648@aol.com. [196]

Sandi Gordon is married and has four children. Diagnosed with Parkinson's disease at age 30, she has written two books that share her story and faith. Sandi also does motivational speaking. Contact: 677 Cranbrook, Kirkwood, MO 63122. (314) 821-4906. PSBooksINC@aol.com. [124, 170]

Kathleen Hagberg is married, the mother of three adult children, a human interest newspaper columnist, author of a book of children's verses and children's stories, and a Director of Children's Ministries. Contact: 41 Bittersweet Trail, Wilton, CT 06897. (203) 762-0541. [97]

Mary Hake is a wife, mother of two grown daughters, whom she homeschooled, and a writer and copyeditor. She is active in her church and *Oregon Christian Writers*. Contact: 320 E. Elmore St., Lebanon, OR 97355-3901. (541) 258-8210. haket@ptinet.com. [77]

Mary Ann Hamilton is editor of *Colorado Post-Polio Connections Newsletter* for 13 years. As a member of the *Colorado Post-Polio Support Groups*, she has helped put on five successful state conferences for polio survivors. Contact: mhamil1185@aol.com. [70]

Bonnie Compton Hanson, writer/speaker, has authored several books, plus hundreds of published poems and articles, including in *Chicken Soup for the Pet Lover's Soul*. Contact: 3330 S. Lowell St., Santa Ana, CA 92707. (714) 751-7824. bonnieh1@worldnet.att.net. [18, 27, 208]

Adell (Dollie) Harvey, the author of 10 books, is mother of eight and wife of the director of *Missionary Gospel Fellowship*. She is in demand as a humor and family life speaker. Contact: 1300 N. Berkeley Ave., Turlock, CA 95380. [25, 54]

Marilyn J. Hathaway writes inspirational messages gleaned from sighting God in marketplace moments. Her family spans four generations of perpetual activity, joy, triumph, and tribulation. As a community volunteer, the sources are endless. Contact: 2101 Mariyana Ave., Gallup, NM 87301. (505) 722-9795. [16, 195]

Marilyn Willett Heavilin is a wife, mother, and grandmother. She has authored five books and speaks internationally on family life, prayer, Biblical issues, and dealing with loss. Contact: PO Box 1612, Redlands, CA 92373. (909) 792-6358. Roses1nDec@aol.com. [40, 116]

Deborah Holt enjoys writing poetry, short articles, and stories. When not busy raising two teenagers, one dog, and a yard of dandelions, she indulges her quiet passion for reading and good conversation. Contact: 12850 Wiregrass Lane, Jacksonville, FL 32246. deb_holt@hotmail.com. [19]

Whitney Von Lake Hopler writes and edits for many Christian publications. She has served as an editor for *The Salvation Army's* national magazines, and recently published her first novel, *Wild Canvas.* Whitney and husband, Russ, enjoy daughter, Honor. Contact: WhitneyVLH@aol.com. [68]

Grace Witwer Housholder, award-winning journalist and author of *The Funny Things Kids Say Will Brighten Any Day*, says children and laughter are gifts from God. Enjoy! Contact: 816 Mott St., Kendallville, IN 46755. (219) 347-0738. http://www.funnykids.com. [199, 247]

Michele Howe has published over 300 articles and is a curriculum writer for *Group Publishing* and *Christian Service Brigade.* She also reviews for *Publishers Weekly.* Her book, *Bible Stories, Food, and Fun* will be published next fall. Contact: 6154 South Otter Creek Road, LaSalle, MI 48145. jhowe@monroe.lib.mi.us. [80]

Valerie Howe is a wife, mother of five children, speaker, and author. She speaks on both Christian parenting and women's issues. Contact: PO Box 141, Lebanon, MO 65536-0141. (417) 532-1009. FAX: (417) 532-1009. vhowe@llion.org. [122]

Jo Huddleston has written three books and numerous articles that have appeared in such magazines as *Guideposts* and *Decision.* Jo is a book reviewer and conference workshop speaker. Contact: PO Box 1683, Auburn, AL 36831-1683. johudd@earthlink.net. [9]

Armené Humber is a communicator and writer who encourages and inspires women. She teaches career transition classes for the *Women's Opportunities Center* at University of California, Irvine. Contact:11166 McGee River Circle, Fountain Valley, CA 92708. (714) 775-6705. armhumber@aol.com. [67, 95, 143]

Kristen Johnson Ingram lives at the edge of the woods in Springfield, OR, with her husband, and a cat and dog. She has three children, seven grandsons, and a great-granddaughter. She has written 13 books and about 1800 magazine and newspaper articles. [231]

Pauline Jaramillo is a journalist and freelance writer. Her published works include: research, profile, and personal experience articles; political issues, short stories, one-act plays, and poetry. She is bicultural and bilingual (Spanish/English). Contact: P.O. Box 225, Rimforest, CA 92378. sorm@earthlink.net. [94]

Betty J. Johnson, wife, mother, writer, and speaker has had over 30 articles and stories published in various magazines and books. She enjoys grandmothering, golfing, biking, leading small groups, and mentoring. Contact: 5755 Autumn Brush Ct., Parker, CO 80134. (303) 841-3383. BJJParker@aol.com. [55, 162, 265]

Jewell Johnson, wife, mother of six adult children, registered nurse, and freelance writer specializing in articles on prayer and personal experiences. Contact: 4210 W. Madison, Springfield, MO 65802. (417) 869-9317. [108, 130]

Veda Boyd Jones, an award-winning author of 19 books, writes inspirational romance novels for adults and historical fiction and biographies for children. She and her husband Jimmie live in the Ozarks with their sons, Landon, Morgan and Marshall. [235]

Rebecca Barlow Jordan is a bestselling author of three books, with sales of over 1500 greeting cards, articles, calendars, and stories; a minister's wife, mom, marriage leader, and women's teacher/speaker. Contact: 318 Jamie Way, Greenville, TX 75402. (903) 454-1185. rebecca@webwide.net. [92, 184]

Ellie Kay, author of *Shop, Save and Share*, is an international speaker, local television personality, humorist, and "half-witted mother of five." Married to an AF fighter pilot, she's from "everywhere and nowhere." Contact: PO Box 229, Ft. Drum, NY 13603. Halfwit5@juno.com. [5, 198]

Kelly King enjoys spending time with her family, Vic, Conner, and Courtney. She loves teaching God's Word to teenagers as well as writing and speaking. Contact: 9201 Dena Lane, Oklahoma City, OK 73132. VWKDKING@aol.com. [225]

Karen Kosman is a wife, mother and grandmother, *CLASS* graduate, writer. Published in Kathy Collard Miller's books, *God's Vitamin "C" for the Hurting Spirit*, and *God's Unexpected Blessings*. Contact:15402 Ashgrove Dr., La Mirada, CA 90638. (714) 670-9017. ComKosman@aol.com. [62, 155]

Marilyn Krebs is originally from California and ministered with her husband in Rochester, NY for 10 years. They have five daughters and four grandchildren. She enjoys reading, and writing her first novel. Contact: 106 Bluefield Rd, Starr, SC 29684. (864) 296-3732. [12]

Lynn Kuntz, wife and mother of four, has written award-winning fiction and nonfiction for a number of newspapers and magazines, co-written screenplays for several award-winning children's comedy-drama productions and the movie, *Dakota*, and is author of two children's books. [237]

June LaCelle: Publishing credits include *Decision Magazine* and *Wesleyan Advocate*. Mrs. LaCelle lives and writes near Rochester, NY. She delights in grown children and growing grandchildren. Contact: 2 Greenwood Cliff, Fairport, NY 14450. (716) 223-2839. junel@rochester.infi.net. [13, 50]

Muriel Larson, author of 17 books and thousands of published writings and songs, is a professional writer, counselor, and speaker, and has taught at writers' conferences across the nation. Contact: 10 Vanderbilt Circle, Greenville, SC 29609. (864) 244-4993. MKLJOY@aol.com. [126]

Marita Littauer, professional speaker for over 20 years, author of nine books, president of CLASServices Inc., an organization that provides resources, training, and promotion for speakers and authors. P.O. Box 66810, Albuquerque, NM 87109. (800) 433-6633. www.classervices.com. [262]

Rayeann Longwell is a freelance writer specializing in short stories, poems, and skits. She and her husband, Jeff, are involved in marriage ministry, and enjoy traveling, camping, and Broadway musicals. Contact: 6497 N. Delta, Kansas City, MO 64151. Longwell@sound.net. [125]

Rita J. Maggart is a floral designer and author/illustrator of *In the Growing Places*. Her inspirational speaking teaches, "There's an artist in each of us, come find the artist in you!" Contact: 512 Neilwood Dr., Nashville, TN. 37205. (615) 353-1177. [140, 214]

Gracie Malone is an author, freelance writer, Bible study teacher, and conference and retreat speaker. For 25 years, she has mentored women, developed leaders, and established small group ministries. Contact: 1109 Churchill Ln., Greenville, TX 75402. (903) 454-8155. gmalone@ix.netcom.com. [52, 86]

Ruth E. McDaniel is a Christian writer, full-time caregiver, witness for the Lord, mother of three, and grandmother of eight. [164, 177]

Marticia Burns McKinney is a writer specializing in the Christian marketplace. She has contributed to *Brio*, *Homeschooling Today*, and other magazines. She is the mother of one son.Contact: 2100 Roswell Rd., Ste. 200C, Marietta, GA 30062. (770) 423-1129. [152]

Cindi McMenamin, a professional journalist, is a pastor's wife, mother, author, and conference speaker. She specializes in teaching God's Word and encouraging women to develop intimacy with Christ. Contact: 25653 Lola Court, Sun City, CA 92586. (909) 679-1174. hcmcmen@pe.net. [236, 255]

Kathy Collard Miller is a wife, mother, author of over 35 books, including *God's Abundance*, and a speaker. She has spoken in 22 states and 3 foreign countries. Contact: PO Box 1058, Placentia, CA 92871. (714) 993-2654. Kathyspeak@aol.com. [169, 251, 259]

DiAnn G. Mills, is a wife and mother of four adult sons in Houston, Texas. She is a Christian writer and church librarian. Author of short stories, articles, devotionals, and two novels. Contact: 14410 Dracaena Ct., Houston, TX 77070. millsdg@flash.net. [28, 245]

Rosalie J.G. Mills, freelance writer and speaker, has been published in *God's Abundance* and by *Plastow Publications*. She is currently co-authoring a book chronicling God's healing and restoration in her life. Contact: (818) 548-8981. rmills7777@aol.com. [240]

Sharon P. Moore is a wife, mother of five adult children, grandmother of three toddlers, secretary, poet, writer, speaker, and Bible study leader. Contact:10221 N. 14th Ave.-C, Phoenix, AZ 85021. (602) 861-9308. gsmoore@uswest.net. [88, 165, 238]

Fern Ayers Morrissey: Christian mother of four, grandmother of eight, aspiring poet, diarist, premier pen pal with correspondents spanning seven countries/ 50 years; loves literature, Russian language, classical music. Husband says she can cook, too! Contact: 3836 Oak Ridge, St. Louis, MO 63121. [114]

Lynn D. Morrissey: author (first book-*Seasons of a Woman's Heart*; stories in *God's Abundance, God's Unexpected Blessings, Why Fret That God Stuff?, Teens Can Bounce Back*); CLASSpeaker (prayer-journaling & women's topics); classically trained vocalist. Contact: 155 Linden Ave., St. Louis, MO 63105-3839. (314) 727-8137. lynnswords@primary.net. [61, 87, 171]

Jan Nations, managing producer in radio, also produces tapes for pastors. Her own line of greeting cards for healing of divorce generated many interviews. Jan's writing has been published by *Multnomah*. Contact: 7866 Brandy Circle, Colorado Springs, CO 80920. (719) 531-7625. [151, 153]

Deborah Sillas Nell lives with her husband, Craig, and daughter, Sophia. Deborah is a writer, artist, and counselor. Contact: 735 McAllister St., Hanover, PA 17331. (717) 637-4065. [139]

Mary Beth Nelson, married to Walter for fifty years, is published in *God's Unexpected Blessings, Why Fret That God Stuff*, inspirational magazines, in newspaper articles, and books reviews. She writes music, poetry, and for children. Contact: Box 326, Clarendon, TX 79226. [233]

Donna Mesler Norman is a freelance writer, speaker and soloist, who enjoys creating children's stories, classical music, and travel to anywhere. She and her husband reside in a lakefront chalet nestled deeply in the woods of eastern Missouri. Contact: (314) 745-7914. [107]

Karen O'Connor is an award-winning author and a sought-after speaker, specializing in topics of personal and spiritual growth. Karen has appeared on national radio and television and leads women's retreats. Contact: (619) 483-3184. wordykaren@aol.com. [248]

Susan Titus Osborn is a contributing editor of *The Christian Communicator*. She has authored 18 books and numerous articles. She has taught at over 110 writers' conferences across the U.S. Contact: 3133 Puente Street, Fullerton, CA 92835. (714) 990-1532. Susanosb@aol.com. Web site: christiancommunicator.com. [66, 266]

Glenda Palmer is the author of a story in *Chicken Soup for the Kid's Soul*, plus devotionals, greeting cards, songs, and 16 children's picture books. She is co-founder of *The Write Touch* classes and instructor for *The Institute of Children's Literature*. [249]

Jane Parrish is a wife, mother, and grandmother. As a Precept Bible study teacher she has had the privilege of teaching II Timothy at *St. James Bible Institute* in Kyiv, Ukraine. Contact: 837 Guenevere Dr., Ballwin, MO 63011. ljparr@swbell.net. [229]

Golden Keyes Parsons, *Matters of the Heart Ministries*, speaker/writer/musician, specializes in women's and mother/daughter conferences. Teams up with pastor/husband to lead couples' conferences. Contact: PO 764, Red River, NM 87558. (505)754-1742. bgpar@taosnet.com. [14]

Sheryl Patterson, wife and mother of three, enjoys writing and gardening in the majestic Sierra mountains. A graduate of *Life Bible College*, she enjoys speaking and leading worship, and co-authors a weekly devotional column. Contact: 317 Polaris Circle, Bishop, CA 93514. (760) 872-2832. [142]

Katy Penner, retired missionary, nurse and teacher with missions, Congo government and University of Saskatchewan, published one book, writing memoirs—*Diamonds in the Sand.* Contact: #217-489 Hwy. 33 W., Kelowna, BC V1X 1Y2. (250) 765-4941. [90]

Vickie Phelps is a freelance writer living in the piney woods of East Texas with her husband, William. Her articles have been published in several Christian periodicals including, *Lutheran Woman Today, Christian Standard,* and *Women Alive.* Contact: V1950phel@aol.com. [267]

Betty Chapman Plude is a freelance writer and speaker. She is the author of *A Romance With North San Diego County Restaurants,* numerous articles, and two newsletters. Contact: 834 Cessna St., Independence, OR 97351. (503) 838-4039. pludeea@open.org. FA X(503) 838-3239. [138]

Dr. Kathryn Presley is a wife, mother, and grandmother. An Associate Professor of English, she has published numerous poems, short stories, and is currently completing her first novel. She has been keynote speaker for ladies' retreats and other women's groups for 30 years. Contact: Route 1, Box 312, Somerville, TX 77879. (409) 535-4394. [47, 65, 154]

Margaret Primrose is a retired employee of *Nazarene Publishing House* who was office editor of *Come Ye Apart* magazine. She has authored two children's books and numerous devotionals and other pieces. [135]

Paquita Rawleigh, a bilingual poet-writer, published her work on *Shadows & Light, Best of 90,* received five awards from *International Society of Poets,* and has spoken in a foreign country. Contact: 6318 Westview, Riverside, CA 92506. (909) 780-9203. prrawleigh@juno.com. [49, 58, 213]

Carolee Reisch is the mother of three grown daughters, newspaper/radio copy writer, poet, children's ministry curriculum writer, public speaker/Bible teacher, current student of *Moody Bible Institute.* Contact: PO Box 123, Halifax, PA 17032. creisch@epix.net. [59]

Shirley Reynolds is a freelance writer who finds inspiration through her work at a center for the homeless. Her note pad is never empty! Contact: 5228-170th Pl. S.W., Lynnwood, WA 98037. KAReynolds@juno.com. [219]

Karen L. Riley is Promotional Director for the radio ministry, *The Christian Working Woman.* With a background in marketing, she writes, designs, and produces communication materials. Contact: 725 E. Illinois Street, Wheaton, IL 60187. [147]

Laura Sabin Riley is a wife, mother, author, and a passionate speaker. Laura is the author of *All Mothers Are Working Mothers,* a devotional book for stay-at-home moms (*Horizon Books*), and numerous short stories. Contact: PO Box 1150, Yuma, AZ 85366. RileysRanch@juno.com. [244, 252]

Lucinda J. Rollings, freelance writer, mother of two adult children and grandmother of Amanda and Jessica. Lucinda and her husband work with *Awana Clubs International,* a Christian youth organization, as event coordinators for Central and Southern Indiana. Contact: awana.ec.ind@juno.com. [136]

Suzy Ryan lives in Southern California with her husband and three small children. Her articles have appeared in *Today's Christian Woman, Woman's World,*

Bounce Back Too, Christian Parenting Today, The American Enterprise, and *Focus on the Family.* Contact: KenSuzyR@aol.com. [186, 246, 258]

Fran Caffey Sandin is a wife, mother of two young adult children, a new grandmother, a registered nurse, and a freelance writer who co-authored the best-selling book, *Courage for the Chicken Hearted.* Contact: 105 Edgewood Drive, Greenville, TX 75402. [48, 206, 243]

Cynthia Schnereger lives in Boise, ID, with her husband, Jim, and two sons, Jason and Joshua. Her writing ministry includes Bible studies, news and feature articles, and vignettes. She is a regular contributor to *Light and Life Magazine.* Contact: Writer4him@aol.com. [56]

Doris Schuchard is a wife and mother of two children. She enjoys writing in the areas of family issues and educational curriculum. She recently moved from Kansas City to Atlanta and plans to keep focusing on inner beauty in her new surroundings. [137]

Vesta-Nadine Severs author of young adult novel, *Lucinda,* plus three other books. She taught in five schools *How to Write a Book.* Over 160 articles were published from east coast to Taiwan and India. Contact: vnsevers@juno.com. [148]

Luci Shaw is writer-in-residence at *Regent College,* Vancouver, a poet, lecturer, and author of 17 books of poetry and prose including *Water My Soul.* Contact: 4909 Lewis Ave. Bellingham, WA 98226. (360) 650-1515. Shawbiz@aol.com. *I Can't See Him. Is He There?, Rainbow in Winter, Contrasts,* and *What I Put in My Raincoat Pocket* from *Horizons: Exploring Creation* © Luci Shaw, 1992. Used by permission of the author. [20, 78, 79, 103]

Linda Evans Shepherd is a national speaker and author of *Encouraging Hands-Encouraging Hearts,* as well as *Share Jesus Without Fear* with Bill Fay. She is the mother of two and married for 20 years. Contact: athttp://www.sheppro.com. [6, 85, 123]

Doris Smalling is a wife, mother of three grown children, adult Sunday School teacher, published poet, author, and public speaker. Contact: 1137 N. Harrison CT, East Wenatchee, WA 98802-4684. (509) 884-5002. dpsmalling@aol.com. [113, 182]

Annette Smith is a wife, mother of two, speaker, registered nurse, and author of the book *The Whispers of Angels: Stories To Touch Your Heart.* Contact: PO Box 1221, Groveton, TX 75845. (409) 642-2229. ranann@inu.net. [273]

Debra West Smith is a wife and mother of two teenagers who enjoys history, travel, handbells, and teaching Sunday School. Work includes books in the *Hattie Marshall Frontier Adventures* and articles for *Lifeway Christian Resources.* Contact: dlwsmith@juno.com. [221]

Glenda Smithers lives in Kingsville, MO. She is a preschool director, Sunday school teacher, public speaker, and author of three children's missions books. [43]

Rachel St. John-Gilbert is a professional laugher and freelance writer. Her work has been published in *Better Homes and Gardens.* Fun-loving husband, Scott, and seven-year-old son, Trevor, keep her equitably humbled and encouraged! [160]

Ina Strain is a wife, mother, and former missionary to Viet Nam, staff member for the *Radio Kids Bible Club,* and high school teacher. Her husband John was co-founder for *Hume Lake Christian Conferences.* Contact: 65 Pheasant Run, Edison, NJ 08220. (732) 321-0237. [149]

Patty Stump is a writer, Bible study teacher, Christian counselor, and frequent speaker at retreats, conferences, and special events. She communicates messages relevant for today, grounded in Scripture, with humor, encouragement, and insights. Contact: PO Box 5003, Glendale, AZ 85312. (602) 979-1441. [134, 176, 211]

Lea Tartanian, a medical secretary, writer, and a member of *Toastmasters*, has written for 23 publications. Her goals are to publish inspirational books, conduct journaling workshops, and be a motivational speaker. Contact: 3012 Phyllis Street, Endwell, NY 13760. (607) 754-3671. [222]

Jane S. Foard Thompson is a worship leader, speaker, and writer. She and her husband, Jack, served eight years as missionaries in Honduras. Their speaking and music ministry extends across the U.S., C.A., and Europe. Contact: 3206 Teal Ave, Sarasota, FL 34232. [44, 202]

Joyce E. Tomanek, wife, mother, ham operator, crafter, organic gardener, cancer survivor, and writer. Her book, *Sonlight Beneath the Clouds*, about surviving and living abundantly, is nearing completion. Contact: 549 Traves Cove NW, Clarkesville, GA 30523. (706) 754-5030. [45]

June L. Varnum is the author of articles and devotions, amateur photographer, and speaker. She has taught Sunday school and led Bible studies, prayer groups, and retreat workshops. Contact: P.O. Box 236, Loyalton, CA 96118. (530) 993-0223. email: jvarnum@psln.com. [119]

Ann M. Velia teaches Bible studies through her church and writes a devotional column for her local newspaper. She and her husband, Jim, recently celebrated their 34th anniversary. Contact: 4248 Mission Bell Avenue, Las Cruces, NM 88011. (505) 521-3460. [23, 60, 277]

Brenda Waggoner is a licensed professional counselor and author of *The Velveteen Woman*. She leads *The Velveteen Woman Seminar* on becoming REAL as we find ourselves unconditionally loved by God. Contact:16301 CR 558, Farmersville, TX 75442. (972) 782-7680. fbwaggoner@aol.com. [89, 279]

Lori Wall is a single parent of three children, and the in-house playwright for Pasadena's *Exodus Theatre Troupe*. She is self-publishing a poetry book to minister to AIDS victims. Contact: PO Box 41-701, Los Angeles, CA 90041. (213) 257-0274. [209]

Phyllis Wallace hosts the *Woman to Woman* radio talk show, produced by *Lutheran Hour Ministries* and aired on over 350 stations. Guests share hope in Christ through discussions of life issues impacting women. Personal appearances: [314] 951-4140. LLLWALLACP@LHM.org. [24, 46]

Mary Whelchel is founder and speaker of the radio program, *The Christian Working Woman*, heard on over 500 Christian stations. She has written 10 books and has an active speaking ministry. Contact: (630) 462-0552. [146]

Elizabeth Wilt is an enthusiastic wife, mother, pharmacist, speaker, and author! She has written four unpublished books: *Insights of the Invisible, Glimpses of Glory, Mirrors of Majesty*, and *Windows of Wonder*. Contact:16708 George Franklyn Drive, Independence, MO. 64055. (816) 373-2308. [131]

Cassandra Woods is a writer and speaker who enjoys encouraging others to become all that God created them to be. She is a wife and the mother of three children. Contact: P.O. Box 13311, Birmingham, AL 35202. CWjoy@aol.com. [132]

Martha B. Yoder left the nursing profession because of post-polio problems and began to write. The multiple handicaps within her family provided much material through which she can encourage others. Contact: 1501 Virginia Ave., Harrisonburg, VA 22301. [159, 261]

Jenny Yoon is a third grade teacher. She is also a graduate student at *Biola University*. She enjoys singing, playing guitar, and the outdoors. Contact: 5424 Arbor Rd. G-26, Long Beach, CA 90808. Jihyunn@aol.com. [15]

Jeanne Zornes speaks and writes with humor, compassion, and Biblical support through *Apple of His Eye Ministries*. She's written six books, including *When I Felt Like Ragweed, God Saw A Rose* (Shaw). Contact: 1025 Meeks, Wenatchee, WA 98801. [275]

Credits

Some stories in *Seasons of a Woman's Heart* come from other sources, which are credited below. The pages on which these stories can be found are listed in brackets at the end of each entry.

The Good Fight, Bearing One Another's Burdens, and *The Three Locks* from *Clippings from My Notebook,* Corrie ten Boom, Thomas Nelson Publishers, TN, 1984. Used by permission. [7, 26, 74]

God's Better "Yes" and *Sounds of Silence* from *My Life Is In Your Hands,* Kathy Troccoli, Zondervan Publishing House, MI, 1997. Used by permission. [11, 190]

Not One Ray of Light, What Does God Ask of You?, God's Prerogative, and *Playing Favorites* from *Diamonds in the Dust,* Joni Eareckson Tada, Zondervan Publishing House, MI, 1993. Used by persmision. [17, 64, 180, 216]

When Things Go Wrong from *His Imprint, My Expression,* Kay Arthur, Harvest House Publishers, OR, 1993. Used by permission. [22]

The Potter and the Clay, The Faithfulness of God, and *The Grace of Patience* from *Abiding in Christ,* Cynthia Heald, NavPress Publishing Group, CO, 1995. Used by permission. [35, 210, 274]

Letting Go of Loss, The Sacrament of Surrender, and *A Space for Worship* from *Dear Abba: Finding the Father's Heart through Prayer,* Claire Cloninger, Word Publishing, TN , 1997. Used by permission. [51, 203, 268]

Let's Face It, The Eyes of the Heart, Ah, Sweet Repose, Flirting with Danger, Storm Warning, Sing Out Your Lungs, You're Family, Monday Musings, and *I Remember It Well,* from *We Brake For Joy!,* Patsy Clairmont, Barbara Johnson, Marilyn Meberg, Luci Swindoll, Sheila Walsh, and Thelma Wells, (c) by Women of Faith, Inc., Zondervan Publishing House, MI, 1998. Used by permission. [57, 133, 141, 161, 183, 232, 239, 278]

With Christ in the Storm from *Whispers of Hope Journal,* Beth Moore, LifeWay Press, TN, 1998. Used by permission. [69]

Everything I Need and *Forgiving Everything* from *Basket of Blessings,* Karen O'Connor, WaterBrook Press, CO, 1998. Used by permission. [84, 185]

Aged to Perfection and *With an Everlasting Love* from from *Courage for the ChickenHearted,* Becky Freeman, Susan Duke, Rebecca Barlow Jordan, Gracie Malone, and Fran Caffey Sandin, Honor Books, OK, 1998. Used by permission. [52, 86]

Patterns for God and *The Tapestry of Life* from *By His Pattern,* Gwen Ellis, Tyndale House Publishers, Inc., IL, 1998. Used by permission. [93, 158]

Your Fishing Net, Values, and *Children Are Priority* from *A Mother's Heart,* Jean Fleming, NavPress Publishing Group, CO, 1982. Used by permission. [99, 218, 257]

A Child's Cry from *Let's Make a Memory,* Shirley Dobson, Word Publishing, TN, 1983. Used by permission. [106]

You Are an Overcomer, You Are Useful, You Are a New Creation, from *Reflecting His Image,* Liz Curtis Higgs, Thomas Nelson Publishers, TN, 1996. Used by permission. [128, 178, 194]

The Cheerful Giver and *Faith's Influence* from *Let Prayer Change Your Life,* Becky Tirabassi, Thomas Nelson Publishers, TN, 1990. Used by permission. [144, 272]

Speaking Straight to Jesus and *O Come, Let Us Adore Him* from *Prayer: Conversing With God,* Rosalind Rinker, Zondervan Publishing House, MI, 1970. Used by permission. [150, 276]

Trusting the Unseen from *Shaping A Woman's Soul,* Judith Couchman, Zondervan Publishing House, MI, 1996. Used by permission. [163]

Roses or a Right Heart? from *Perennial,* Twila Paris, Zondervan Publishing House, MI, 1998. Used by permission. [166]

Lifting the Veil, The Flame of Joy, and *Be Still and Know* from *God's Joyful Surprise,* Sue Monk Kidd, Guideposts Associates, Inc., NY, 1987, Reprinted by HarperCollins Publishers, Inc. Used by permission. [172, 234, 253]

The Prayer of Helplessness from *Adventures in Prayer,* Catherine Marshall, Ballantine Books, a division of Random House, Inc., NY, 1976. Used by permission. [188]

Working for Jesus and *"Gentle Me," Lord,* from *Heartstrings: Finding a Song When You've Lost Your Joy,* Jill Briscoe, Tyndale House Publishers, Inc., IL, 1997. Used by permission. [192, 212]

Adjusting Your Focus from *Loving God with All Your Mind,* Elizabeth George, Harvest House Publishers, OR, 1994. Used by permission. [197]

Overcoming the Power of the Past from *Night Wrestling,* Leslie Williams, Word Publishing, TN, 1997. Used by permission. [200]

Strong and Courageous from *As Silver Refined,* Kay Arthur, WaterBrook Press, CO, 1997. Used by permission. [201]

Lover of Hospitality from *It Takes So Little to Be Above Average,* Florence Littauer, Harvest House Publishers, OR, 1983. Used by permission. [207]

A Time for Awakening from *Time Began in a Garden,* Emilie Barnes with Anne Christian Buchanan, Harvest House Publishers, OR, 1995. Used by permission. [224]

An Inward Singing from *Decision Magazine,* January, 1992, Karen Burton Mains, *Billy Graham Evangelistic Association,* MN, 1992. Used by permission. [230]

Unity from *Gift from the Sea,* Anne Morrow Lindbergh, Pantheon Books, division of Random House, Inc., NY, 1955. Used by permission. [264]

Managing the Unmanageable from *Do Plastic Surgeons Take VISA?,* Kathy Peel, Word Publishing, TN, 1992. Used by permission. [270]

Other Books by Starburst Publishers®

(partial listing—full list available on request)

Seasons of a Woman's Heart—A Daybook of Stories and Inspiration
Edited by Lynn D. Morrissey

A woman's heart is complex. This daybook of stories, quotes, scriptures, and daily reflections will inspire and refresh. Christian women share their heartfelt thoughts on Seasons of Faith, Growth, Guidance, Nurture, and Victory. Including Christian women's writers such as Kay Arthur, Emilie Barnes, Luci Swindoll, Jill Briscoe, and Florence Littauer.
(cloth) ISBN 1892016036 **$18.95**

*The **God's Word for the Biblically-Inept**™ series is already a bestseller with over 100,000 books sold! Designed to make reading the Bible easy, educational and fun! This series of verse-by-verse Bible studies, Topical Studies, and Overviews mixes scholarly information from experts with helpful icons, illustrations, sidebars and time lines. It's the Bible made easy!*

The Bible—God's Word for the Biblically-Inept™
Larry Richards

An excellent book to start learning the entire Bible. Get the basics or the in-depth information you are seeking with this user-friendly overview. From Creation to Christ to the Millenium, learning the Bible has never been easier.
(trade paper) ISBN 0914984551 **$16.95**

Revelation—God's Word for the Biblically-Inept™
Daymond R. Duck

End-time Bible Prophecy expert Daymond Duck leads us verse-by-verse through one of the Bible's most confusing books. Follow the experts as they forge their way through the captivating prophecies of Revelation!
(trade paper) ISBN 0914984985 **$16.95**

Daniel—God's Word for the Biblically-Inept™
Daymond R. Duck

Daniel is a book of prophecy and the key to understanding the mysteries of the Tribulation and End-Time events. This verse-by-verse commentary combines humor and scholasticism to get at the essentials of Scripture. Perfect for those who want to know the truth about the Antichrist.
(trade paper) ISBN 0914984489 **$16.95**

Health and Nutrition—God's Word for the Biblically-Inept™
Kathleen O'Bannon Baldinger

The Bible is full of God's rules for good health! Kathleen Baldinger reveals scientific evidence that proves the diet and health principles outlined in the Bible are the best for total health. Learn about the Bible Diet, the food pyramid, and fruits and vegetables from the Bible! Experts include: Pamela Smith, Julian Whitaker, Kenneth Cooper, and T. D. Jakes.
(trade paper) ISBN 0914984055 **$16.95**

Men of the Bible—God's Word for the Biblically-Inept™
D. Larry Miller

Benefit from the life experiences of the powerful men of the Bible! Learn how the inspirational struggles of men such as Moses, Daniel, Paul, and David parallel the struggles of today's man. It will inspire and build Christian character for any reader.

(trade paper) ISBN 1892016079 **$16.95**

Women of the Bible—God's Word for the Biblically-Inept™
Kathy Collard Miller

Finally, a Bible perspective just for women! Gain valuable insight from the successes and struggles of such women as Eve, Esther, Mary, Sarah, and Rebekah. Interesting icons like: Get Close to God, Build Your Spirit and Grow Your Marriage will make incorporating God's Word into your daily life easy.

(trade paper) ISBN 0914984063 **$16.95**

What's in the Bible for™ Teens?
Mark R. & Jeanette D. Littleton

From the creators of the *God's Word for the Biblically-Inept™* series comes a brand new series called *What's in the Bible for . . .™*. The first release is a book that teens will love! *What's in the Bible for™ Teens?* contains topical Bible themes that parallel the challenges and pressures of today's adolescents. Learn about topics like Bible Prophecy, Relationships, and Peer Pressure in a conversational and fun tone. Helpful and eye-catching "WWJD?" icons, illustrations, and sidebars included.

ISBN 1-892016-05-2 **$16.95**

On The Brink
Daymond R. Duck

Subtitled: *Easy-to-Understand End-Time Bible Prophecy.* From the author of *Revelation* and *Daniel—God's Word for the Biblically-Inept™*, *On The Brink* is organized in Biblical sequence and written with simplicity so that any reader will easily understand end-time prophecy. Ideal for use as a handy-reference book.

(trade paper) ISBN 0914984586 **$11.95**

The **God's Vitamin "C" for the Spirit™** *series has already sold over 250,000 copies! Jam-packed with stories from well-known Christian writers that will enlighten your spirits and enrich your life!*

God's Vitamin "C" for the Spirit™
Compiled by Kathy Collard Miller & D. Larry Miller

Subtitled: *"Tug-at-the-Heart" Stories to Fortify and Enrich Your Life.* Includes inspiring stories and anecdotes that emphasize Christian ideals and values by Barbara Johnson, Billy Graham, Nancy L. Dorner, and many other well-known Christian speakers and writers. Topics include: Love, Family Life, Faith and Trust, Prayer, and God's Guidance.

(trade paper) ISBN 0914984837 **$12.95**

God's Vitamin "C" for the Spirit™ of Women
Compiled by Kathy Collard Miller

Subtitled: *"Tug-at-the-Heart" stories to Inspire and Delight Your Spirit.* A beautiful treasury of timeless stories, quotes, and poetry designed by and for women.

Well-known Christian women like Liz Curtis Higgs, Patsy Clairmont, Naomi Rhode, and Elisabeth Elliot share from their hearts on subjects like Marriage, Motherhood, Christian Living, Faith, and Friendship.
(trade paper) ISBN 0914984934 **$12.95**

God's Chewable Vitamin "C" for the Spirit™ of Moms
Delightful, insightful, and inspirational quotes combined with Scripture that uplift and encourage women to succeed at the most important job in life—Motherhood.
(trade paper) ISBN 0914984-942 **$6.95**

God's Vitamin "C" for the Hurting Spirit™
Compiled by Kathy Collard Miller & D. Larry Miller
The latest in the best-selling *God's Vitamin "C" for the Spirit* series, this collection of real-life stories expresses the breadth and depth of God's love for us in our times of need. Rejuvenating and inspiring thoughts from some of the most-loved Christian writers such as Max Lucado, Cynthia Heald, Charles Swindoll, and Barbara Johnson. Topics include: Death, Divorce/Separation, Financial Loss, and Physical Illness.
(trade paper) ISBN 0914984691 **$12.95**

More of Him, Less of Me
Jan Christiansen
Subtitled: *A Daybook of My Personal Insights, Inspirations & Meditations on the Weigh Down™ Diet.* The insight shared in this year-long daybook of inspiration will encourage you on your weight-loss journey, bring you to a deeper relationship with God, and help you improve any facet of your life. Each page includes an essay, Scripture, and a tip-of-the-day that will encourage and uplift you as you trust God to help you achieve your proper weight. Perfect companion guide for anyone on the Weigh Down™ diet!
(cloth) ISBN 1892016001 **$17.95**

The Fragile Thread
Aliske Webb
From the author of the critically acclaimed, *Twelve Golden Threads* (over 75,000 sold), comes a novel of one woman's journey through a mid-life transformation as she decides to open a quilt shop in a small town. The novel portrays Aggie, a woman taking risks, facing self-doubts, and reaching out to others. She rediscovers her values, beliefs, and spiritual foundation when a megacorporation threatens to take over her small town.
(cloth) ISBN 0914984543 **$17.95**

God's Abundance
Edited by Kathy Collard Miller
Over 100,000 sold! This day-by-day inspirational is a collection of thoughts by leading Christian writers such as Max Lucado, Patsy Clairmont, Jill Briscoe, Billy Graham, Liz Curtis Higgs, and Naomi Rhode. *God's Abundance* is based on God's Word for experiencing a simpler, yet more abundant life. Learn to make all areas of your life—personal, business, financial, relationships, and even housework—a "spiritual abundance of simplicity."
(cloth) ISBN 0914984977 **$19.95**

Promises of God's Abundance
Kathy Collard Miller

Subtitled: *For a More Meaningful Life.* The Bible is filled with God's promises for an abundant life. *Promises of God's Abundance* is written in the same
way as the best-selling *God's Abundance.* It will help you discover these
promises and show you how simple obedience is the key to an abundant life. Scripture, questions for growth, and a simple thought for the
day will guide you to a more meaningful life.
(trade paper) ISBN 0914984-098 **$9.95**

God's Unexpected Blessings
Edited by Kathy Collard Miller

Over 50,000 sold! Learn to see the unexpected blessings in life. These
individual essays describe experiences that seem negative on the surface but are something God has used for good in our lives or to benefit
others. Witness God at work in our lives. Learn to trust God in action.
Realize that we always have a choice to learn and benefit from these
experiences by letting God prove His promise of turning all things for
our good.
(cloth) ISBN 0914984071 **$18.95**

Why Fret That God Stuff?
Compiled by Kathy Collard Miller

Subtitled: *Stories of Encouragement to Help You Let Go and Let God Take Control
of All Things in Your Life.* Occasionally, we all become overwhelmed by
the everyday challenges of our lives: hectic schedules, our loved ones'
needs, unexpected expenses, a sagging devotional life. *Why Fret That
God Stuff* is the perfect beginning to finding joy and peace for the real
world!
(trade paper) ISBN 0914984-500 **$12.95**

Purchasing Information:

www.starburstpublishers.com

Books are available from your favorite bookstore, either from current
stock or special order. To assist bookstores in locating your selection be
sure to give title, author, and ISBN#. If unable to purchase from the
bookstores you may order directly from STARBURST PUBLISHERS.
When ordering enclose full payment plus shipping and handling as follows: Post Office (4th Class)—$3.00 (Up to $20.00), $4.00 ($20.01–
$50.00), 8% ($50.01 and Up); UPS—$4.50 (Up to $20.00), $6.00
($20.01–$50.00), 12% ($50.01 and Up); Canada—$5.00 (Up to $35.00),
15% ($35.01 and Up); Overseas (Surface)—$5.00 (Up to $25.00), 20%
($25.01 and Up). Payment in U.S. Funds only. Please allow two to three
weeks minimum (longer overseas) for delivery. Make checks payable to
and mail to: STARBURST PUBLISHERS, P.O. Box 4123, LANCASTER,
PA 17604. Credit card orders may also be placed by calling 1-800-441-
1456 (credit card orders only), Mon-Fri, 8:30 A.M. to 5:30 P.M. Eastern
Standard Time. Prices subject to change without notice. Catalog available for a 9 x 12 self-addressed envelope with 4 first-class stamps.